Invasion

Invasion

How America Still Welcomes
Terrorists, Criminals, and Other
Foreign Menaces to Our Shores

Michelle Malkin

Since 1947
REGNERY
PUBLISHING, INC.
An Eagle Publishing Company • Washington, DC

First paperback edition published 2004

Library of Congress Cataloging-in-Publication Data

Malkin, Michelle.
    Invasion : how America still welcomes terrorists, criminals, and other foreign menaces to our shores / Michelle Malkin.
    p. cm.
Includes bibliographical references and index.
    ISBN 0-89526-075-1
    1. United States—Emigration and immigration—Government policy. 2. Immigrants—Government policy—United States. 3. Internal security—United States. 4. Deviant behavior—United States. I. Title.
    JV6483.M29 2002
    325.73—dc21
                                2002010845

Published in the United States by
Regnery Publishing, Inc.
An Eagle Publishing Company
One Massachusetts Avenue, NW
Washington, DC 20001

Visit us at www.regnery.com

Distributed to the trade by
National Book Network
4720-A Boston Way
Lanham, MD 20706

Printed on acid-free paper
Manufactured in the United States of America

10 9 8 7 6 5 4 3 2 1

Books are available in quantity for promotional or premium use. Write to Director of Special Sales, Regnery Publishing, Inc., One Massachusetts Avenue, NW, Washington, DC 20001, for information on discounts and terms or call (202) 216-0600.

For Mom and Dad, my inspiration
For Jesse, my foundation
For Veronica, our future

Contents

Introduction

The nineteen hijackers who invaded America on September 11, 2001, couldn't have done it without help from the United States government. We unlocked our doors, spread out the welcome mat, and allowed these foreign visitors to plot death and destruction in the comfort of our home. And they could do it again in a heartbeat.

The United States Congress, pressured by ethnicity lobbyists, corporations, the travel industry, and open-borders activists, aided the September 11 terrorists by losing track of foreign students and visitors overstaying their visas. To this day, no such tracking systems have been implemented.

Federal lawmakers also created visa programs and airline-sponsored regulations that aided the terrorists' travel. Those programs remain in place today.

State Department officials established policies that expedited the terrorists' visa applications. Those policies remained in place months after the attack.

And Immigration and Naturalization Service inspectors waved the terrorists through while ignoring their previous overstays and incomplete paperwork. The agency's incompetent, negligent, and corrupted management remains in place today, while Congress debates folding it into the proposed Department of Homeland Security.

The September 11 invaders weren't the first to benefit from criminal-friendly immigration policies and practices. America's historic generosity toward the salt of the earth has been exploited ruthlessly by the scum of the earth. Since the first World Trade Center bombing in 1993, more than forty Islamic radicals convicted or tied to terrorism have exploited all forms of entry into the country, legal and illegal. Six of these Islamic militants were naturalized United States citizens at the time they committed their terrorist acts, eleven were legal permanent residents, twelve were illegal immigrants, thirteen were tourists, and two were students.[1]

And terrorists are just some of the enemies invading our shores.

Angel Maturino Resendiz, who used dozens of aliases, including "Rafael Resendez-Ramirez," and became known as the "Railway Killer" after he murdered twelve Americans, entered the United States illegally dozens of times from Mexico. Though Resendiz had a rap sheet a mile long, he was repeatedly released from custody.

The federal government's failure to track criminals such as Resendiz jeopardizes the men and women in blue assigned to protect Americans. Among the cop-killers who should have been deported but freely roamed our streets:

— a Hungarian rapist who gunned down a veteran Los Angeles homicide detective on the verge of retirement

- an El Salvadoran alcoholic who shot a female rookie cop from Los Angeles in the face
- a Mexican drug dealer who gunned down a young Washington state trooper during a routine traffic stop
- a Jamaican convict who shot a Virginia officer point-blank in the head during a foot chase

Our immigration authorities have deliberately granted citizenship or legal permanent residence to hundreds, if not thousands, of other known brutal thugs, including:

- a Haitian death squad leader known as "The Devil"
- an Ethiopian war criminal who hung naked women upside down from poles and beat them with wire
- a Cuban psychiatric ward "nurse" who tortured political prisoners with wet electric prods wired to their temples and genitals

Millions who do aspire to live the American Dream—instead of destroying it—wait in line for years to gain legal entry and citizenship. Meanwhile, instead of protecting our borders and weeding out national security threats, immigration officials

- release criminal aliens into the community to demonstrate "efficiency"
- smuggle drugs and people
- peddle fake documents
- trade visas for money and sex
- punish and intimidate whistleblowers

In June 2002, President Bush unveiled a plan to create a cabinet-level homeland security agency into which the INS would be folded. But this cosmetic reorganization distracts attention from the millions of illegal aliens who continue to stream into America despite massive government spending on immigration enforcement.[2]

There are currently fewer than four hundred Border Patrol agents along the four-thousand-mile border between Canada and the United States—less than one agent for every ten miles.[3] Although there are an estimated 9 to 11 million illegal aliens living in the United States,[4] the INS has only twenty thousand detention beds for illegal aliens awaiting deportation[5] and fewer than two thousand agents assigned to interior enforcement.[6] At least 314,000 illegal aliens who have been ordered deported—including six thousand Middle Easterners—have evaded the INS and remain on the loose.[7]

When we do track down illegal aliens, our clogged deportation system, exploited by corrupt immigration lawyers and illegal alien advocates, makes it almost impossible to send them back to their homelands. Regina Norman Danson, who impersonated a Ghanaian queen threatened with a forced clitorectomy, won the celebrity endorsements of Julia Roberts and Hillary Clinton and remains in this country. So do convicted foreign child molesters, burglars, and other violent felons who found sympathizers in the secretive immigration court system. Others who have played the persecution card:

- a Palestinian bomb-builder who entered the United States illegally through Canada and claimed political asylum based on alleged persecution by Israelis

- a Pakistani militant who claimed political asylum based on his status as an ethnic minority, then went on a shooting spree at the Central Intelligence Agency headquarters in McLean, Virginia

— the mastermind of the deadly 1993 World Trade Center bombing, who traipsed into the country on a fake Iraqi passport without a visa, claimed political asylum, and was released by federal immigration authorities because New York officials didn't have enough space to detain him

— an Egyptian national who fled his native country after being arrested on charges of molesting his seven-year-old cousin, claimed religious persecution after illegally crossing the border into the United States from Mexico, and then brutally molested and murdered his twelve-year-old California neighbor

How do we protect ourselves from foreign homicidal evil-doers and the hapless bureaucrats who let them roam across our fruited plain? To start, ordinary Americans must realize that their government has failed to carry out its most basic constitutional duty: to "provide for the common defense."

Many fine books have been written about the historical, economical, and cultural impact of immigration. This book, written while America plunged into the first year of its War on Terror, expounds on a very simple theme: *Immigration policy must be treated as a national security issue.* Despite the deaths of thousands of Americans at the hands of foreign menaces on our own soil, our government refuses to take it seriously.

The public deserves informed analysis of whether our fraud-ridden, vote-pandering immigration policies—designed for the sake of winning electoral support from minority communities—continue to come at the expense of public safety and the national interest.

Even after September 11, the mainstream media has buried its head in the sand—preferring to run scores of cookie-cutter sob stories about illegal aliens "unjustly" detained instead of focusing on the still rising costs to society of an immigration system run amok. The pages of *Invasion* spotlight the immigration nightmares that the media elite downplay and ignore. *Invasion* contains a new perspective:

- As a first-generation American, I am the new face of the immigration debate.
- I am sick and tired of watching our government allow illegal line-jumpers, killers, and America-haters to flood our gates and threaten our safety.
- I am sick and tired of watching ethnic minority leaders cry "racism" whenever Congress attempts to shore up our borders.
- And I am especially sick and tired of business leaders, lobbyists, and lawmakers from both major parties caving in—and selling out our national security.
- I believe in immigrant profiling. I believe we should discriminate in favor of foreigners yearning to live the American Dream—and against foreigners yearning to destroy it.

The voice of New Americans who support our government's constitutional imperative to provide for the common defense is sorely missing from the current debate on immigration policy in the post–September 11 era. I believe naturalized Americans and their families—such as my own—can play a leading role in the movement to defend and reclaim our borders from aliens who despise our sacred institutions. It is our sworn duty and obligation.

Invasion was inspired in part by two of the most patriotic, level-headed, and hard-truth-telling Americans I know: my mom and dad. As the daughter of legal immigrants from the Philippines, I have never taken for granted the rights and responsibilities that come with citizenship. The oath my parents took (in English, by the way) when they were naturalized in 1989 resonated even more powerfully with me after September 11:

> I hereby declare, on oath, that I absolutely and entirely renounce and abjure all allegiance and fidelity to any foreign prince, potentate, state, or sovereignty of whom or which I have heretofore been a subject or citizen; that I will support and defend the Constitution and laws of the United States of America against all enemies, foreign and domestic; that I will bear true faith and allegiance to the same; that I will bear arms on behalf of the United States when required by law; that I will perform noncombatant service in the Armed Forces of the United States when required by the law; that I will perform work of national importance under civilian direction when required by the law; and that I take this obligation freely without any mental reservation or purpose of evasion; so help me God.[8]

Patriotism surged after the September 11 attacks—but not among some ethnic advocacy groups that would claim to represent my immigrant family. Along with Arab-American, Hispanic-American, and other hyphenated groups who favor lax immigration policies, these groups characterized attempts to protect our borders from all enemies, foreign and domestic, as an unnecessary "backlash."

They were joined by profit-driven immigration lawyers, university officials, corporate executives, and vote-driven political strategists in both major parties, who refuse to put the national interest above their own narrow interests.

What these misguided opponents must understand is that the demand for a more discriminating immigration policy—one that welcomes American Dreamers and bars American Destroyers—is rooted in love of country, not hatred of foreigners.

In my ten years as a newspaper journalist, I've heard from thousands of readers—including countless legal immigrants—who are fed up with a system that rewards criminal aliens at the expense of law-abiding citizens. I've interviewed dozens of immigration officials who are sick of rule-bending at the expense of public safety, and want the whole truth of the government's failed enterprise to be exposed. *Invasion* speaks for, and to, this vast audience of liberty-loving Americans.

My mom and dad taught me to be proud of my country, to appreciate its blessings, and to try and give back to it. I can never repay my parents for the risks and hardships they endured to guarantee a better life for their children in America. But if *Invasion* contributes in some way to the education of my fellow citizens and the enhancement of national sovereignty, it will serve as a small token of gratitude to both my country and my parents, who provided me the golden gifts of life, liberty, and the pursuit of happiness.

Part I: The Terrorist Welcome Mat

Chapter 1

What Would Mohamed Do?

"Crave death. . . . Make sure that nobody is following you. . . . Bring knives, your will, IDs, your passport. . . . Pray: 'Oh God, you who open all doors, please open all doors for me, open all venues for me, open all avenues for me.' "

These were some of the handwritten instructions found in September 11 ringleader Mohamed Atta's abandoned luggage.[1] If he could send a message from hell—where he surely went after he piloted American Airlines Flight 11 into the World Trade Center—Atta would have good news for his band of homicidal brothers around the world: The doors to America are still wide open.

One year after the terrorist attacks, the avenues for death and destruction remain virtually unobstructed.

When we assess the security of our borders, our immigration laws, and our tourism policies, we must view them through the cold eyes of a terrorist killer. We must ask at every turn: *What would Mohamed do?* How would he exploit our entry points, evade detection, and blend into the American mainstream? What would an instruction manual for Atta's future conspirators trying to reach our shores look like?

Top-secret intelligence wouldn't be needed to compile such a field guide. Everything a terrorist needs to know about infiltrating this country is readily available from newspapers, television broadcasts, the Internet, and government publications.

Invading America: A Post–September 11 Checklist

Pick Your Passageway: Air, Sea, or Land

Exploit airport insecurity

At Los Angeles International Airport, inspectors report that supervisors instructed them not to respond to concerns from airlines about illegal immigrants elsewhere in the airport because it would distract them from their number one mission: processing passengers.[2] Sound too dangerous to be true?

A February 12, 2002, memo issued by the Los Angeles acting deputy port director Michael Cochran ordered inspection agents: "Unless there is some special, extenuating circumstance, we are not to respond to calls from airlines requesting that we examine the documents of suspected illegal aliens.... [Even] if something 'special' does come up, i.e., suspected terrorists, kidnapping, slavery or other, we should not go and arrest groups of people."[3]

One disgusted LAX inspector's reaction to the orders: "God help the American public."[4]

At JFK International Airport in New York City, harried airport inspectors admit they don't even look at visas before stamping their approval nor do they request required documentation, because it would take too much time.

At Miami International Airport, too, the daily crush of passengers causes immigration inspectors to compromise security measures against their better judgment. More concerned with appearances than public safety, top Miami INS bureaucrats—still employed by the agency in sensitive positions—released criminal alien visitors from their custody in order to relieve overcrowding and create a false impression of efficiency for visiting members of Congress.

Former and current agents say they felt like "stamp monkeys." They blame managers for appeasing the airline industry instead of enforcing the law, and report that even after September 11, they were urged by supervisors not to waste time checking terrorist watch lists.

As if these dangerous compromises aren't enough to deal with, there are also the untold numbers of illegal aliens who have infiltrated high-security areas at more than a dozen American airports (at least 450 had been rounded up by the end of April 2002 as part of the federal government's "Operation Tarmac" crackdown). And then there's the entrenched incompetence of security workers.

In March 2002, a *USA Today* investigation found that undercover government testers at thirty-two of the nation's airports were able to sneak knives through security checkpoints 70 percent of the time, simulated explosives 60 percent of the time, and guns 30 percent of the time between November 2001 and February 2002 while the airports were on highest alert.[5] A follow-up test by the Transportation Security Administration in May 2002 at thirty-two airports nationwide found that one in four times, screeners failed to detect simulated weapons (including guns, dynamite, and bombs). In Cincinnati, Jacksonville, and Las Vegas, screeners failed to detect potentially dangerous items in at least half the tests. At Los Angeles International Airport, the failure rate was 41 percent.[6]

No doubt terrorists and their sympathizers received word of these security holes with evil glee.

Slip through the seaports

At least two terrorist conspirators—Los Angeles International Airport millennium bombing plotters Abdelghani Meskini and Abdel Hakim Tizegha—entered the United States by hitching rides on ships from Algeria.

In the spring of 2002, INS officials knew of four Pakistani, five Mexican, and four Turkish crew members who similarly jumped ship. Despite heightened security measures taken after September 11, all of the fugitive sailors escaped from cargo ships after docking in Norfolk, Virginia. The INS admitted that at this one port alone, crews of forty foreign cargo vessels have been allowed ashore without proper authorization since December 2001.

While most returned, the Pakistanis bailed out on March 15, 2002, and caught cabs and buses to cities across the country. The Mexicans abandoned their ship a week later. The Turks slipped off a week after that. As of July 2002, none of the Mexicans and Turks had been caught, and only two of the Pakistanis had been found.

On April 2, 2002, another crew almost eluded the INS. In Hawaii, nine Chinese men who had been rescued from a burning Indonesian oil tanker fled from the hotel where they were staying and into the population. Donald Radcliffe, district director for the INS office in Honolulu, said the agency didn't take them into custody because "we thought they'd play by the rules."[7]

Island residents snitched on the crew members, who were hiding somewhere on Oahu, and the fugitives turned themselves in a week later. Soon after, they requested asylum and remained in federal custody pending hearings.

A less comfortable, but often effective, means of travel is the stowaway alternative. In May 2002, the United States Coast Guard alerted federal, state, and local law enforcement officials that it had received intelligence information that "twenty-five Islamic extremists" linked to the al Qaeda network had entered America on prominent commercial cargo vessels through the ports of Miami, Florida; Savannah, Georgia; and Long Beach, California.[8] According to Senator Bob Graham of Florida, the suspects allegedly dressed as stevedores, wearing orange vests and hard hats to avoid detection.[9]

In October 2001, a suspected Egyptian-born terrorist was discovered inside a cargo container on a ship bound from Italy to Canada. He had a satellite phone, a cell phone, and a laptop computer. Italian authorities believe the stowaway was an al Qaeda operative.[10]

Only about 3 percent of all cargo containers on ships coming into the United States are inspected.[11] In January 2002, the Customs Service announced a "container security initiative" to pre-screen high-risk containers at high-volume megaports overseas. But eight months after the September 11 attacks, the New Jersey *Bergen Record* reported that the INS still had no patrols monitoring major seaports in the United States for stowaways.

Michael O'Hanlon of the Brookings Institution concluded that neglecting inspection of cargo containers "may be our single greatest vulnerability that we have not yet made much progress toward addressing."[12]

Walk around the rubber orange cones

Porous. Weak. Ineffective. Swiss-cheese. Those are the polite adjectives used by our own immigration officials to describe

America's four-thousand-mile border to the north and our two-thousand-mile border to the south. The September 11 hijackers all came through the front door, but illegal immigration through Canada and Mexico is the passageway of countless terrorist brethren.

Many northern border stations remain unguarded at night. To dissuade potential foreign threats from crossing, agents leave out *rubber orange cones*.[13] In Pembina, North Dakota, illegal border-crossers drive around a twelve-foot steel barricade with a laughable warning that reads "Avoid Heavy Penalty" and asks intruders to check in when they see the nearest guards. The 917-mile stretch of border in the Grand Forks sector has about one field agent for every thirty-eight miles.[14]

In Blaine, Washington, retired deputy chief Border Patrol agent Eugene Davis estimated that "there has been no effort to locate 95 percent" of aliens apprehended in his region over the past decade and released pending deportation hearings. "They have simply been allowed to disappear in the United States. No one knows whether a number of these missing persons are trained terrorists who will eventually emerge to perpetrate more acts of terrorism against innocent United States citizens."[15]

In the Detroit sector, which encompasses some eight hundred miles of water boundaries with Canada, patrol boats are scarce and cameras were "falling apart" prior to September 11, according to veteran border agent Mark Lindemann.[16] Many sectors will receive new camera equipment to help detect border crossers, but as seasoned agents quip, they've never met a camera that can climb down from a pole and take an illegal alien into custody.

At the Buffalo-Niagara bridges along the United States–Canada border, an average of 23,400 cars, trucks, buses, and trains cross every day—more than 8.5 million last year. Nearly 99 percent of that traffic enters the country without inspection.[17]

William Dietzel, a retired supervisor of customs inspections in Buffalo, notes: "If people knew the actual number of cars, trucks, and train cars that are opened up and searched thoroughly for weapons and terrorists, it would scare them."[18]

Despite recent efforts to step up security, the story remains the same in the south. Bin Laden–funded operatives can pay cheap prices for escorts, join global smuggling rings, bribe corrupt immigration officials, or ride the rails undetected from Mexico along with hundreds of thousands of other "undocumented workers."

These law-breakers have grown so accustomed to our high tolerance for illegal immigration that some are actually suing the United States for not providing water stations on their illegal journeys into our country.[19] INS commissioner James Ziglar responded to demands that America provide better travel amenities to immigration outlaws along the Mexican border by announcing the activation of a half-dozen "rescue beacons" – thirty-foot-tall, solar-powered towers with flashing strobe lights and "alarm buttons" illegal aliens can use to summon help.[20] (Next step: free continental breakfasts and pillows with mints?)

We don't have borders. We have the world's longest backdoor welcome mats. Just watch out for those pesky rubber cones and remember to bring your own bottled water.

Game the System: Marriage Fraud, Asylum, or Amnesty

Once a terrorist of Mohamed Atta's ilk has made it to our shores, there are numerous ways for him to stay in the United States.

Get hitched

You can't buy love, but if you can persuade an American to marry you, you can buy yourself invaluable time, legal residence, and eventual citizenship. Marriage fraud, says Richard Gottlieb, officer in charge of the North Carolina INS, is "like the path of least resistance."[21] Once you make it into this country, you're bound to find a willing American citizen to play a treacherous version of "Who Wants to Marry a Militant?"

Convicted 1993 World Trade Center conspirator El Sayyid A. Nosair marched down the aisle with Karen Ann Mills Sweeney, an American-born convert to Islam, just as he was facing possible deportation for overstaying his visa.[22] As a result, he secured legal permanent residence status and later became a naturalized American citizen.

So did Osama bin Laden's personal secretary, Wadih el Hage, who married an American in 1985 and became a naturalized citizen in 1989. Khalid Abu al Dahab, who plotted the 1998 U.S. embassy bombings in Africa, struck gold after marrying three American women, and finally obtained U.S. citizenship.

Ali Mohammed, another top terrorist aide to bin Laden who was convicted for his role in the embassy bombings, also became an American citizen after marrying a woman he met on a plane trip from Egypt to New York.[23]

Eight Middle Eastern men who plotted to bomb New York landmarks—Fadil Abdelgani, Amir Abdelgani, Siddig Ibrahim Siddig Ali, Tarig Elhassan, Abdo Mohammed Haggag, Fares Khallafalla, Mohammed Saleh, and Matarawy Mohammed Said Saleh—all obtained legal permanent residence by marrying American citizens.

So did Zuhaier Ben Mohammed Rouissi, a Tunisian national with ties to top terrorist suspects. He paid Christy Layne of Canton, Ohio, $1,100 to marry him after his tourist visa lapsed.[24] Lebanon-born Chawki Youssef Hammoud hooked up with Jessica Yolanda Fortune in 1994. Hammoud's marriage afforded him a green card windfall—and the cover to operate a cell that allegedly smuggled cigarettes to raise cash for the terrorist Hezbollah organization. Fortune was convicted of marriage fraud in October 2001.

Hammoud's brother, Mohammed, married three different American citizens. After arriving in the United States on a counterfeit visa, receiving a deportation order, and filing an appeal, he wed Sabina Edwards and sought a green card. Suspicious INS officials refused to award him legal status after this first marriage was deemed bogus in 1994.

Undaunted, he married Jessica Wedel in May 1997, and while still wed to her, paid the already married Angela Tsioumas to marry him in Detroit. The Tsioumas union netted Hammoud temporary legal residence, and they settled in Charlotte, North Carolina, where law enforcement officials say they operated an elaborate smuggling and terrorist-related ring.[25]

Tsioumas, who bragged to others that she would "marry any of them for the right price,"[26] entered a plea agreement in March 2002 on charges of conspiracy. The Hammoud brothers went on trial in May 2002 for their role in skirting immigration laws, cigarette smuggling, and money laundering in support of terrorism.[27] They were found guilty on all counts in June 2002.[28]

Say the magic words: "political asylum"

Our most generous historic offer to the world's politically oppressed—shelter from tyranny—is routinely used against us by our enemies. Uttering "political asylum" is the immigration equivalent of "Open sesame."

Among the foreign America-haters who invoked asylum: convicted murderer Mir Aimal Kansi and World Trade Center bomb plotters Ramzi Yousef and Sheik Omar Abdel Rahman.

Untold numbers of asylum claimants are released on their own recognizance, and promptly disappear. Asylum hearings are often delayed for a year or more. Fraud is, yes, rampant. In fact, it is so "out of control," a GAO report noted in early 2002, that investigators found a 90 percent rate of fraud in a preliminary review of five thousand petitions for asylum. A more detailed follow-up review of 1,500 of those petitions could locate only one that was bona fide.[29]

Among those who attempted to take advantage of our generosity: Mohdar Mohamed Abdoulah, a former San Diego State University student from Yemen suspected of aiding and befriending at least three of the September 11 hijackers. In May 2000, he filed what federal prosecutors now charge is a false asylum application claiming to be a persecuted minority from Somalia. After his arrest in May 2002, Abdoulah spoke of "the hatred in his heart" for the United States government, and railed that the United States brought "this on themselves," according to federal prosecutors. [30]

Could Emma Lazarus, who wrote the famous sonnet affixed to the Statue of Liberty, ever have imagined our nation embracing the likes of Abdoulah and other terrorist travelers when she beckoned to the poor "wretched refuse" of foreign shores?

Wait it out

"If you get into this country, temporary is permanent," says former INS investigations chief Jack Shaw. "If you're in, you stay... and you wait for the next legalization program or amnesty to come along."[31]

That's what convicted 1993 World Trade Center bomber Mahmud Abouhalima did. He arrived in the United States with a tourist visa in 1985. After his six-month visa expired, he joined millions of other illegal aliens in this country who entered legally and then simply overstayed without fear of detection or punishment. He was rewarded with legal permanent residence thanks to an amnesty for illegal immigrants granted by Congress in 1986, and he obtained his green card in 1988.

For illegal overstayers, border-crossers, ship-jumpers, and even *known terrorists*, federal law provides another escape route: the 245(i) program.[32] Illegal aliens in any of these categories who have found an employer or spouse to petition for their residency status need only pay a measly $1,000 fee to "adjust their status" and gain permanent residence without leaving the United States. Usually, these alien lawbreakers would be forced to leave the United States and reapply for visas in their home countries (which involves fresh background checks by consular offices with access to their native criminal records).

Many would be barred from returning to America for up to ten years. But under 245(i), passed by Congress with bipartisan support, more than half a million foreigners forked over the token fine between 1994 and 1997 and avoided legal hassles. The program was supposed to be temporary, but immigrants' rights groups lobbied successfully for extending the deadline. Based on INS data, analysts for the Federation for American Immigration Reform estimated that one-quarter of all legal immigrants being "admitted" to the United States are actually people who came here illegally and are adjusting their status largely as a result of 245(i).[33] Congress was heading toward permanent extension of the program before September 11 — and President George W. Bush joined Democrats in crusading for this mini-amnesty even *after* the terrorist attacks.

For those foreign law-breakers who don't bother with the paperwork, the rewards are generous: Driver's licenses. Taxpayer identification numbers. College tuition breaks. Banking privileges. Health care. Meanwhile, the risks of getting caught, detained, and deported are negligible. There are only two thousand INS agents assigned to interior enforcement (chasing after illegals once they've entered the country). And there are only twenty thousand detention beds to hold aliens—if the INS ever bothers to take them.

On Memorial Day weekend in 2002, with the nation on high terror alert, the agency shrugged its shoulders when New York City police tried to turn in seven illegal aliens from the Middle East who had been arrested with false identification cards in a dilapidated van near a major tunnel. "These men posed no terrorist threat or, for that matter, any threat to the community," an INS spokesperson told the *New York Post,* which broke the story.[34] The agency ordered furious cops to release the men who were all *admitted illegal aliens!*

Even if they're ordered deported, illegal aliens are usually let go on their own recognizance after posting minimal bonds and are never seen again. Those who actually show up for hearings can still game the system through endless appeals to soft-on-crime judges. The system favors aliens' rights over citizens' safety.

Senior Border Patrol agent Mark Hall, whose union represents officers who patrol the United States–Canadian border in Michigan and Ohio, summed it up for Congress: "When illegal aliens are released, we send a disturbing message. The aliens quickly pass on the word about how easy it is to enter this country illegally and remain here. This practice is devastating to our sound border enforcement strategy."[35]

Travel First-Class: Visas and Tickets, Please

Would you believe getting a visa from the State Department is easier than getting a Visa credit card?

The visa-vending machine

In the six months following the attacks, the State Department issued more than fifty thousand new tourist, business, and student visas to non-Israeli visitors from the Middle East—and another 140,000 new visitor visas to individuals across southern Asia, a haven for al Qaeda.[36]

In addition, more than nine thousand people born in the Middle East (excluding Israel) and more than nineteen thousand from South Asia received immigrant visas between September 2001 and February 2002.[37] In the last five years alone, nearly 1.5 million visitors and immigrants from fifteen nations where Osama bin Laden's network has a large presence streamed into the United States.[38]

Between January 2000 and November 2001, nearly 4,800 Arab and Muslim young men from al Qaeda strongholds entered the United States legally on temporary visas issued by the State Department. After the September 11 attacks, the Justice Department was able to track down *fewer than half* of those men for questioning.[39] Welcomed with open arms, thousands more of these Middle Eastern guests continue to walk through the front door and disappear without a trace.

Now, suppose a known bin Laden operative brazenly tried to apply for a visa today under his true identity. Would you believe he might still have a chance of getting in? State Department form DS-156—the official nonimmigrant visa application—asks the following questions: "Do you seek to enter the U.S. to engage in export control violations, subversive or terrorist activities, or any other unlawful purpose? Are you a member of a terrorist organization as currently designated by the U.S. Secretary of State?"

According to the form, "A YES answer does not automatically signify ineligibility for a visa."[40] That's right. "Mere" membership in a terrorist organization is no bar to coming to America for pleasure, education, business—or bloody subversion.

After September 11, it seemed America might get serious about stemming the flow of visitors from al Qaeda–friendly countries. "Arab, Muslim Men to Get Tougher U.S. Visa Screening," announced the *Washington Post*.[41] The new security measures introduced in November 2001 included longer wait times for FBI background checks on Arab and Muslim male applicants from twenty-five countries: Afghanistan, Algeria, Bahrain, Djibouti, Egypt, Eritrea, Indonesia, Iran, Iraq, Jordan, Kuwait, Lebanon, Libya, Malaysia, Morocco, Oman, Pakistan, Qatar, Saudi Arabia, Somalia, Sudan, Syria, Tunisia, the United Arab Emirates, and Yemen.

But even as the security measures were being introduced, American diplomats in Saudi Arabia rushed to assure Middle Eastern tourists that visa eligibility criteria had not changed. The State Department stressed that a supplemental application form for young Arab and Muslim males aged sixteen to forty-five was temporary. And despite the fact that fifteen of the nineteen September 11 hijackers obtained their visas in Saudi Arabia, and three of them skipped the usual interview process through the Visa Express program[42] so prevalent there, the program remained in place nine months after the attacks.[43]

If the next Mohamed Atta can't get the overseas visa-vending machine to work by legal means, foreign-born officers working in American consulates are ripe targets for bribery. United States consular officer Arcelia Betansis, a Mexican-born, naturalized American citizen stationed in Juarez, Mexico, was convicted in April 2002 for accepting bribes and gratuities in return for expediting visa approvals for 497 people, including drug traffickers.[44] Yemeni national Abdullah Noman, who was arrested in October 2001 and pled guilty in May 2002, used his position as a United States consular officer in Saudi Arabia to sell false visas to hundreds of illegal immigrants from the Middle East. Federal authorities have no idea where these immigrants are.

Said Assistant United States Attorney Lee Vilker: "Once they slip into the country, it's almost impossible to track them down."[45] In July, the State Department disclosed that federal authorities were seeking twenty-nine aliens suspected of bribing U.S. embassy workers in Qatar for visas. The scheme allegedly involved a total of seventy-one Middle East nationals and at least two U.S. embassy workers (one a Jordanian national, the other a U.S. citizen). Also among the alleged participants: two bogus visa-holders who reportedly lived with the September 11 hijackers the summer before the attacks.[46]

A Heinz 57 variety of visas

> Attention terrorists: Are you having a hard time getting into England? How about France? Or even Canada? Tired of being turned down for a visa? Why not try the United States of America, where our motto is: "No visa, no problem"? We have already given out thousands of visas to people who can't get admitted to other countries. Terrorists like you. And you. So what are you waiting for? Yes. Whether you're a suicide bomber, a shoe bomber, or even the big man himself—you can't be denied. U.S. visas: Everywhere you terrorists want to be.[47]

That was how comedian Jay Leno spoofed America's lax entrance policies earlier this spring. He and his sketch-writers are closer to the truth than they could possibly imagine. We peddle visas and green cards (for permanent legal residents) like used cars: cheap, quick, and sleazy. In 2000, 10 million visitors arrived on short-term tourist visas, while another 2.5 million traveled here on business visas, and millions more obtained longer-term visas and green cards.[48]

In April 2002, the INS proposed eliminating the minimum six-month stay guaranteed to tourists with B-1 business and B-2 pleasure visas (which eighteen of the nineteen September 11 hijackers had legally obtained to gain initial entry into America). But as Cleveland immigration lawyer Jeffrey Moeller asks: "Whether you give them thirty days or six months, who cares? Once they've crossed the border they have the capacity to disappear."[49]

With a total of fifty-seven categories of immigrant and non-immigrant visas—many of which are for sale to the highest foreign bidder—bin Laden–funded terrorists have myriad paths to choose from. Here are just a few:

Buy a high-tech ticket

Data from the United States Department of Labor reveals that four Muslim charities under federal investigation for ties to terrorism applied for high-tech, or H-1B visas, on behalf of at least sixteen workers over the past few years.[50] Three of the charities—the Global Relief Foundation of Bridgeview, Illinois, the Holy Land Foundation for Relief and Development in Richardson, Texas, and the Benevolence International Foundation of Palos Heights, Illinois—had their assets frozen by the Treasury Department after the September 11 attacks. The fourth, Islamic Relief Worldwide in Burbank, California, accepted $50,000 from an alleged bin Laden front group at its British office, according to Treasury officials.[51]

The H-1B program grants nonimmigrant visas to nearly 200,000 "temporary" foreign workers every year to fill high-tech positions. The cost to applicants is $1,000 per visa, which allows a foreigner to stay in the United States for up to six years—and later apply for permanent residency. Applicants are required to have at least a bachelor's degree in a field related to their proposed employment. This foreign employment program, launched in 1992, has quickly evolved into another all-purpose visa giveaway. Fashion models, artists, and "essential support personnel" for foreign entertainers or athletes are among the "highly skilled" workers eligible for H-1B status.[52]

Leaving aside the questionable rationale for such a large for-
eign-worker program at a time when the technology industry is
undergoing layoffs,[53] H-1B fraud is out of control and poses a
substantial national security threat in the War on Terror. The
GAO found that the INS had no reliable system for tracking
H-1B applications. As a result, immigration officials exceeded
the legal cap on H-1B visas by untold thousands.

INS employees told the GAO that "because of pressure to
adjudicate cases quickly, they did not routinely use investigations staff to look into potentially fraudulent applications
because doing so would take more time and reduce the number
of applications they could complete."[54] In addition, H-1B workers from China were recently charged with conspiring to steal
sensitive technology from American companies and selling it to
firms in their native land.[55]

The Bush administration has no plans to bar H-1B applicants from terrorist-friendly nations, or otherwise to curtail the
program.

Diversity lottery: Play to win
Thanks to Massachusetts senator Ted Kennedy, tens of thousands of foreigners can gamble for a shot at one of America's
highly coveted permanent resident immigrant visas ("green
cards") every year. Senator Kennedy essentially championed the
visa lottery as a way for Irish illegal immigrants to gain amnesty.[56] But it has become yet another way for individuals from
al Qaeda–friendly nations to get their foot in the door.

During the past five years, 7,409 lottery visas were awarded
to applicants from Iraq, Iran, Syria, Libya, Sudan, and Afghanistan.[57] In June 2002, the State Department announced that in
the most recent lottery, terrorist-friendly Saudi Arabia and
Egypt drew 38 and 1,551 lucky winners respectively; al Qaeda

stronghold Yemen had 44 diversity lottery recipients. Afghanistan claimed 45 winners; official state sponsors of terrorism Iraq, Iran, Sudan, Libya, and Syria clinched a total of 2,259 lottery winners.[58]

Egyptian immigrant Hesham Mohamed Hadayet underscores the danger of blindly granting visa lottery tickets to foreigners from America-hating regions of the world. On July 4, 2002, Hadayet shot two people to death and wounded three others at the El Al Israel Airlines ticket counter at Los Angeles International Airport. How did he get here and stay here? He entered legally in July 1992 on a six-month visa. After overstaying, he filed for permanent residency, but was denied in 1996 for reasons that the INS says are "unclear." The INS began deportation procedures, but in 1997 the gunman won permanent residency status through his wife—one of the thousands of lucky winners from the Middle East who obtained a visa through the Diversity Lottery program.[59]

The next Visa Lottery drawing is scheduled for fall 2002. A spokeswoman told me the State Department's Bureau of Consular Affairs has no plans to bar entrants from terrorist-sponsoring nations.[60] Good luck, Mohamed.

The so-called "Diversity Visa Lottery," part of the 1990 Immigration Act, is conducted by the State Department and allots up to 55,000 such visas to individuals from mostly non-Western countries around the world, including Iraq, Iran, Syria, Libya, and Sudan, and other terrorist havens across Africa and Asia.

There is no application fee or special application form. The only eligibility rules are a clean criminal record, a clean bill of health, and a high school diploma/equivalent or two years of work experience. Illegal immigrants in the United States are eligible. Winners can apply for residency for family members. Despite photo and signature requirements, fraud is rampant.

Study with the enemy

September 11 terrorist Hani Hanjour and 1993 World Trade Center bomber Eyad Ismoil entered America legally with F-1 student visas, then dropped out of sight after failing to enroll or complete their required coursework. Among the more than one million foreigners who now hold student visas in the United States, how many others are sleeper terrorists who have slipped through the cracks and disappeared?

In May 2002, federal prosecutors cracked down on a separate student visa fraud ring involving 130 foreigners accused of paying substitutes to take English-language proficiency exams to meet their visa requirements. Nearly sixty Middle Eastern men and women in thirteen states were arrested. One of the suspects had flight manuals, photos of people outside the World Trade Center, and a date book with only one entry: September 11. Another suspect also had apparent flight training materials in his car.[61] Yet another alleged bogus test-taker linked to the ring, Saudi national Saleh Ali Almari, came here on a student visa and enrolled at Marymount University in Arlington, Virginia, in the fall of 2000, but did not take classes.[62]

Between 1989 and 1995, nearly one hundred Middle Easterners paid bribes to community college teachers and administrators in San Diego—the home base for at least two of the September 11 terrorists—in exchange for counterfeit admission papers and grades, which allowed them to get student visas. The mastermind of the scheme, Iranian-American businessman Sam Koutchesfahani, pled guilty to visa fraud in 1998, along with officials from six colleges. But the whereabouts of his "students," who poured a total of $350,000 into the plot, remain frighteningly unknown.[63]

Elite U.S. colleges and universities continue to help train students from America's most hostile enemy countries. Iran, Iraq,

Libya, Syria, and Sudan—all listed by the State Department as state sponsors of terrorism—sent nearly ten thousand students to the United States on academic visas between 1991 and 1996.

Many of these students enrolled in programs that could be used to build biological, chemical, and nuclear weapons.[64] Not until May 2002 did the federal government announce plans to intensify screening of foreign student visa applicants seeking to study nuclear and missile technology, aircraft propulsion, information security, and marine technology.[65] In addition to these thousands of students from official state sponsors of terrorism, al Qaeda–friendly countries send thousands more. In the 2000–2001 school year, Saudi Arabia sent more than 5,000 students; Mohamed Atta's native Egypt sent nearly 2,300.[66]

The lack of a comprehensive, mandatory tracking system to ensure that foreign students show up at their designated schools and leave after graduation makes the F-1 program a wide portal for terrorists. To this day, the government has no idea how many of the one million foreigners admitted into America on student visas are actually going to school in compliance with their visas.

In May 2002, INS commissioner James Ziglar and Attorney General John Ashcroft trumpeted the launch of a new Internet-based foreign student tracking system scheduled to be implemented in July 2002. But participation in the system by more than seventy thousand American schools—many of whose leaders oppose the tracking system as an administrative nuisance—will be *voluntary*.[67] The INS is hoping for full mandatory participation by the end of January 2003. But just a few weeks after the ambitious announcement by Ziglar and Ashcroft, the Justice Department's Inspector General raised "serious concerns about the INS's ability to fully implement" the system on time.[68]

Two wings and a prayer

As with every other major visa category, terrorists and other individuals with ties to terrorism have slipped through the religious worker visa program. Among those in the United States with religious-based visas: 1993 World Trade Center bombing mastermind Sheik Omar Abdul Rahman, and four Palestinian men who worked for the Holy Land Foundation for Relief and Development and the Islamic Association for Palestine — both Muslim charities that have been tied by the State Department to the terrorist organization Hamas.[69]

The religious worker visa program allows thousands of foreigners to fly to America to fill domestic shortages among ministries, nunneries, and other religious professionals. In 1998, some eleven thousand foreigners received these "R" visas. In 2000, the GAO highlighted persistent lapses in policing applications for fraud during the past decade. "Neither INS nor [the] State [Department] knows the overall extent of fraud in the religious worker visa program," the GAO reported.[70] Federal investigators discovered fraud rings involving churches and other religious institutions based in Colombia, Fiji, and Russia.[71]

There are no plans to prevent the R visa program from being used in the future as a Radical Muslim Cleric Immigration plan.

Cashing in

Foreigners from some al Qaeda–friendly countries (including Egypt and Pakistan) can enter the U.S. if they fork over a $150,000 investment and agree to manage U.S.-based businesses. Well-funded terrorists would be wise to choose this visa option. These E-2 "investor treaty" visas take as little as two days to process and can be renewed indefinitely. Investors can bring their spouses, children, and key employees with them.

In March 2002, an INS internal memo noted that $300 million was transferred into the United States illegally under another investor program, and that "open questions remain as to the background of the vast majority of the alien beneficiaries of this program."[72] This EB-5 immigrant investor visa law allows up to ten thousand wealthy foreigners and their families each year to buy immigrant visas in exchange for business investments. The law says the down payment must be at least $500,000.

But former INS officials-turned-private-consultants—such as former INS general counsel Paul Virtue—successfully lobbied for loosened financial rules.[73] Supposedly, the EB-5 program uses the promise of citizenship to attract substantial overseas investment to aid struggling American businesses.

But the benefits of this economic development plan have gone mostly to former immigration officials, who formed lucrative limited partnerships to cash in on their access. Immigrant investors paid token fees to these partnerships. The partnerships secured promissory notes for the remainder of the foreign investments, which were forgiven after investors received their permanent green cards. Former INS employees, working for these partnerships, aggressively lobbied their old colleagues to accept the dubious financial arrangements. As a result, aliens were paying a fraction of the required minimum investment, and almost all of the monies went to the general partners and the companies who set up the limited partners. A *Baltimore Sun* investigation found "only a tiny fraction of the money ever made it to the companies seeking assistance."[74]

Worse, the INS admitted in a report to Congress that it "is unable to quantify the incidence of fraudulent activity in the EB-5 program."[75]

Despite recent reforms, the scam continues around the world. The program is well known in the Middle East. Here is what one immigration firm, Acker Choquette Advocates, based in Dubai, United Arab Emirates, promises immigrant investor applicants on its Web site: "Financing is available, with low initial cash investment of US $136,000.00. Minimum physical presence in the US is all that is required, along with the intent to remain a permanent resident."[76]

No visa necessary

Jay Leno was joking, but it's the truth: American visas are everywhere terrorists want to be. For those terrorists who can't get a visa, though, there's still no need to despair. You can leave home without it and still fly into our country legally.

Travel without a visa

The "Transit Without a Visa" program was created in 1952 to help with the resettlement of World War II refugees, most of whom had no identity or travel documents to obtain visas. But half a century after its inception, this obsolete humanitarian program has morphed into a lucrative marketing gimmick for the travel industry. The program waives visa requirements for passengers who are ostensibly passing briefly through the United States on their way to final destinations abroad. During the past three years, more than 5 million airline passengers— accounting for roughly 5 percent of all foreign nationals entering the country through airports—were routed here under the Transit Without a Visa program.[77]

Airlines are responsible for guarding and escorting passengers in transit, and are supposedly liable for damages when they cannot confirm that program participants have actually departed the country. But since the INS does not keep arrival and departure records on a majority of these passengers, the airlines are unaccountable.[78]

In fact, FBI and INS agents suspect that private guards hired by major airlines at Los Angeles International Airport smuggled visa-less Middle Eastern passengers elsewhere into the United States as part of organized rings.[79] In June 2002, a federal immigration inspector and two private airport security guards were arrested and indicted by a federal grand jury for allegedly taking part in an alien-smuggling conspiracy that allowed travelers transiting from the Philippines (where al Qaeda has spread) to slip out of Los Angeles International Airport without visas.[80]

A report by the Justice Department Inspector General after the September 11 attacks warned of continuing lapses in the transit program and concluded that the agency "must take immediate action... to enhance national security."[81] But representatives of the transportation industry argued that terminating the program would be "inconvenient to the traveler" and would result in a loss of business for the airlines.[82] As of July 2002, no action had been taken to curtail the Transit Without a Visa program.

Visa Waiver program

Another 17 million visitors to the United States didn't need to bother with visas last year. Pushed vigorously by the hurry-up-and-move-'em-through lobby (the airline, travel, and tourism industries), the Visa Waiver program allows tourists from twenty-eight countries to come to the United States for tourism or business for ninety days or less without obtaining the key entry document used to screen out foreign threats.

To "facilitate low-risk travel" to the United States, foreign participants in the program need only bring valid passports. Before the ninety-day time period is up, many travelers simply apply for an extension of their stays—or illegally overstay—then settle in comfortably for permanent visits. As with every other "low-risk" visa program created to ease entry into the country, fraud is rampant and largely unchecked. Some 100,000 passports issued by Visa Waiver countries have been stolen in recent years.[83] Belgium has more lost or stolen passports than any other Visa Waiver program participant but has retained its eligibility.[84]

Worse, federal investigators found that even after September 11, INS inspectors at four international airports—Miami, Dulles–Washington, D.C., Honolulu, and John F. Kennedy in New York City—were failing to check for stolen and fraudulent passports; they were also failing to check visa-less passengers' names on terrorist watch lists.[85]

So, America-haters abroad: Just follow in the footsteps of suspected al Qaeda members Zacarias ("20th hijacker") Moussaoui and Richard (the Shoe Bomber) Reid, and get yourself a passport from France or the United Kingdom. Or one of the other twenty-eight approved nations: Japan, Germany, Italy, Netherlands, Australia, Spain, Switzerland, Ireland, Sweden, Belgium, Austria, New Zealand, Denmark, Norway, Finland, Iceland, Slovenia, Luxembourg, Portugal, Singapore, Uruguay, Liechtenstein, Monaco, Andorra, Brunei, and San Marino.[86]

That's the ticket.

———————————

Remember the spiritual exhortation that the terrorist hijackers were instructed to recite before their deadly mission: "Oh God, you who open all doors, please open all doors for me, open all venues for me, open all avenues for me."

One year after the September 11 attacks, Mohamed's prayer is still being answered. From our consular offices to our airports, seaports, and land borders, and from our visa policies to our asylum policies to our naturalization policies and deportation policies, every front, back, and side door to America has been left swinging in the wind. Our government remains ill-equipped, incapable, and unwilling to keep out, track down, and remove foreign law-breakers. We remain paralyzed by political correctness, greed, and schizophrenia about enforcing our immigration rules.

Before the next Mohamed traipses through the door and leads more hordes of America-haters on another mission of death and destruction, we must decide once and for all:

— Will we stop putting tourism dollars over national security?

— Will we stop putting diplomatic interests over national security?

— Will we stop putting customer service over national security?

— Will we stop putting ethnic votes over national security?

— Will we stop putting alien rights over national security?

Only when we put national security first can we defeat the Mohamed Attas of the world.

Chapter 2

Pandering While Osama Plots

"Every last one of the September 11 hijackers entered the country legally with visas.... This means that... the assumption that lax border enforcement toppled the twin towers is inaccurate, and that the government's recent efforts to tighten the screws on foreigners without evidence of terrorist involvement may be pointless. It should come as no surprise that immigrants—especially those with dubious legal standing—quickly became the scapegoats of the September 11 attacks."[1]

—**Dallas Morning News** columnist Ruben Navarrette, November 29, 2001

Those who oppose post–September 11 efforts to crack down on illegal immigration perpetuate a perilous myth. They believe we can continue to ignore "good" illegal immigrants streaming across the borders (e.g., Mexican workers) without compromising our ability to screen out the "bad" illegal immigrants (e.g., Middle Eastern terrorists).

Navarrette and others echoing his views must take off their blinders and look far beyond the visa status of the nineteen hijackers. They ignore the fact that illegal alien day laborers hanging out in front of convenience stores and government offices helped at least seven of the hijackers—Hani Hanjour, Khalid

29

Almihdhar, Majed Moqed, Salem Alhazmi, Ziad Jarrah, Abdulaziz Alomari, and Ahmed Saleh Alghamdi—obtain fraudulent state photo identification in Virginia.

Navarrette and his allies ignore the simple truth that high tolerance for illegal immigration helps foreign conspirators blend in and carry out their plans. And they ignore this obvious reality: We can't win the War on Terror by focusing solely on the narrow circumstances of one infamous day.

Mohamed Atta's predecessors have stormed America through every available open door: front, side, and back. According to a May 2002 study by the Center for Immigration Studies, of forty-eight Islamic militants involved in terrorist conspiracies in America during the past decade, only one-third were here legally on temporary visas as students, tourists, or business travelers—as most of the September 11 hijackers were when they committed their terrorist acts.

Another seventeen were lawful permanent residents or naturalized American citizens. And the rest?

One-fourth were illegal aliens who overstayed their visas, snuck across the border, arrived as stowaways on ships, or entered the country using false passports. Still others applied for political asylum or were granted amnesty after illegal stays (see Appendix A). In all, twenty-one of the forty-eight Islamist terrorists violated our immigration laws at some point in the last ten years.

Illegal aliens, the center's research director Steve Camarota noted, "have taken part in almost every major attack on American soil perpetrated by Islamist terrorists, including the first attack on the World Trade Center, the Millennium plot, the plot to bomb the New York subway, and the attacks of 9/11."[2]

Yet, one year into our War on Terror, politicians in both major parties continue to pander to the forces of political correctness at the expense of national security. Democrat and Republican strategists in Washington are consumed by the desire to court ethnic blocs, most of which advocate a soft-on-crime approach to illegal immigration. In a bipartisan show of politically correct pandering, President George W. Bush joined Democratic Senate Majority Leader Tom Daschle in pushing for a mini-amnesty program for illegal border-crossers and visa-overstayers—mostly from Mexico—who refuse to return to their own countries for background checks while applying for permanent legal residence.

It is one thing for Mexican officials to downplay the criminal nature of their country's illegal immigrants to the U.S., as President Vicente Fox often does. But when our own immigration authorities echo that line, it is an alarming dereliction of duty. Just one day after the September 11 terrorist attacks, Atlanta's INS deputy district director Fred Alexander was quoted reassuring "undocumented" day laborers who plan to build a shelter in Marietta, Georgia: "It's not a crime to be in the U.S. illegally. It's a violation of civil law."[3]

Not only is illegal entry into this country a criminal misdemeanor subject to fines and imprisonment and punishable as a felony after repeat violations, it is also a federal felony to recruit, hire, harbor, and encourage illegal aliens.[4] (See Appendix B.)

Yet, in May 2002, INS commissioner James Ziglar echoed Alexander's lax attitude. He assured the Mexican government that America would continue to allow millions of Mexicans to break our laws: "No one likes the idea that people came into the country illegally, but it's not practical or reasonable to think that you're going to be able to round them all up and send them home," Ziglar said during a joint press conference with Mexican officials at the Tucson, Arizona, Border Patrol station.[5]

Meanwhile, labor, ethnic, and religious groups are demanding a broad amnesty law that would formally legalize all 9 to

11 million illegal aliens currently residing in the country. They launched a nationwide mail-in campaign in May 2002 that will climax just before the November 2002 elections, when organizers will dump mountains of pro-amnesty postcards on the White House and Congress.

And in almost every state in the union, ethnic activists continue to lobby for a host of public accommodations for illegal immigrants, including driver's licenses, banking privileges, college tuition breaks, protection from police action, health care, and even American taxpayer–subsidized water stations to ease their illegal journeys across our borders.

Politicians of both major parties lack the will to tell them "no" and risk losing a few votes.

Illegals Helping Terrorists

A month before the September 11 attacks, hijackers Hani Hanjour and Khalid Almihdhar hopped into a van and headed to the parking lot of a 7-Eleven store in Falls Church, Virginia. That's where scores of Hispanic day laborers—the kind that immigration advocacy groups refer to euphemistically as "undocumented"—hang around looking for work. Like moths to a light, the al Qaeda operatives flocked to these alien outlaws for unwitting assistance in their murderous plot.

When Hanjour and Almihdhar pulled into the 7-Eleven lot in August 2001, they weren't scouting for someone to move furniture or mow lawns. They were looking for a different service, widely known to be available from illegal immigrant day laborers in the area. They wanted quick and easy help in fraudulently obtaining Virginia state photo identification cards, which they presumably used to board American Airlines Flight 77 at Washington Dulles International Airport the next month.

The first two laborers they encountered declined to participate in their scheme. But Hanjour and Almihdhar didn't have to wait too long. Luis Martinez-Flores, an illegal alien from El Salvador who had been in this country undetected since 1994, approached the van and agreed to help, according to court records.[6]

Martinez-Flores accompanied the terrorist pair to a nearby Department of Motor Vehicles office. At the time, Virginia had an extraordinarily lax policy for issuing IDs and drivers' licenses. No proof of residence was necessary if a Virginia resident signed residency certification forms or notarized affidavits vouching for the applicant. Martinez-Flores supplied the terrorists with fake addresses for their residency forms (using one of his old addresses) and falsely certified that the pair lived there. He stayed with them while the forms were processed and approved. After receiving their ID cards, Hanjour and Almihdhar drove Martinez-Flores back to the 7-Eleven, withdrew $100 from the store's ATM, and gave him the cash.[7]

Armed with their new fraudulent ID cards establishing them as Virginia residents, Hanjour and Almihdhar went back to the DMV the very next day and helped obtain state IDs for two of their terrorist conspirators, Majed Moqed and Salem Alhazmi, who would later accompany them on the fatal flight into the Pentagon. Hanjour and Almihdhar used the same bogus address Martinez-Flores had lent them; the applications were approved promptly. Hanjour returned to the DMV a third time and again used Martinez-Flores's address to help hijacker Ziad Jarrah successfully obtain a Virginia ID.[8] The FBI believes Jarrah was at the controls of United Airlines Flight 93 when it crashed into a field near Shanksville, Pennsylvania.

Fellow hijackers Abdulaziz Alomari and Ahmed Saleh Alghamdi also enlisted illegal aliens to gain fraudulent Virginia state IDs. They drove a van to the parking lot of a DMV office in Arlington, Virginia, and started approaching Hispanic men for assistance with residency forms. Victor Lopez-Flores, an illegal alien from El Salvador, and Herbert Villalobos, a legal permanent resident from El Salvador, agreed to help the terrorists. They all rode together to the office of a local attorney whose secretary, Kenys Galicia, notarized identity and residency forms falsely stating that Alomari and Alghamdi lived in Virginia. Villalobos and Lopez-Flores accompanied the terrorists back to the DMV office, which approved and issued ID cards. Alomari and Alghamdi paid Villalobos $50. Lopez-Flores received $80. Galicia, who had notarized fraudulent forms for illegal aliens for at least one year before encountering Alomari and Alghamdi, received $35, court records indicate.[9]

On September 21, 2001, ten days after the terrorist attacks, the Virginia DMV announced that it would no longer accept residency certification forms as proof of residency.[10] Federal investigators later learned that the majority of hijackers owned driver's licenses or state photo ID cards from other states as well. Thirteen of the nineteen had Florida licenses or IDs; a few held licenses or cards from more than one state, including California, Arizona, and Maryland; and some received duplicate cards from the same state within months of September.[11]

In the wake of September 11, Americans across the country supported measures to prevent identification and drivers' license fraud by illegal immigrants. But they were met with fierce resistance from Hispanic advocacy groups who immediately attacked these efforts as putting an undue burden on the driving "rights" and safety of illegal immigrants. Ignoring the lessons of September 11, many public officials continue to bow to the aliens-first crowd. Incredibly, some state legislatures are following the lead of another state that attracted terrorist suspects because of its lenience toward illegal aliens: Tennessee.

DWI: Driving While Illegal

In April 2001, the Volunteer State rolled out the welcome mat for illegal day laborers, terrorists, and other foreigners seeking state ID cards or driver's licenses. Goaded by local Hispanic interest groups such as Latinos Unidos, League of United Latin American Citizens (LULAC), and the Nashville Hispanic Chamber of Commerce, a bipartisan coalition of Tennessee legislators voted to abolish requirements that driver's license applicants furnish Social Security numbers, and expanded the documents accepted by state license examiners for identification if the applicant was not an American citizen.

While citizens and legal aliens could still be forced to produce Social Security numbers, any "undocumented" applicant could bypass the requirement by signing an affidavit stating that he or she has "never had a Social Security number." Despite the obvious opportunity for fraud and bribery, let alone the corrosive impact of rewarding thousands of law-breaking aliens with driving privileges, Republican governor Don Sundquist signed the bill into law.[12]

"We are very happy," said Israel Arreguin of Latinos Unidos. "It's going to benefit all of us."[13]

A few months later, tens of thousands of out-of-state illegal immigrants swamped the state's motor vehicle agencies. "There were waits of five and six hours," said Dana Keeton, a spokeswoman for the Tennessee Department of Public Safety. The National Guard was even called in to control unruly crowds. Alarmed legislators rushed to amend the law. But the changes, adding a few easily navigated hurdles to establish residency, were nominal. And the illegals kept swarming in from all over the country. After obtaining Tennessee driver's licenses, many easily obtained driver's licenses from other states.[14]

Among those who attempted to take advantage of Tennessee's alien licensing racket were five Middle Easterners from New York City. How did they know about the Volunteer State's policy? Maybe they read the *New York Times*, which trumpeted the new trend in alien document services in Tennessee, North Carolina, and other states on its front page on August 1, 2001: "In U.S. Illegally, Immigrants Get License to Drive."[15] Just a few weeks after the story appeared, Abdelmuhsen Mahmid Hammad traveled to Memphis and obtained a fraudulent license with the help of state examiner Katherine Smith and her "friend" and middleman, Khaled Odtllah. Hammad was in the country illegally with an expired visa.[16]

Authorities say his cousin, Sakhera Hammad, obtained a fraudulent Tennessee license in October 2001. Four months later, Abdelmuhsen Mahmid Hammad drove back to Memphis with a carful of Middle Eastern immigrants seeking licenses from Smith. One, who held a Venezuelan passport, had illegally crossed the border from Mexico into California. Another was an illegal alien from Egypt. Federal investigators, tipped off by a New York FBI agent, arrested the entire group. Authorities said there were possible connections between two of the license scammers and the September 11 hijackers. A World Trade Center repair pass, giving access to six underground levels in one of the towers, was found in Sakhera Hammad's possession. It was dated September 5.[17] All five of the men pled guilty to charges of fraud, but denied ties to terrorism. Odtllah was released in late June 2002; three of his acquaintances remained in custody pending deportation.

Did Smith know something more about these shady characters? Were these aliens planning to use their Tennessee IDs to board flying bombs, too? We'll never know. Smith died on February 10, 2002, in a suspicious car crash inferno—deemed intentional arson by the FBI—the day before she was to appear at a detention hearing. Investigators found gasoline on her clothes; witnesses said there was only slight damage to the car.[18] "This was not a traffic fatality," Tennessee Highway Patrol Captain Jimmy Erwin concluded.[19]

Yet another dead body, another dead American, warning us to close terrorist-friendly loopholes in our immigration policy.

Some states have since moved to tighten residency requirements and documentation requirements for noncitizens.[20] One of these states was Florida, where Mohamed Atta gained a license simply by showing his Egyptian driver's license—and where visa holders could obtain licenses that were valid even after their visas had expired.[21] In the wake of September 11, Florida, Arizona, and New Jersey all passed legislation to coordinate driver's licenses to expire with immigration visas. Minnesota also moved to adopt similar rules. Pennsylvania dropped foreign birth certificates and non–United States driver's licenses as acceptable forms of proof of identity.

But elsewhere, politicians refused to listen. Two states—Utah and North Carolina—continue to allow applicants to prove their identity using a taxpayer identification number (TIN) rather than a Social Security number. (The feds have offered TINs to anyone who cannot get a Social Security number—namely, illegal aliens—since 1996.) As a result, North Carolina has issued nearly 400,000 licenses to drivers with no valid Social Security number, including an unknown number of illegal aliens, who were instead assigned a bogus 999-99-9999 identifier.[22]

"We have no legal authority to question people, we don't have the responsibility or the authority to question if they're in this country legally or illegally," said Judy Hamaker-Mann, director of driver's licenses for Utah, in defense of the policy. "Utah takes the position that we try and get people licensed to make sure they have the skills and the knowledge to drive and make passage safely."[23] Wayne Hurder, director of driver's license certification for North Carolina, echoes that rationalization: "Until somebody stops the flow of illegal immigrants, they're going to be here; they're going to be driving," Hurder said. "We're better off if we provide some incentive for them to get automobile insurance and learn the laws of driving."[24] But the flow won't be stopped until incentives like the ones Hurder and Hamaker-Mann offer are cut off.

In February 2002, New Mexico governor Gary Johnson signed a measure helping aliens from Mexico and other foreign countries obtain driver's licenses in his state. Like Tennessee, Utah, and North Carolina, New Mexico now accepts documents other than Social Security numbers as proof of identification. Although the governor stressed that the law would benefit legal rather than illegal aliens, the fine print of motor vehicle agency regulations specified that one of the alternative documents that the state will now accept from applicants is the *matricula consular*—a Mexican ID card issued primarily to illegal immigrants living in the United States.[25] Mexican consul Juan M. Solana attended the signing celebration at Governor Johnson's side.

In April 2002, the Missouri House of Representatives passed a bill allowing illegal aliens to obtain licenses without providing Social Security numbers.[26] While Virginia reversed its lax residency requirements, Washington State's legislature decided not to force license applicants to prove residency.[27] In Mississippi, a measure died that would have caused all noncitizens' licenses to expire in a year.[28] In California, the Mexican American Legal Defense and Educational Fund sued the state in May 2002 claiming a bill to allow illegal immigrants to obtain driver's licenses inadvertently became law last year and must be implemented by the Department of Motor Vehicles.[29] And political leaders in Tennessee stubbornly defended their pro–illegal alien "reform" under the guise of making the roads safer. Governor Sundquist rejected the notion that states have any responsibility for ensuring that their licensing policies comply with national immigration laws.

"It's the federal government's role to worry about who is a citizen and who is not a citizen," Governor Sundquist sniffed during a meeting of the National Governors Association on homeland security.[30]

Meanwhile, Hispanic advocacy groups criticized efforts to rescind the law. "It just makes me ill," said Dilka Roman, president of Tennessee's League of Latin American Citizens. "I've seen so much good come out of this law, with people getting insurance and learning the rules of the road. It would be a tragedy and a giant step backwards to change it now."[31]

Those who support licensing illegal immigrants cast it as a public safety issue, arguing that illegal aliens are more likely to learn the rules of the road and less likely to flee the scene of an accident if they have a driver's license. One of the lessons of September 11, however, is that licensing illegal aliens *undermines* safety by giving terrorists a ticket to the American mainstream. As Minnesota Public Safety commissioner Charlie Weaver argued: "A driver's license is a gateway to guns, airplanes, pilot schools, checking accounts, and credit cards."[32]

It is a master key, in other words, for foreign terrorists who – like the Mexican day laborers who hang around on street corners near DMVs in states from Virginia to California – have "just come here to work."

Tennessee, Utah, North Carolina, and New Mexico are currently the only states that accept documents other than Social
Security numbers as the principal proof of identity for obtaining driver's licenses. But other states are likely to join them.
Before the terrorist attacks, there were campaigns in fifteen
states to ease illegal aliens' path toward obtaining driver's
licenses. Illegal alien advocates vow to keep up the fight. "There
was a lot of knee-jerk, emotional response" after September 11,
complained Lynda Callon, a supporter of drivers' licenses for
illegal aliens who works with immigrants at the Westside Community Action Network in Kansas City, Missouri. "But this issue
is not going to go away."[33]

Banking on Greed

The nineteen hijackers would not have been able to kill three
thousand Americans without access to their complicated web of
finances. So a few weeks after the September 11 terrorist
attacks, President Bush issued an executive order freezing the
assets of organizations linked to terrorism. Soon after, Bush
signed the USA Patriot Act, which authorized the Treasury secretary to require the banking industry to obtain information
about accounts opened in the United States by noncitizens.

In July 2002, an FBI official disclosed that the September 11
hijackers were able to open thirty-five American bank accounts
without having legitimate Social Security numbers. Some of the
accounts were opened with fabricated Social Security numbers,
never checked by bank officials. "With no scrutiny from the
financial institutions or government regulators, the hijackers
were able to move hundreds of thousands of dollars from the
Middle East into the United States through a maze of bank
accounts beginning more than a year before their attacks," the
New York Times reported.[34]

But at the same time Bush was taking tough steps to crack down on the finances of foreign menaces and tighten identification security, the American banking industry was throwing its vaults wide open to thousands of illegal aliens. And the Internal Revenue Service was making it easier for illegals to do business inside our borders.

In November 2001, California-based financial giant Wells Fargo proudly publicized its plan to loosen identification guidelines for illegal aliens from Mexico who want to open American checking or savings accounts in its branches spread across twenty-three states. Banks usually require foreign customers to show passports or driver's licenses as primary forms of ID, with credit cards and Social Security numbers as backup documents. Now, as a result of heavy lobbying from the Mexican government and Hispanic-American activists, Wells Fargo accepts the *matricula consular* as a primary form of identification.

Any Mexican national living abroad (read: any illegal Mexican immigrant living in the United States) can get the card simply by supplying proof of Mexican citizenship, such as a birth certificate or voting card, and paying a $29 fee. While most Wells Fargo customers must supply Social Security numbers or taxpayer identification numbers in addition to two forms of ID, those who show *matricula consulares* can instead present a signed form from the Internal Revenue Service verifying their foreign residency. The IRS emphasizes that it will not share the information with the INS.

Tony Lew, an INS spokesman in Los Angeles, told the *Los Angeles Times* that the agency has no problem with Wells Fargo's new policy. "Our priorities are to go after illegal immigrants involved in committing crime," he said. "If they are law-abiding citizens, we don't have the resources to go looking for them."[35] Apparently, Lew doesn't understand that *illegal* aliens are, by definition, neither "law-abiding" nor "citizens."

Backed by the feds, bank officials eager to cash in on the huge illegal alien market—and score a few politically correct brownie points—are pulling out all the stops to lower the bar for "undocumented" Mexican customers.

"We welcome you to come to one of our branches where we won't question your legal status," Wells Fargo vice president John Murillo crowed at a Spanish-language news conference.[36] U.S. Bancorp moved quickly to accept Mexican IDs following Wells Fargo's announcement. "Whether someone is legal or illegal is not for us to determine," Alice Perez, Hispanic marketing manager for U.S. Bancorp, told the *Chicago Daily Herald*.[37]

Other financial institutions accepting the Mexican consular cards include Firstar banks, Harris Bank, Union Bank, Metro-Bank, and American branches of the Puerto Rico–based Banco Popular. And in February 2002, Bank of America joined the crowd and opened up shop directly inside a Mexican consular office in Santa Ana, California. The Spanish-language newspaper *La Opinión* estimated that $20 million had been deposited in new bank accounts in just the first three months since the programs began.[38]

The Mexican Foreign Ministry has encouraged its forty-eight consulates in the United States to promote acceptance of the *matricula consular* for broad identification purposes, not just as a means to open bank accounts. Immediately following Wells Fargo's lead were local governments in Arizona, Texas, and California, including Orange County and San Francisco, which now accept the consular cards as identification so that illegal aliens jailed for "minor offenses" such as speeding will not be deported. In May 2002, the Los Angeles City Council voted to accept the Mexican IDs as part of a six-month "pilot program" allowing illegal immigrants there to borrow books from libraries, attend meetings at City Hall, and receive other city benefits available to legal resident taxpayers.[39]

"Eventually, this will be accepted throughout the United States," claims Miguel Angel Isidro-Rodriguez, head of the Mexican Consulate in Santa Ana.[40] And for the banking industry, Mexico is only the first step. Wells Fargo has said it is open to accepting similar cards issued by other governments.[41]

Meanwhile, the IRS encouraged illegal aliens to line up and receive individual taxpayer identification numbers (TINs) — with the explicit promise not to turn them in to immigration authorities. The alternative numbers, which can be obtained with less proof of identity than a Social Security number, allow illegal aliens to pay taxes. That prompted Michele Waslin, a senior immigration policy analyst with the National Council of La Raza, to say that illegals who apply for TINs just "want to follow the law and be good citizens living in the United States."[42]

If that were really the case, of course, they'd turn themselves in for deportation and wait in line back in Mexico before applying for a visa to come into the United States to work and earn money. A more plausible explanation for the demand for TINs is that they are another safe and smooth avenue toward opening bank accounts despite illegal status. No criminal background check is required before applying for a TIN, which many banks now accept as a primary form of ID.

Just more good news for fugitive foreign criminals, al Qaeda operatives, and other terrorists stationed across the globe and in search of hassle-free banking with no questions asked.

School Daze

The discovery that a few of the September 11 hijackers held expired academic visas led, quite rightly, to increased scrutiny of foreign students living in the country illegally. INS investigators discovered how hard it is to find foreign student dropouts in an operation in San Diego in December 2001. As reported in the *Washington Post*, the INS "sought the records of local universities and found about fifty apparent visa violators from countries linked to terrorism. When they went looking for the students, they located only ten, one of whom had his papers in order. Other students weren't home, had moved or transferred."[43]

But as Congress moved to expedite student tracking systems, and law enforcement authorities began arresting visa violators on campuses across the country, state and federal lawmakers continued to push for measures encouraging illegal aliens to enroll at public universities despite their criminal status.

Texas became the first state to give in-state tuition discounts to illegal aliens in June 2001. Juan Hernandez, director of the Mexican government's presidential office, framed the victory as a civil rights milestone for illegal aliens: "In terms of real access for migrants, this is the equivalent of the reforms in the 1960s and 1970s that allowed qualified African-Americans and Mexican-Americans to enter the nation's best universities." Democrat state representative Rick Noriega, the law's author, shrugged off the legislature's responsibility to uphold federal immigration policies: "We as state lawmakers should not be made to be enforcers for a faulty INS system."[44] In New York, the City University of New York had a longstanding policy of granting in-state tuition discounts to illegal aliens. After September 11, administrators came to their senses and revoked the policy. But bipartisan panderers in the state legislature passed a bill in June 2002 allowing undocumented immigrants throughout the state to pay in-state tuition to attend state and city colleges. Republican governor George Pataki promised to sign the proposal, which is retroactive to the 2001–2002 school year.[45]

In California, the campaign to allow illegal aliens to pay in-state tuition at public universities was led by the Mexican

American Legal Defense and Educational Fund (MALDEF). Democrat Governor Gray Davis signed the bipartisan proposal into law in October 2001. MALDEF hailed the measure as "one more step towards the full integration of immigrants into California's social, as well as economic fabric."[46]

Notice that the group omitted a key word in its press release. MALDEF and company's goal isn't the integration of just any immigrants into American life. Their objective—now spreading across the country from North Carolina to Utah to Washington State, and on Capitol Hill—is to openly integrate *illegal* aliens into the mainstream.[47] Like driver's licenses and bank accounts, access to higher education confers legitimacy on individuals whose very presence violates federal law. Moreover, granting illegals in-state tuition rates creates an intolerable inequity that forces out-of-state U.S. citizens and legal permanent residents to pay higher rates than their law-breaking peers. This deferential treatment conflicts with existing federal immigration law, passed in 1996, which expressly forbids granting "postsecondary education benefits" to illegal aliens in one state unless out-of-state citizens are offered the same benefits.[48]

The embrace of illegal alien students comes at a time when terrorist states and groups are using American universities to enhance their ability to build biological, chemical, and nuclear weapons. As Hillary Mann of the Washington Institute for Near East Policy first reported in 1997, United States weapons inspectors in Iraq discovered documents describing an Iraqi government strategy to send its students abroad—mostly to the United States—specifically to study nuclear-related subjects in order to develop Iraq's weapons programs. Among the visa recipients: a key scientist in Iraq's nuclear weapons program who earned a doctorate in nuclear engineering at Michigan State University; three Iranian scientists involved in developing the Iranian nuclear program; and Eyad Ismoil, a Jordanian who studied engineering at Wichita State University in Kansas and participated in the 1993 World Trade Center bombing.[49]

Mann highlighted alarming security lapses in the admissions process involving students from terrorism-supporting nations. Syrian and Sudanese students were "not subject to any special clearance procedures; Iranian undergraduates and graduate students in all disciplines except nuclear physics and related subjects receive only an intermediate security check, not the more extensive background check required for Iranian graduate students in the nuclear field and nearly all Iraqi and Libyan students." In addition, Mann noted, once these students enter the United States "they are not subject to an effective monitoring or tracking procedure, which means that students can declare that they are studying benign subjects such as social sciences and then concentrate on nuclear physics, chemistry, biology, and engineering without anyone in the U.S. government becoming aware of the change."[50]

To respond to these deficiencies, Mann recommended that America tighten its visa-screening procedures to require its most in-depth background check for all students from states that sponsor terrorism, and deny visas to students from such countries seeking to study "dual use" subjects that could contribute to their countries' development of weapons of mass destruction. Second, Mann argued that Washington should prohibit Iran, Sudan, and Syria from transferring funds to finance their students' studies in the United States—a prohibition that already applies to students from Libya. Third, Mann urged the United States to implement quickly and fully INS recommendations for better monitoring and tracking of foreign students once they are in the country.

Some commonsense reforms belatedly addressed these concerns. In May 2002, the Bush administration unveiled its plans to create a panel that will screen foreign graduate students, postdoctoral fellows, and scientists who apply for visas to study sensitive topics uniquely available on American campuses. But the tracking system is still in its infancy. And these policies will have no effect whatsoever on students who enter the country *illegally*. The INS openly acknowledges this fact. When *Newark Star-Ledger* columnist Paul Mulshine asked agency spokesman Russ Bergeron how many illegal aliens are currently attending college in America, he replied: "There's no way of knowing. Even the schools wouldn't know." Mulshine followed up: "So if an illegal immigrant is studying aviation, no one would know?" Bergeron responded: "That's correct. Or molecular biology or nuclear physics."[51]

Unsafe Sanctuaries

On November 19, 2001, New York City mayor-elect Michael Bloomberg reassured Hispanics and other immigrants of his commitment to preserve the Big Apple as a sanctuary for illegal aliens:

> People who are undocumented do not have to worry about city government going to the federal government. We will provide the services, whether they are health care services or education for their children or anything else we can do, irregardless [*sic*] of the federal government rightly trying to make sense out of our immigration policy.... My job as mayor is to make sure we deliver the city services. It is the federal government's job to make sure we get control of our borders and have an appropriate immigration policy.[52]

Such pass-the-buck pronouncements were stunning coming from the new mayor of a city still covered in rubble because foreign terrorists exploited our immigration policies at every turn. But even more shocking is that Bloomberg was simply following in the footsteps of his much-heralded predecessor, Rudy Giuliani, who had gone all the way to the United States Supreme Court to defend regulations that restrict city employees from informing the INS about illegal aliens (except in limited cases).

New York City's sanctuary policy was created by executive order in 1989 under Democrat mayor Ed Koch and upheld by every mayor since. *City Journal*'s Heather Mac Donald points out that despite the order's crime exception, aliens arrested and charged with crimes by city police are rarely turned over to the INS. Moreover, Mac Donald reports: "The estimated 400,000 illegal aliens in the city exist outside any official tracking system— until, that is, they end up in prison, where they make up an astonishing 24 percent of the state's prisoners."[53]

In 1996, Congress enacted immigration and welfare reform laws that forbade local governments from barring employees from cooperating with the INS.[54] That should have effectively ended sanctuary laws in municipalities across the country. It didn't.

Giuliani filed suit against the feds in 1997, but was rebuffed by a federal district court, which ruled that the sanctuary decree amounted to special treatment for illegal aliens. In 1999, a three-judge United States Circuit Appeals Court also rejected the city's arguments and concluded that the restrictions were nothing more than an unlawful effort to flout federal enforcement efforts against illegal aliens. Backed by prominent Hispanic advocacy groups such as the League of United Latin American Citizens (LULAC), Giuliani took the case to the Supreme Court, which rejected his appeal in January 2000. Despite the loss, he vowed to uphold the spirit of sanctuary for foreign law-breakers.

The Twin Towers are gone and Giuliani is no longer mayor, but the city's retrograde policy of safe harbors for potential terrorists still stands.

The 1996 federal reform measures that New York City has defied also gave local governments the ability to request that their law enforcement officers be deputized to act on behalf of the INS and assist in efforts to stem illegal immigration.[55] But the few efforts to use the law before September 11 were beaten back by immigrant advocates' cries of "racism." *Government Executive* magazine reports that in 1998, for example, Ruben Ortega, then the chief of police in Salt Lake City, proposed deputizing his officers so they could arrest illegal immigrants allegedly involved in the drug trade. "But Hispanic groups said Ortega's plan would lead to racial profiling," the magazine noted, "and the Salt Lake City Council defeated the proposal."[56]

In March, the state of Florida resurrected such efforts and announced a plan to work with the feds to deputize and train some thirty-five police officers, sheriff's deputies, and Florida Department of Law Enforcement agents in federal immigration policies and procedures. But instead of welcoming the measure as a way to supplement limited INS resources in the war on terror, spokesmen for the governors of New York, New Jersey, Illinois, and Michigan—all states with large numbers of immigrants—said they were not considering agreements along the Florida model, according to the *New York Times*.[57]

In April, news outlets leaked the contents of a memo drafted by the Justice Department's Office of Legal Counsel, which concluded that states and localities, as "sovereign entities," have the "inherent authority" to enforce immigration laws. The opinion cited a 1984 Tenth Circuit Court of Appeals ruling (*United States v. Salinas-Calderon*) that a state trooper had the "general investigative authority" to explore possible immigration violations.[58]

While Florida, South Carolina, and Virginia greeted the news enthusiastically, the mere possibility of such cooperation among law enforcement organizations caused an uproar among Hispanic activists, civil liberties groups, and politically correct police chiefs. Officials in San Diego and Salt Lake City balked at the potential costs and damage to "community relations." Los Angeles city attorney Rocky Degadillo protested that "immigrants from around the world come to this city to pursue their dreams...those dreams should not be quashed if we are forced to enforce immigration laws at the local level."[59]

Maria Jimenez, a civil rights activist with the American Friends Service Committee in Houston decried the ruling with incredible insensitivity toward the families of the thousands of Americans killed on September 11. "We're again the victim of 9-11," she said. "This is another fallout of that terrible day."[60]

In the wake of September 11, the need for improved cooperation among local, state, and federal authorities in enforcing immigration laws is greater than ever. Yet sanctuary cities across the country continue to declare themselves safe refuges where local government officials will do everything in their power to protect illegal aliens—and thwart INS investigations of foreign threats.

Take San Francisco, which has had a sanctuary policy since Dianne Feinstein was mayor in the 1980s. Anna Brown, an inspector with the San Francisco Police Department's hate crimes unit, told the *San Francisco Examiner* that despite the terrorist attacks, "We do not make inquiries on people's immigration status."[61]

Los Angeles has been a sanctuary for illegals since 1979, when the city police commission issued an order at the city council's behest barring cooperation between local cops and the INS. Known as Special Order 40, the directive also forbade police from questioning anyone they arrest about their immigration status until after criminal charges have been made. As the *Los Angeles Daily News* recounts: "The intention of the special order was to eliminate any fear that illegal aliens might have had about calling police when they needed help, but the effect has been to make L.A. an asylum for illegal aliens, a place where all could come to escape the law."[62]

Longtime anticrime activist Hal Netkin of Van Nuys, California, points out the absurd consequences of the order: "While a police officer may do a complete 'make' on suspects stopped for minor traffic infractions, incredibly, they are not allowed by this LAPD policy to inquire on the immigration status of suspected felons when there is probable cause."[63] Protecting illegals in this manner has only served to undermine public safety for all residents—citizens and noncitizens alike. Illegal alien vendors, day laborers, Mexican gang members, and document counterfeiters walk the streets of L.A. without fear of arrest.

The climate is tailor-made for foreign terrorist cells and fugitive criminal aliens to turn these naïve sanctuaries into living hells.

A Criminal "Adjustment"

On February 2, 2002, Democratic House Majority Leader Dick Gephardt gave a short speech on Hispanic radio stations. He was responding to President Bush's joint address to Congress on the War on Terror. While Gephardt claimed that Democrats "want to work together to improve homeland security and protect our borders," he called in the same breath for Congress to continue rewarding illegal aliens with special protections.

"We need to expand and extend programs like 245(i)," Gephardt said.[64] Senator Edward Kennedy echoed the call for a "meaningful extension" of the 245(i) program. The provision, championed most vocally by Hispanic activists, lets illegal aliens "adjust" their unlawful status and eventually become legal permanent residents without leaving the United States.[65]

It applies not only to illegal aliens who snuck across our border, but also to eight other categories of aliens, including foreign crewmen who illegally jumped ship and aliens who entered the country legally but overstayed visas, violated the terms of their visas, or broke employment rules.[66]

And buried in the fine print of the law is another shocking category of potential beneficiaries: *"Any alien who has engaged, is engaged, or at any time after admission engages in any terrorist activity."*[67] In late March 2002, researchers for the Washington, D.C.–based Federation for American Immigration Reform made an unsettling discovery that underscores the danger of this amnesty program. Among those with pending applications under 245(i) was one of the most prominent detainees taken into custody after September 11, an illegal visa overstayer from Lebanon named Rabih Haddad.

Haddad, who traveled in and out of the country for fourteen years and settled his family in Ann Arbor, Michigan, helped found the Chicago-based Global Relief Foundation. The Muslim charity was shut down by the Bush administration after September 11 because of long-held suspicions of funding terrorist organizations.

The foundation glorifies "martyrdom through jihad," and according to federal prosecutors, maintained contacts with Wadih el Hage, Osama bin Laden's former personal secretary, who was convicted in the 1998 bombings of two American embassies in Africa.[68] Haddad filed his 245(i) request in the last-minute rush of applications last spring—on April 30, 2001, the very last day of eligibility.

Asim Ghafoor, a lawyer and spokesman for the Global Relief Foundation, said that despite government efforts to remove Haddad, his 245(i) request was still pending as of June 2002. "It's the last leg we have to stand on," he told me.[69] In a separate interview, Ghafoor explained that Haddad's lawyers were intimately aware of the 245(i) loophole and the politics that enabled Haddad to apply. "Bush was sucking up to the Hispanic vote," Ghafoor said.[70]

Joining Gephardt and Kennedy, President Bush voiced support for the 245(i) program in a speech to the Hispanic Chamber of Commerce in Washington, D.C.:

> I've told the Congress that I want to make sure that the Mexican citizen here is well respected, and we will. We'll respect people in our country. And one way to do that is to pass 245(i), which will allow for families to be reunited. If you believe in family values, if you understand the worth of family and the importance of family, let's get 245(i) out of the United States Congress and give me a chance to sign it.[71]

This so-called "family values" legislation is nothing more than a law enforcement evasion program—a political pandering tool that undermines the fight against terrorism. Under normal circumstances, a green card applicant in the United States would be required to go back to his home country and submit to criminal background checks at a State Department consular office. Under Section 245(i), however, illegal aliens who are "physically present" in the United States and seeking a visa status change can remain in the country and submit their applications to the INS without having to leave the U.S.[72]

As former American Immigration Lawyers Association president H. Ronald Klasko pointed out in a summary comparing the consular application process with the 245(i) program: "Police certificates from all countries where the foreign national lived for six months or more since age 16 are required in consular cases. They are not required in adjustment of status cases."[73]

Supporters in both parties claim that 245(i) applicants will undergo adequate screening. Fingerprints must be submitted for checks against the FBI's criminal database. But as we will see in Chapters 4, 9, and 10, the INS has a long history of bungling fingerprint checks. Moreover, INS agents will have no access to criminal records in an applicant's home country. And as overwhelmed as some consular offices might be, they are not nearly as backlogged as the INS.

Spouses and children of applicants are also covered under 245(i). All the program requires is that an illegal alien find an employer or family member to sponsor his or her visa petition within a certain time period, and then pay a $1,000 "penalty" fee to the government for the final "adjustment."[74] It is estimated that the program may have taken in $1.4 billion, but the INS has never fully accounted for the fees.[75]

Where does this cash go? Much of it is supposedly deposited in the Justice Department's detention account to pay for incarcerating aliens in INS custody. This gimmick recklessly politicizes appropriations for what should be one of the agency's basic functions. The funding mechanism forces the INS to support the decriminalization of illegal immigration in order to generate revenue.

The 245(i) provision's initial sunset date was 1997; eligibility for the original program ended on January 18, 1998. In the meantime, reforms passed in 1996 attempted to crack down on alien law-breakers. Under the 1996 Illegal Immigration Reform and Immigrant Responsibility Act, illegals who had been in the United States for more than six months faced three- to ten-year bars to reentering if they left the country to obtain visas and attempted to return.[76] Immigration advocacy groups clamored for a restoration of the 245(i) provision to spare illegals from the new law. The National Immigration Forum disseminated sob stories, such as this one, describing individuals who would be aided by the return of Section 245(i):

> Norma entered the U.S. illegally from Mexico. She settled in North Carolina and married a U.S. citizen. They have been married over two years, have a child, are expecting another this fall and have recently purchased a new home for their growing family. Norma and her husband are torn on what to do about her immigration status. As the wife of a citizen, she qualifies for an immigrant visa. However, if she returns to Mexico to obtain her visa, she would be barred from reentering the U.S. for 10 years. Norma does not want to leave her husband, her children, or her home for 10 years. Restoration of 245(i) would allow this family to stay together.[77]

Caving in to intense lobbying efforts from Hispanic interest groups, Congress revived Section 245(i) for a limited period to protect illegal aliens such as Norma from having to face the consequences of their actions. Under the so-called Legal Immigration Family Equity (LIFE) Act amendments enacted in December 2000, the original eligibility cutoff date was extended temporarily to April 30, 2001.[78]

In Washington, however, there is no such thing as temporary. Not even a month after the new cutoff date expired, the House of Representatives adopted a bill to extend the mini-amnesty for yet another four months.

Five days before the terrorist attacks on America, the Senate approved an amended version of the bill — and expanded it to include approximately 200,000 more illegal aliens not previously eligible for the program. The bill would extend until November 30, 2002, the period for illegal aliens to remain in the United States while they apply for permanent residency.

Conservative Republicans led by Representative Tom Tancredo of Colorado, who chairs the House Immigration Reform Caucus, successfully fought efforts to attach the Section 245(i) extension bill to border-security and defense-appropriations legislation. But in 2002, pressure continued to build for restoring the program permanently—pressure not only from Democrats and Hispanic lobbying groups, but also from a Republican White House desperate to attract Hispanic voters in 2004.

Once again, Representative Tancredo and his caucus members fought the bipartisan onslaught. But the Bush-led juggernaut was insurmountable. Despite a barrage of calls from angry constituents, native-born and naturalized alike, the House passed the provision—tucked into the Enhanced Border Security and Visa Entry Reform Act of 2002—by a 275-137 margin, barely (by one vote) meeting a two-thirds vote requirement. Ninety-two Republicans voted for the bill; 123 opposed it. Twenty-two members skipped the vote.

It took Democratic senator Robert Byrd of West Virginia to state the obvious: "It is lunacy—sheer lunacy—that the president would request, and the House would pass, such an amnesty at this time. That point seems obvious to the American people, if not to the administration."[79] He helped strip the 245(i) provision from the Senate version of the border security bill.

In May 2002, President Bush signed the Enhanced Border Security and Visa Entry Reform Act without the 245(i) provision attached. But he vowed "to work with Congress" to pass it separately. Demonstrating either woeful ignorance or strategic deception, Bush asserted that extending the 245(i) amnesty will "help us meet the goals of legitimate commerce and important travel. And at the same time, it'll help us keep the country secure."[80] Soon after, Senate Majority Leader Daschle introduced a 245(i) bill that would extend the application deadline another two years—and only close the terrorist amnesty loophole for those applying after April 30, 2001.[81]

This is more than sheer lunacy. It's "bipartisan" politics at its most treacherous.

The Mother of All Amnesties

Not satisfied with the de facto amnesty that the Section 245(i) plan provides, illegal alien advocates continue to clamor for an all-out, open amnesty program for the rest of the estimated 9 to 11 million illegal aliens in the United States. Politicians in both parties are leading them on.

Just weeks after September 11, Gephardt, Senate Majority Leader Tom Daschle, Secretary of State Colin Powell, and INS commissioner James Ziglar rushed to assure Mexico about their bipartisan desire to "regularize" illegal aliens. In May 2002, labor, religious, and ethnic advocacy groups launched a mailing campaign in support of a general illegal alien amnesty. The campaign is dubbed "a million voices for legalization." Its organizers plan to dump mounds of postcards on the White House and Congress before the November elections.[82]

The last time Washington granted mass amnesty—as part of the 1986 Immigration Reform and Control Act—supporters promised that it would stem the future flow of illegal aliens. The 1986 act created two separate amnesty programs, a general program and a targeted agricultural program. But as INS analysts who studied immigration patterns from 1987 to 1997 discovered, rewarding illegal behavior only resulted in more illegal behavior.[83]

By 1997, each of the 2.7 million illegal aliens who had been amnestied had been replaced by a new illegal alien. These figures understate the total effect of the amnesty, because they don't count the relatives of the "regularized" aliens who later joined their family members.

Among those who benefited from the 1986 act was convicted World Trade Center bomber Mahmud Abouhalima, who arrived in the United States with his wife from Germany on a tourist visa in 1985. He stayed in the country after it expired. Instead of being tracked down and deported, he was rewarded with legal permanent residence after the 1986 amnesty became law. He obtained his green card in 1988 and spent the next five years in Brooklyn, driving a taxi, preaching Islamic extremism, training secretly for jihad, and plotting the 1993 bombing of the World Trade Center.

As *Time* magazine reported, Abouhalima claimed he worked for seven months on a farm in South Carolina:

"But his wife told a *Time* reporter that she can remember no travels outside the New York metropolitan area except for one trip to Michigan to visit friends. 'The amnesty program was a joke,' says Duke Austin, a spokesman at the Immigration and Naturalization Service. 'Since documentation wasn't required, the burden was on the government to prove the aliens were not farmers. Fraud was widespread and enforcement virtually impossible.' "[84]

Anti-amnesty watchdogs told the *Dallas Morning News* that the program "was so riddled with fraud that even applicants who didn't know that strawberries don't grow on trees qualified." Phil Martin, an expert on agriculture economics at the University of California at Davis, went further. "It was the biggest immigration fraud ever in the United States," he said.[85]

Blanket amnesty legitimizes illegal immigration by absorbing and absolving millions of law-breakers with no questions asked. The implications for the war on terrorism are obvious. Amnesty would not only reward those who "work hard" and "pose no threat," but would also incorporate into our country's mainstream tens of thousands of illegal aliens from terrorism-sponsoring countries in the Middle East and elsewhere. Al Qaeda couldn't ask for a nicer gift.

Bordering on Insanity

In late May 2002, INS chief James Ziglar unveiled a new border safety initiative: pepperballs.

That's right. To assist overwhelmed Border Patrol agents dealing with some of the most sophisticated immigration law-breakers from around the world, Ziglar is equipping them with what the Associated Press described as "plastic containers filled with debilitating pepper."[86]

If you don't feel safer, you're not supposed to. The new initiative, which also includes building light towers and sending horses and hovercraft down to remote areas on the southern border, isn't intended to improve our safety. It's for the safety and reassurance of illegal aliens who fear drowning, getting lost, or getting shot while entering America in violation of our immigration laws.

The same week Ziglar announced the plan, as if to underscore its naïveté and sheer lunacy, federal agents arrested two Egyptian nationals for allegedly trying to smuggle illegal Middle Eastern immigrants into New Jersey by way of Mexico. For a fee of $8,000, court documents say, the suspected smuggling ring flew customers on tourist visas to Brazil, then sent them to

Guatemala, through Mexico, and finally across the southwest border into America.[87]

Another international crime ring, led by Iraqi native George Tajirian, guided aliens from all over the world into the United States—usually across the Rio Grande or through El Paso, Texas, checkpoints—and arranged transportation and lodging for them once inside.[88]

According to federal prosecutors, Tajirian charged up to $15,000 a head—chump change for deep-pocketed terrorist enterprises. During Tajirian's trial, which resulted in a thirteen-year prison sentence, prosecutors introduced evidence that Tajirian was responsible for smuggling individuals with known ties to subversive or terrorist organizations as well as individuals with known criminal histories. All told, law enforcement officials believe Tajirian may have smuggled more than one thousand Middle Eastern aliens across the southwest frontier.

These are just two rings, operating over just a few years, that were caught. Odds are, thousands more Middle Easterners have illegally crossed undetected. And it's important to note that the Middle East has no monopoly on terrorists. Latin America is home to many terrorist organizations, some of which reportedly have substantial income from the drug trade. Al Qaeda is said to have a base on the border of Brazil, Argentina, and Paraguay.[89]

In addition, the Colombia-based Marxist groups Revolutionary Armed Forces of Colombia (FARC) and the National Liberation Army (ELN) are both officially designated as terrorist organizations by the United States Department of State. They engage in drug trading, bombings, kidnapping, extortion, hijackings, and guerrilla and conventional military action against Colombian political, military, and economic targets.[90]

There have been minor improvements in border security since September 11. Agents have increased their working hours and canceled annual leave. There is talk of consolidating the INS and Customs Service. The Enhanced Border Security and Visa Entry Reform Act raises the pay of Border Patrol agents and gives the INS authority to hire two hundred new investigators and two hundred inspectors. In addition, the Department of Defense sent 1,600 National Guard troops to aid agents along both borders.

But Homeland Security chief Tom Ridge has emphasized that the mobilization of the National Guard is temporary. "Because of the relationship we have and continue to develop and enhance every day with our friends in Mexico, the last thing we want to do is militarize the borders between friends. We want them open, we want them mutually beneficial, and that is simply a temporary measure," Ridge said.

Huge security holes remain. Long stretches of both our northern and southern borders are virtually unpatrolled, including several unofficial crossings between Big Bend National Park in Texas and the sparsely populated Mexican states of Chihuahua and Coahuila. For years, people there have been illegally crossing back and forth between the United States and Mexico, according to the *San Francisco Chronicle*. The nearest official crossing is more than one hundred miles away at Presidio, Texas.

"The border is porous," conceded Simon Garza Jr., chief United States Border Patrol agent in the area. "We just don't have enough manpower to cover it."[91]

Manpower — or willpower?

Hispanic interest groups willfully ignore countless ways in which the illegal-friendly policies they support increase our vulnerability to future terrorist attacks.

Yet, politicians are pressing forward with aggressive "outreach" campaigns for their votes. In Texas, two Democratic gubernatorial candidates held an unprecedented, televised election debate completely in Spanish. House Minority Leader Dick Gephardt—a Missouri Democrat—took a Spanish-language immersion course in Cuernavaca, Mexico. Meanwhile, Bush advisor Karl Rove, the Republican National Committee, and the National Republican Senatorial Committee pulled out all the stops to woo Hispanic voters. The GOP sent leaders to the Berlitz school for Spanish lessons, held "Hispanic Day" events, convened a "Latino Summit" in Los Angeles, launched a Spanish language television show, and, as Rove put it, made the Latino vote "our mission and our goal" requiring effort of all Republicans "in every way and every day working to get that done."

Minority outreach like that is well and good, but kowtowing to pro–illegal alien activist groups is not. There's a fine line between reaching out and selling out our national security for votes.

Chapter 3

The Profiteers

"Capitalists will sell us the rope with which to hang them."
—widely attributed to Vladimir Lenin

Our immigration enforcement priorities didn't fall into chaos by accident. America's homeland security system is a mess largely because a conglomerate of special interests helped make it so. We've seen how vote-pandering and political correctness on illegal immigration aided the terrorist invasion in America. Now, let's look at the groups who put profits and social agendas ahead of national security.

Speed Demons

Terrorists clearly benefited from the $590 billion travel and tourism industry's need for speed in rushing passengers through our consular offices and ports of entry.

Despite showing incomplete paperwork, September 11 hijacker Khalid Almihdhar breezed through New York's JFK

Airport, where harried INS officials blame pressure from the airline industry for their sloppiness. Almihdhar, along with fellow hijackers Abdulaziz Alomari and Salem Alhamzi, used another time-saving device handed to them by our very own State Department—the tourism-driven Visa Express program, which allowed visa applicants in Saudi Arabia to save time by bypassing regular screening.[1]

And 1993 World Trade Center plotter Ahmad Ajaj, indicted "20th hijacker" Zacarias Moussaoui, and suspected shoe-bomber Richard Reid all took advantage of the travel industry–supported Visa Waiver program, which allows travelers from certain countries to enter the United States without a visa.

History of Haste

The pressure to expedite passage of foreign travelers has its roots in a 1990 amendment to the Immigration and Nationality Act, which required INS officers to process foreign visitors arriving at air or seaports of entry "within 45 minutes of their presentation for inspection."[2] The Air Transport Association and Travel Industry Association of America, responding to hours-long lines at international airports, led the campaign for the new clearance standard. A five-dollar user fee was imposed on incoming foreign travelers to fund more INS inspectors to meet the requirements of the law.[3]

But the INS workforce has not kept pace with the onslaught of visitors—and national security is the sacrificial lamb. At the nation's busiest international airports, the time limit gives inspectors as little as twenty to thirty seconds to spend on each passenger's paperwork.

One Miami airport inspector, Patrick Pizarro, quit in disgust after September 11, partly because of his frustration with the congressionally mandated policy of rushing foreigners through

to appease the travel lobby's speed demons. In a scathing farewell
e-mail to colleagues, he wrote:

> I'm not by myself, believe me, when I say that I just feel like
> a body with a stamp, charged with making sure the passen-
> gers make it in and out the [inspections] area as quickly as
> possible. A stamp monkey. Everyone feels that way.... We let
> people in every day that we know we shouldn't. We do this
> job with too many hands behind our backs, and we're only
> born with two![4]

Jan C. Ting, a former high-ranking INS official and currently an
immigration law professor at Temple University, came to similar conclusions about the customer service–driven visa approval
and inspection processes:

> Any suggestion that we should take our time and tell our
> Foreign Service officers to look at these visa applications
> and not to issue them if they have any reservations [is
> opposed by the tourism lobby]. The travel industry opposes
> any enforcement of immigration laws that threatens its cash
> flow. Airlines, hotels, restaurants and theme parks want the
> government to keep issuing tourist visas quickly, without
> hassling applicants.[5]

The I-94 form—INS's tracking record issued to all foreign visitors—requires applicants to provide complete, truthful, and leg-
ible information about where they will stay in the United States
during their visit. September 11 hijacker Khalid Almihdhar,
here on a business visa, wrote: "Marriott in New York City." No
street address. No hotel room. No phone number. No indication
about which of the ten Marriott hotels in the Big Apple he

meant. If only an INS agent at JFK Airport had taken the time to ask.

The information might have come in handy when federal authorities realized that they had let in a known terrorist with links to both the East African embassy and *U.S.S. Cole* bombings. But swamped immigration inspectors had let it go. Soon after his admission to the country, FBI agents launched a futile search for Almihdhar. They found him two months too late—when he wrapped up his "business" trip by piloting American Airlines Flight 77 into the Pentagon.

Another plotter who was waved through in a hurry: Lafi Khalil, a Palestinian who was later arrested along with Gazi Ibrahim Abu Mezer in Brooklyn, New York, for planning to bomb the New York City subway system. In November 1996, Khalil received a C-1 transit visa from an American consular officer in Israel so that he could pass through the United States on his way from Israel to Ecuador.

A month after receiving his transit visa, Khalil arrived at New York's JFK International Airport. He presented his passport with the United States visa to an INS immigration inspector, who mistakenly admitted Khalil to the United States on a B-2 tourist visa. This allowed Khalil to stay in the country for six months rather than the twenty-nine days authorized by his original transit visa. The INS inspector, Joubert Dupuy, blamed the forty-five-minute inspection limit for his mistake, but candidly admitted that even if he had seen the C-1 visa designation, he would not have followed the INS field guide and asked Khalil to show an airline ticket to his final destination because it would have taken too much time.[6]

The Enhanced Border Security and Visa Entry Reform Act of 2002 included a provision repealing the forty-five-minute inspection limit at airports, but added a little-noticed clause

requiring the INS to staff ports of entry with the "goal of providing immigration services... within 45 minutes of a passenger's presentation for inspection."[7] In other words: no relief from
the speed demons.

Express Visas and Quickie Travel

The problem of rushed and overburdened immigration inspectors is compounded by America's Swiss-cheese visa policies. The
visa is supposed to be our country's best method for keeping out
criminals and terrorists. Law enforcement agents consider it the
most important screening mechanism for homeland security. Yet,
ethnic panderers in Congress and moneygrubbing corporate lobbyists have spent the past decade poking holes in the system to
allow expedited visa issuance and visa-free entry with the Visa
Express program and the Visa Waiver program.

Among the cheerleaders of the Visa Waiver program is Senate
Majority Leader Tom Daschle of South Dakota. Daschle's wife,
Linda, is a veteran aviation industry lobbyist who has represented the Air Transport Association, the American Association
of Airport Executives, and Northwest and American Airlines—
all of whom back the Visa Waiver program.

In a speech to travel lobbyists in 2000, Senator Daschle threw
his full support behind permanent authorization of the program.
"It means less unnecessary confusion for our international visitors, less unnecessary expense for our consular offices in 'low-
risk' nations, and more time and resources that can be shifted to
places they are really needed," Daschle asserted.[8] The program
became permanent later that year.

Supporters promised that removing visa requirements would
not compromise national security, because INS agents would
check passports of Visa Waiver participants against terrorist
watch lists. But as the Justice Department's inspector general

found, INS agents have consistently failed to perform these checks—even after September 11.[9] One JFK port official noted the checks made it difficult to meet the congressionally mandated forty-five-minute time limit.[10]

Passport fraud compounds the problem. For example, 1993 World Trade Center plotter Ahmad Ajaj tried to enter the United States through the Visa Waiver program after pasting his photo onto a Swedish passport.[11] Ajaj's luggage contained numerous videocassette tapes and manuals describing methods of manufacturing explosives.[12]

Fortunately, Ajaj was caught, but the lax manner in which the program is run helped ease the way for visitors such as Zacarias Moussaoui, the French citizen indicted for conspiracy related to the September 11 hijackings, and suspected shoe-bomber Richard Reid, who didn't need a visa to board a plane from London bound for the United States in December 2001.

William Norman, president of the Travel Industry Association of America, continues to defend the Visa Waiver program as a "vital tool" for "facilitating" travel from "low-risk" nations.[13] But with the al Qaeda terrorist network spread among seventy nations—across the Middle East, into Western Europe, and throughout southeast Asia—what is a "low-risk" nation in the post–September 11 world?

For rank-and-file immigration employees, the elevation of travel interests over security has caused endless frustration. INS supervisors at Miami International Airport openly chastised primary inspectors for checking medical and supporting documents, and for interrogating tourists who had overstayed their visas. "Supervisors would stand over your shoulder with a watch in their hand, saying you needed to hurry up," former INS inspector Fernande Bayda told reporter Bob Norman of the *Miami New Times*. "So we only had time to deal with people who were so obvious anybody could catch them. The sophisticated criminals — the counterfeiters, the smugglers, the terrorists — [supervisors] didn't even want to know who they were."[14]

The bottom line: more travel, more tourists, more terrorists, and nearly three thousand dead Americans. What does the industry have to say for itself?

Responding to post–September 11 criticism of the travel industry's apathy toward national security, Air Transport Association spokesman Michael Wascom sniffed: "We are in the business of moving people, not to enforce the law."[15]

The University Pimps

Higher education, we now know, has provided several terrorists smooth passage to America. September 11 hijackers Mohamed Atta and Marwan Al Shehhi entered on visitor visas, but enrolled in flight schools while awaiting "change of status" approval for student visas.

Atta and Al Shehhi's colleague, Hani Hanjour, entered the country on a student visa, but ditched classes and disappeared without a trace. Fellow hijacker Ahmed Alghamdi also entered on a student visa that had expired by the time of the attacks. Eyad Ismoil, the truck bomb driver in the 1993 World Trade Center attack, entered with a student visa to study at Wichita State University and then overstayed illegally.

Hundreds of thousands of foreign students have used their entry to gain permanent residence in America. Between 1971 and 1991, more than 3 million people received student visas, and 393,000 of them eventually adjusted their immigration status and obtained green cards, economist George Borjas reported in *National Review*.[16]

Yet, education officials, who reap an estimated $12 billion a year[17] from foreign students, continue to balk at the idea of adequately policing foreigners who pose potential and proven national security threats.

At the time of the September 11 attacks, roughly 600,000 foreign students were enrolled in United States colleges and universities.[18] Among them were thousands of individuals from terrorism-supporting nations. Last year alone, more than 3,700 citizens of Libya, Sudan, North Korea, Iran, Iraq, Syria, and Cuba—all state sponsors of terrorism—obtained student visas. When California senator Dianne Feinstein asked INS officials to tell her the status of some 16,000 students from terror-sponsoring nations who passed through American colleges during the past decade, she received a frightening answer: They didn't know.[19]

Why not? Because like the national foreign visitor tracking database, a foreign student database proposed long ago was aborted by special interests who were in stubborn denial about our vulnerability to murderous terrorists in students' clothing.

After the 1993 World Trade Center bombing, Congress launched a small student tracking system called CIPRIS—the Coordinated Interagency Partnership Regulating International Students. The Internet-based pilot system collected biographical data, addresses, and information about the academic status of foreign students and scholars studying in nearly two dozen southeastern schools. CIPRIS, which was spearheaded by INS official Maurice Berez, was scheduled to be implemented nationwide in 2003.

Throughout the late 1990s, then–FBI director Louis Freeh and a national panel of counterterrorism experts pushed for quick installation of CIPRIS and for tougher restrictions on student visas. But representatives of the education industry stood in the way:

— Gary Althen, director of the Office of International Students at the University of Iowa and past president of the National

Association of Foreign Student Advisers (NAFSA), asserted that "the fundamental question about CIPRIS is not whether its technological approach to 'regulating' students and scholars will work, but whether it ought even to be attempted."[20]

— "There is no evidence that foreign students constitute a terrorism threat," said Victor Johnson, a policy analyst at NAFSA. "There's no reason to single them out."[21]

— "It's hard to help students if you are wearing the hat of a policeman," complained Jan Sandor, assistant director of international education at the University of Georgia.[22]

— "The program is being implemented with undue haste," the American Camping Association howled. "When insufficiently tested systems are brought on line, the ensuing chaos could disrupt American campuses, summer camps that depend on foreign counselors, families counting on au pairs, businesses expecting trainees, resorts that depend on summer work exchanges and short-term language programs that operate in a very competitive international market."[23]

— "This will send a message that we really don't want international students," worried Kathy Steiner-Lang, director of the International Office at Washington University.[24]

The education lobby sought to undermine the law any way it could. NAFSA officials reportedly leaned on the INS to remove Maurice Berez, the agency's chief CIPRIS advocate, from the project. (Berez was removed in the fall of 1998.)

Next, administrators protested a ninety-five-dollar student fee that would have funded CIPRIS; they complained that collecting the fee would be unduly burdensome. In February 2000, after immense pressure from NAFSA and higher education officials, twenty-one senators, led by former senator Spencer Abraham (and including then–Missouri senator John Ashcroft), persuaded the INS to delay fee collection—effectively stopping CIPRIS in its tracks.[25]

Congress amended the law in October 2000 to shift fee-collection duties to the INS. In the meantime, university lobbyists continued to oppose efforts by intelligence and immigration officials to introduce foreign student fingerprinting and information-sharing measures to screen out terrorist threats. NAFSA lobbyists called for an outright repeal of CIPRIS as recently as August 2001, and some schools refused to collect the required student data. Opponents claimed that tracking "constituted an unreasonable barrier to foreign students who seek legitimately to pursue their higher education."[26]

While Washington was dithering, four of the September 11 terrorists exploited the higher education loopholes and taught us a deadly lesson.

The Complaints Continue

On the surface, the education lobby has changed its tune. "As the terrible events of September 11 made clear, one person who can enter the United States with the intent to commit a terrorist act is one too many," NAFSA executive director Marlene Johnson asserted. "The nation's higher-education community is fully committed to helping Congress to achieve reforms that will strengthen our nation's capacity to protect the United States from the threat of terrorism."[27]

NAFSA, the Association of International Educators; the American Council on Education; the American Association of Community Colleges; the American Association of State Colleges and Universities; and other major educational organizations endorsed renewed student tracking provisions included in the Enhanced Border Security and Visa Entry Reform Act, which was sponsored by Senators Feinstein and Jon Kyl of Arizona and signed into law in May 2002. Hundreds of educational institutions are cooperating with federal authorities to share information about foreign students as required by the USA Patriot Act.

But the show of solidarity is tenuous at best. Within weeks of the September 11 attacks, educational special interests helped defeat a temporary student visa moratorium plan floated by Senator Feinstein. "I believe that we need a temporary six-month moratorium on the student visa program to give the INS time to remedy the many problems in the system," Feinstein said in a September 27, 2001, press release. "This may be controversial, but there has to be recognition that this is an unprecedented time in the country and our national security depends on our system functioning to ensure that terrorists do not take advantage of the vulnerabilities in the student visa program."[28] By November 2001, after receiving a typhoon of complaints from Ivy League universities, English-language schools, and international education lobbyists, Feinstein abandoned the mild proposal.[29]

School officials also lodged steady criticisms of Bush administration efforts to prevent foreign nationals from studying certain subjects that could bear on the development of weapons of mass destruction. "We oppose restrictions, limits on student visas of any kind," said Glen Gaulton, vice dean for research and research training at the University of Pennsylvania.[30]

Moreover, individual colleges continue to attack plans for the new student tracking system, which is a watered-down version of CIPRIS. "I believe you should manage academics as an academic environment [sic], not under government deadlines and schedules that disrupt the educational process," said Catheryn Cotten, the director of Duke University's international office.[31]

"That's a lot of extra work for us, and we get nothing from it," carped Jane Havis, foreign student advisor at Rensselaer Polytechnic Institute in Troy, New York.[32]

Peter Briggs, Michigan State University's director of the office for international students and scholars, complained about the "public perception that border security outweighs the benefits of international education." He made clear his distaste for putting the nation's immigration laws above the interests of his foreign students. "Do I really want to report a brilliant student who is doing their [*sic*] dissertation research, but fails to turn in a certain form?" he asked a reporter. "I don't long in my heart to report people to the Immigration and Naturalization Service."[33]

Victor Johnson, now associate executive director for public policy at the Association of International Educators, sang the same tune the education lobby belted out six years ago about the original student visa tracking system when he declared the new January 30, 2003, deadline dead in the water. "That is a considerably earlier deadline than [INS officials] had led us to believe would be instituted, and I am quite confident they know it cannot be met," Johnson said. "Schools take this very seriously," he said. Uh-huh. "They want to be in compliance with federal law, but they are not going to be able to meet that January 30 deadline."[34]

For intransigent university pimps, homeland defense remains a nuisance—not a duty.

Border Busters

Were it not for protests from business groups worried about border traffic congestion eating into their profit margins, illegal visa overstayers such as September 11 terrorists Mohamed Atta, Hani Hanjour, Nawaf Alhamzi, Satam al Suqami, and Marwan Al Shehhi might have been tripped up by a database system designed to track foreigners.

Section 110 of the 1996 Illegal Immigration Reform and Immigrant Responsibility Act mandated creation of a comprehensive foreigner tracking system. It was strongly recommended by the bipartisan United States Commission on Immigration Reform, headed by the late congresswoman Barbara Jordan of Texas. Such a database would have alerted immigration officials whenever temporary alien visitors failed to leave the country under the terms of their visas.

But Big Business, joined by the Canadian and Mexican governments, as well as pro–illegal immigration activists, resisted. And to this day, the United States remains the only major industrialized nation that has no way of knowing exactly how many foreign guests are breaking its immigration laws, who they are, and where they may be living, working, or lurking. (See Appendix C.)

Leading the opposition was a group called Americans for Better Borders. This deceptively named organization of influential Americans was founded with a singular purpose: to sabotage the federal law that would have created a national, automated entry-exit system for all foreign visitors by the fall of 1998.

United by their common interest in ramming as many cars and trucks through the border as possible with as little hassle as possible from immigration officials, the corporate and alien lobbies formed an umbrella organization to undermine the 1996 tracking law. Among the most prominent members of the group: the United States Chamber of Commerce, Ford Motor Company, the American Trucking Association, the American Immigration Lawyers Association, and business and cultural alliances with Mexico and Canada.[35]

Americans for Better Borders paid lip service to national security concerns, but worked feverishly behind the scenes to prevent implementation of the tracking system. First, they pressured Congress to "temporarily" suspend the Section 110 deadline until March 30, 2001. Next, they set their sights on completely repealing the law.

Peter Iovino, a representative of Ford Motor Company, and Randel Johnson of the Chamber of Commerce—both cochairs of Americans for Better Borders—wrote in a fall 1999 letter to then-president Bill Clinton: "Section 110 at land ports of entry would cause massive traffic congestion along our borders, bringing personal and business travel at many border points to a halt."[36] The group enlisted the bipartisan aid of lawmakers from border trade–dependent states—led, most notably, by former Democratic representative John LaFalce of New York and former Republican senator Spencer Abraham of Michigan—who made numerous attempts to kill Section 110.

In June 2000, Clinton signed legislation passed by the House and Senate that offered a "compromise" solution. The automated tracking system envisioned in the 1996 law was scrapped in favor of a consolidated foreign visitor information database to be phased in gradually by 2005; the 2000 law killed the requirement that new information be collected at the border. The amended plan also created a government-industry task force to study (read: bury) border security issues.

Republican representative Lamar Smith of Texas, who had fought valiantly to preserve the original 1996 law, tried to put a positive spin on the new scheme. He called it "a giant step toward the U.S. being able to exercise its right as a sovereign nation to say who may enter and how long they may stay."[37] But a press release from the American Immigration Lawyers Association made the true effect of the new law clear: "Elimination of Entry-Exit Controls Reflects Realities," the immigration lawyers crowed. The agreement "effectively revokes Section 110 of the 1996 immigration law."[38]

While the sham task force "studied" the issue, terrorists exploited our unguarded borders. A report from Canada's Special Senate Committee on Security and Intelligence called Canada a "venue of opportunity" for terrorist groups, "a place where they may raise funds, purchase arms and conduct other activities to support their organizations and their terrorist activities elsewhere.... Our geographic location also makes Canada a favorite conduit for terrorists wishing to enter the United States, which remains the principal target for terrorist attacks worldwide."[39]

Among the Canadian-based suspects with ties to September 11 hijackers is Nabil al-Marabh, a reputed bin Laden operative who lived in Toronto during the late 1990s. He reportedly transferred about $15,000 to at least three men arrested in the United States for roles in the September 11 attacks.[40] He is also suspected of having provided some of the hijackers with fake identification cards.[41] Although Canadian authorities failed to confirm a link between al-Marabh and the September 11 terrorists, a dozen residents who lived in his Toronto apartment complex say they saw September 11 hijackers Mohamed Atta and Marwin Al Shehhi there.[42]

In June 2001, INS agents caught al-Marabh entering the United States at the Niagara Falls border crossing in the back of a tractor trailer, false Canadian passport in hand. Case officers urged an INS adjudicator to keep him in custody until his deportation hearing because they feared he would flee. Despite a warrant for his arrest issued by the Boston Police Department and intelligence reports that he was associated with bin Laden, the INS released al-Marabh on a $10,000 bond. Al-Marabh never showed up for his August 3 scheduled hearing and was finally arrested by the FBI outside Chicago on September 19, 2001.[43] At the time he was arrested, al-Marabh had a commercial driver's license that permitted him to drive trucks carrying hazardous materials.[44] He faces deportation to Syria in October 2002.

Despite the explosive growth of terrorist groups within its own borders due to liberal immigration and visa policies, the

Canadian embassy continued to express "concerns" about America's plan for a national entry-exit control system. While pledging to help us in the War on Terror, the Canadian government stressed its obsessive need to "improve traffic flow at our borders."[45]

At least the Mexican government is up front about its intentions. President Vicente Fox champions the complete dissolution of all borders in the Western Hemisphere (though this hasn't stopped him from deporting Central Americans who enter Mexico through its border with Guatemala). "When we think of 2025, there is not going to be a border" between the United States and Mexico, Fox bragged soon after his December 2000 inauguration. "There will be a free movement of people just like the free movement of goods."[46]

Juan Hernandez, a dual United States–Mexico citizen who heads Fox's Office for Mexicans Living Abroad, says the country looks forward to the day when "borders are irrelevant."[47] And Fox's foreign minister, Jorge Castañeda, has repeatedly refused to endorse border security reform without a blanket amnesty of all illegal aliens from Mexico living in the United States.[48] "It's the whole enchilada or nothing," Castañeda demanded at a National Association of Hispanic Journalists conference last year.[49]

Among Mexico's strange bedfellows: the AFL-CIO, the Big Business defenders on the *Wall Street Journal*'s editorial page, pandering strategists in both the Republican and Democratic Party leadership seeking Hispanic votes, and the agricultural lobby—which, spearheaded by the American Farm Bureau, has helped sabotage enforcement of federal sanctions against employers who hire and harbor illegal farm workers.

As for Americans for Better Borders, the group seemed to moderate its stance immediately after September 11, and accepted the inevitable implementation of an entry-exit system. "We believe that our borders can and should be a line of defense against those who pose security threats to this country," the group claimed.[50] Nevertheless, the business leaders echoed the Canadian border busters' call for Congress to "be willing to modify" its statutory deadlines for implementing immigration security measures so as not to "impact negatively on cross-border commerce and travel."[51]

Such are the deadly priorities of the corporate profiteers.

The Alien Bar Association

From crusading for wide amnesty for illegal aliens, to opposing asylum and deportation overhauls, to undermining the foreign student database, to blocking the national entry-exit system, the American Immigration Lawyers Association has obstructed tighter borders — and national security — every step of the way.

AILA is the national bar association of more than 7,500 attorneys and law professors who practice and teach immigration law.[52] It has been a powerful lobbying network against all major immigration reforms during the past four decades.

Until September 11, AILA focused on repealing major provisions of the 1996 immigration reform law, including the three- and ten-year bars to reentry for illegal border-crossers and illegal visa-overstayers. AILA also advocated on behalf of aliens who vote illegally, alien smugglers, and illegal immigrants who make false claims of United States citizenship. The organization cashes in on its legal expertise with a popular line of "how-to manuals," "multimedia toolboxes," "comprehensive sourcebooks," "easy-to-use directories," and "informative client brochures" that teach members how to navigate, evade, and undermine enforcement of immigration laws. A popular item for sale on the merchandise section of AILA's Web site is a $10 poster with the slogan: "No human being is illegal!"[53]

After September 11, AILA acknowledged that "[b]y necessity, our immigration agenda has been changed by the September 11 terrorist attacks."[54] The group joined the education lobby in endorsing the Enhanced Border Security and Visa Entry Reform Act but continued to minimize the security risks of unrestrained illegal immigration. Challenging the usefulness of a foreign tracking system, AILA executive director Jeanne Butterfield snorted: "Will the data tell us that the person who overstayed their visa for a week did so to spend some extra time at Disney World or the Grand Canyon? Or will it tell us that the person who overstayed is intending somehow to do us harm?"[55]

Butterfield similarly derided the usefulness of a student tracking system. "How is keeping out foreign students going to make us safer when we let in thirty million visitors every year?" she asked. "It doesn't make sense."[56] Meanwhile, AILA president Steven Ladik challenged Attorney General John Ashcroft's decision to track down Middle Eastern "absconders" who had ignored deportation orders and remained in the country illegally.

"Many of these abscondees may have been ordered deported because they didn't show up for their deportation hearing. And they get what you call an *in absentia* order of deportation. Now I'm concerned that if they come in contact with law enforcement and they're arrested, I don't want a rush to judgment where they're put on a plane and sent out of the country and they never really receive their due process," Ladik told National Public Radio.[57]

Such is the mindset of immigration lawyers who don't believe law-breaking immigrants are, in fact, "illegal." Whether they are terrorists in training or foreign vacationers who decided to ignore the terms of their visa or fugitive deportees, illegal aliens should not be here *no matter what their alibi.* Information about how many of them are in the country, who they are, and where they might be is not only "useless" to AILA. It is a threat to their agenda of minimizing and obfuscating the true scope and risks of lax immigration enforcement.

Hate Crime Howlers

Ethnic and immigrants' rights groups have played critical roles in attacking commonsense immigration and border security reforms.

After September 11, two leading Arab-American advocacy groups that played the Islam card on immigration and national security issues were the American-Arab Anti-Discrimination Committee—which bills itself as "at the forefront combating defamation and negative stereotyping of Arab Americans in the media and wherever else it is practiced"[58]—and the Council on American-Islamic Relations (CAIR), which says it is "dedicated to presenting an Islamic perspective on issues of importance to the American public."[59] Others include the American Muslim Council, the Islamic Institute, the American Muslim Alliance, the Arab American Institute, and the Muslim Public Affairs Council.

On September 11, Salam Al-Marayati, executive director of the Muslim Public Affairs Council, became enraged during an interview on KCRW-FM in Los Angeles when it was suggested that Muslims were likely behind that morning's attacks. "If we're going to look at suspects, we should look to the groups that benefit the most from these kinds of incidents," he said. "I think we should put the state of Israel on the suspect list because I think this diverts attention from what's happening in the Palestinian territories."[60]

Al-Marayati and his colleagues have been rehearsing these victimology verses for years. After the 1993 World Trade Center bombing, CAIR presented its invaluable "perspective" by listing the trial and conviction of bombing mastermind Sheik Omar

Abdul-Rahman as an "incident of bias and violence" against Muslims.[61] After the 1998 bombings of two United States embassies in Africa, Osama bin Laden's picture was put on a California billboard with the label "The Sworn Enemy" over it. CAIR protested it as offensive to Muslims. When President Clinton ordered missile strikes on bin Laden's training camps, Al-Marayati's group labeled the strikes an "an act of terrorism" and "illegal, immoral, inhuman . . . hate crimes."[62]

Immediately after the September 11 terrorist attacks, CAIR invoked the hate crime mantra again by setting up hotlines and counseling services for alleged victims of "anti-Muslim incidents." Its spokesmen cast every counterterrorism effort by the feds as a threat to Muslims' civil rights. Of the Justice Department's call for Middle Eastern visa holders to volunteer for interviews with law enforcement, CAIR spokesman Ibrahim Hooper said: "We believe it perpetuates racial and religious profiling of American Muslims and Arab-Americans, and that it's an ineffective law enforcement tool that sends a chill through the community."[63]

When the Justice Department ordered that the names of known or suspected terrorists simply be provided to federal, state, and local police nationwide and be entered into existing lookout databases, the Muslim lobby went ballistic. "I really don't understand a government that acts on suspicion instead of facts. America is no longer the land of the free," lamented Abdurahman Alamoudi, president of the American Muslim Foundation.[64] (No stranger to terrorists, Alamoudi endorsed the violent Middle East groups Hamas and Hezbollah in a 2000 speech.)[65]

"It smacks of McCarthyism and other events in history in which heavy-handed government tactics against an entire community have done nothing but ruin innocent lives," said Sarah Eltantawi, of the Muslim Public Affairs Council.[66]

So much for the ruined innocent lives of those who became the victims of the largest, most violent hate crime ever committed on American soil.

Less influential but just as vocal are Asian-American grievance-mongers such as the Asian-American Legal Defense Fund (AALDEF) and the Organization of Chinese Americans, which have also lent their voices in support of illegal immigration and loose enforcement. Their liberal advocacy defies the attitude of the constituency they purport to represent. "Leaders of the Asian groups admitted that most Asians living in the U.S. believe that the government should crack down on illegal immigration," reported James Gimpel and James Edwards, authors of the comprehensive *Congressional Politics of Immigration Reform.*[67]

After September 11, AALDEF paid lip service to mourning the thousands who died during the terrorist attacks—but quickly poured its energy into hyping alleged acts of hate-crime violence against South Asians. AALDEF even snagged $30,000 from the United Way's September 11 fund to provide "legal help and preventative measures against hate violence."[68]

Asian-American and Arab-American groups learned well from their Hispanic counterparts. After September 11, the Mexican American Legal Defense and Educational Fund (MALDEF) protested loudly against Operation Tarmac, a sorely needed INS crackdown on illegal aliens working in secure areas of the nation's airports who are guilty of lying on their employment applications and susceptible to bribery.

"The firing and indictments of hard working, family-oriented Latinos is not helping our war on terrorism, but it is causing grave economic and other hardships on our community," complained MALDEF's regional counsel Marisa Demeo. She also criticized cooperation between local and federal law enforcement authorities to root out illegal aliens as "actions that harm the civil rights of Latinos rather than protect them."[69]

The Hispanic groups are reflexively supported by generic pro–illegal alien organizations such as the Washington, D.C.–based National Immigration Forum and the Southern Poverty Law Center. The latter group has smeared grassroots immigration organizations, such as California's American Patrol, the California Coalition for Immigration Reform, and journalist/author Peter Brimelow's VDARE Web site, as "hate groups" akin to skinheads and neo-Nazis.[70]

Also on board: traditional civil rights activists such as Democratic representative John Conyers of Michigan, who joined Hispanic, Arab-American, and civil liberties groups in assailing the Justice Department's plan to fingerprint Middle Eastern visitors as a "totalitarian" scheme of racial and ethnic profiling that violates the "equal protection clause."[71]

Al Qaeda operatives and other foreign menaces couldn't ask for a better ally than America's "hate" police, whose constant cries of racism help distract from the true purveyors of hate and violence. And as we shall next see, the hate crime howlers, illegal alien advocates, and open-borders lobbyists who profit from looser borders have done so not only at the expense of thousands of Americans who died on September 11, but also at the expense of many other forgotten Americans who have died as a result of lax immigration enforcement.

Part II: More Menaces in Our Midst

Chapter 4

Serial Incompetence

The Angel Resendiz Case

Claudia Benton. Christopher Maier. Leafie Mason. Norman and Karen Sirnic. Josephine Konvicka. Noemi Dominguez. George Morber Sr. Carolyn Frederick. Fannie Byers. Jessie Howell. Wendy Von Huben.

These are the names of twelve innocent Americans who lost their lives because the INS failed to do its job and keep dangerous aliens out of the country. No, they were not among the thousands who died in the September 11 terrorist attacks. They are the little-known victims of an illegal alien from Mexico whose criminal career made a bloody mockery of our borders and our immigration laws.

Angel Maturino Resendiz, who became known as the "Railway Killer," illegally entered the United States on numerous occasions from Mexico beginning at age fourteen. For the next twenty-five years, he racked up arrests and convictions in America ranging from trespassing, destruction of property, burglary, aggravated battery, and grand theft auto to carrying a loaded firearm and false representation of United States citizenship. Government records show that he had at least twenty-five encounters with

United States law enforcement authorities between August 1976 and August 1996, when he was arrested and released for trespassing in a Kentucky railyard.[1]

During that period, he was convicted at least nine times on several serious felony charges. He was deported to Mexico by the INS at least three times and was "voluntarily returned" to Mexico at least four times without formal proceedings. Throughout 1998, the Border Patrol continued its blind catch-and-release policy—apprehending Resendiz seven times and letting him go on his own recognizance despite his massive criminal record and three prior deportations. Created in the name of administrative streamlining and cost-saving, the "voluntary departure" policy allows INS agents or immigration judges to shuttle illegal aliens back to Mexico without having official orders of deportation entered against them. For Resendiz, it was a convenient revolving door. Undeterred, he returned effortlessly to our soil with deadly intentions.

In December 1998, the transient day laborer's fingerprints were identified on a car belonging to Dr. Claudia Benton, a talented Texas neurologist and mother of twin daughters who was sexually assaulted, stabbed, and beaten to death alone in her bedroom while her family was away. Weeks later, Houston police issued a felony warrant for Resendiz's arrest. The FBI entered the information into its national criminal database; the Texas Rangers mounted a search and publicity campaign. Law enforcement officers also contacted INS investigators for help. They requested a border lookout and a "hold" on Resendiz in the INS's internal system. According to a Justice Department investigation,[2] however, no INS official ever made any effort to enter Resendiz's warrant data in the agency's automated fingerprint identification system, called IDENT.

The $65 million IDENT system was created by Congress in 1994 to help the INS keep track of recidivist aliens caught entering the country multiple times, and to identify those who have been previously deported or who have significant criminal histories. The recidivist database contained fingerprints and photos of more than one million illegal aliens who had been apprehended by the INS; the criminal lookout database contained records on about 400,000 aliens who had been previously deported or who had significant criminal histories.

The INS's failure to enter Resendiz — an obvious candidate — into the lookout portion of the IDENT system resulted in brutal, tragic, and needless deaths. Despite outstanding state and federal fugitive warrants in connection to murder and burglary, Border Patrol agents once again "voluntarily released" Resendiz on June 1, 1999, after apprehending him in New Mexico. He was let loose in America to kill four others before turning himself in to United States authorities a month later. He admitted guilt in nine murders, and subsequently confessed to, or was linked by forensic evidence, to several more.

After a Texas jury sentenced Resendiz to death in May 2000 for the murder of Benton, Congress demanded better training and integration of criminal alien databases used by the INS and the FBI. But as of September 11, 2001, no progress had been made in that effort. Bogged down by administrative nitpicking and internecine squabbling between the two agencies, the Justice Department said it needed more time to study the issue. A follow-up report by the department's inspector general released in December 2001 stated that the ultimate integration of the two systems is "well off into the future."[3] To this day the INS and FBI databases remain unlinked.

As the INS clamors for more money and new technology to fight the war on terrorism, these twelve casualties of serial murder — and of serial incompetence — must not be forgotten. Our judicial system may have held Resendiz accountable, but this foreign killer's chief accomplice — the INS — got off scot-free. The senseless deaths of Resendiz's victims show that all the fanciest computer databases and biometric technology in the world won't protect us if negligent immigration bureaucrats don't bother—or don't know how—to use them.

Portraits of Grief

Claudia Benton, thirty-nine, was a gifted scientific researcher who specialized in pediatric neurological diseases. Among her many patients were toddlers Cody Juenke and Nicholas Green, who had a rare genetic disorder called Angelman's Syndrome, which crippled their ability to speak and caused seizures. The parents of Benton's young patients say she was a beacon of hope. A faculty member at Baylor College of Medicine, Benton lived with her husband, George, and young twin daughters in a Houston, Texas, suburb. On December 17, 1998, Benton was asleep alone in her bedroom; her family was on a brief trip to Arizona.

That day, Resendiz jumped off a freight train that ran about one hundred yards from the Bentons' neighborhood and broke into the Benton home by jimmying open the garage door sometime during the night. Police said Benton fought hard against her attacker. One of her arms was dislocated and she suffered numerous defensive wounds to her hands and face. Using a butcher knife, Resendiz stabbed her three times in the back. With a bronze statue he had found on a family mantel, he then clubbed Benton in the head nineteen times. While she lay dying with a fractured skull, he raped her and wrapped her head in a plastic bag. He took off with a banjo, a guitar, a stereo, jewelry, and the family's Jeep.

Investigators later matched DNA taken from Benton's body to DNA samples from the case in Kentucky involving Christopher Maier and his girlfriend. Resendiz's fingerprints were also found on items in the house and on broken Jeep parts left in the garage. Police discovered Benton's body after concerned co-workers reported her failure to show up for a genetics clinic.

Benton's devastated husband quit his job to take full-time care of his daughters, now fifteen. They moved out of the state. His brother John testified at Resendiz's trial and tried to pick up the pieces: "I don't want to say he's lost, but he is. He's got two girls. He wakes them up in the morning. He makes them breakfast. He sends them to school and waits for them to come home from school, alive."[4]

Recalling his wife's contributions, George Benton later said: "She was a woman who loved life, lived every day to the fullest. She was a mother, a wife and a doctor. She loved it all.... Claudia had so much real potential to help people with her research and work as a doctor. So much left to give. We'll never get that now."

In July 2001, the Angelman Syndrome Foundation presented its first Dr. Claudia Benton Award for Scientific Research, in honor of the slain geneticist's contributions to the field.

Christopher Maier was a twenty-one-year-old college junior at the University of Kentucky at Lexington. A member of the Phi Kappa Psi fraternity, he was studying theater design. Maier loved skiing, snowboarding, camping, and animals—and at one point in his brief young life, considered majoring in veterinary science.[5] A few days after classes began in the late summer of 1997, Maier and his girlfriend attended a party at his frat house. They went for a late-night stroll along some railroad tracks near campus.

Resendiz accosted the couple and demanded money. Maier's girlfriend, a twenty-year-old sophomore, later testified that Resendiz threatened them with a weapon and ordered them to "get down." He dragged Maier into some weeds ten feet from the train tracks, and then tied up and gagged the couple using belts, torn clothing, and straps from a fanny pack. "I remember being petrified," Maier's girlfriend later recalled. "We were doing everything he told us to do, praying that he would not hurt us."[6]

Using a fifty-two-pound rock, Resendiz bludgeoned the six-foot, five-inch tall Maier to death. Lexington police would later describe Maier as a true hero who "did everything within his power to help the young lady he was with and paid the ultimate price for that."[7] While Maier lay hogtied and dying, choking on his own blood, Resendiz raped his girlfriend and beat her unconscious. Resendiz left her with stab wounds to the neck and a broken eye socket and jawbone. He covered her with brush and abandoned her for dead.

Maier's girlfriend miraculously survived and became the only known target of Resendiz's killing spree to live to tell about her ordeal. DNA samples connected Resendiz to the scene and she provided crucial eyewitness descriptions that led to his eventual arrest—no thanks to immigration authorities.

Determined to get on with her life, she bravely confronted the man who raped her and killed her boyfriend as the final witness for the prosecution at Resendiz's trial. "I wanted to crawl in a hole and never come out again," she later told members of her sorority in a magazine article recounting the attack, "but that would have meant that I let this monster take me away."[8] She graduated from the University of Kentucky in 2000.

To keep Christopher Maier's memory alive, his classmates, fraternity brothers, and family established an endowed scholarship at the University of Kentucky in his honor. It is awarded every year to a student who best reflects the young man's "passion for theater, generosity of spirit, a caring attitude towards all, as well as a zest for life."[9]

Leafie Mason, eighty-seven, was a native of Hughes Springs, Texas. She, too, had many passions: poetry, wildflowers, and family. After two decades with the Internal Revenue Service in Dallas, she moved back home to care for her sister, Virgie, who had been retarded since birth. Leafie Mason took Virgie out for drives and made every effort to make life comfortable for her sister. In a letter to the *Dallas Morning News* published December 3, 1993, she asked a local columnist for help in finding a special cord to secure her sister's toys safely to her bed railings:

"I've tied toy animals to 72-inch shoelaces and even leather boot laces, but they become twisted and so shortened that she cannot manipulate the toys at all. . . . We used to buy clothesline cord made of nylon that had wire in the center. It was narrow, yet supple, and didn't twist. Every retailer we've contacted tells us that they no longer stock the cord and they don't know whether it's even in production anymore. Does anyone have some of this stuff or know where we can get it?"[10]

Several readers sent Mason the cord she needed, and she passed on her gratitude. Such simple gestures and small-town neighborliness made for a peaceful existence — until October 1, 1998. That's when Resendiz stepped off a freight train and into Leafie Mason's final moments of life.

According to police, Resendiz entered her home — which faced the Kansas City–Southern Rail Line tracks some fifty yards away — through an open window. He picked up an antique flatiron and struck Mason in the head as she slept. She raised her arms in self-defense, but Resendiz overpowered the elderly woman — knocking her from her bed to the floor and beating her until the handle of the iron broke.[11] Resendiz then stole money and jewelry from Mason's purse, and promptly disappeared. But he left a palm print on a window, which the local police chief had wisely removed and preserved as evidence before a thunderstorm hit.

Reflecting on Leafie Mason's brutal death, nursing home aide Jennifer Pippin condemned Resendiz and described the effect it had on her patient—Leafie's sister, Virgie: "He didn't kill just one person. I think he killed two."[12]

On March 6, 2001, Virgie died alone at the Theron Grainger Nursing Home in Hughes Springs. She was eighty-three.[13]

The Reverend **Norman "Skip" Sirnic** and his wife, **Karen**, were a popular couple in the tiny town of Weimar, Texas, halfway between San Antonio and Houston. Both came from high-achieving backgrounds: Skip, forty-six, was a high school valedictorian, an honors graduate of Trinity University in San Antonio, and a Vanderbilt Divinity School scholar. An ordained minister since 1977, he led the Weimar United Church of Christ and was known for his humility and compassion. Wife Karen, forty-seven, had a degree in biochemistry from Texas A&M and conducted research for her alma mater. She also served as the church secretary for her husband's tight-knit congregation and sang in the church choir.

The Sirnics were known for their kindness, community activism, and avid gardening. Passionflowers, sunflowers, roses, tomatoes, and green beans filled their parsonage garden. Church member Helen Boysen described her pastor as a humble and funny man: "It was almost as if he talked with us about God and the Bible and the way the Bible instructs us to live. He brought the Bible alive for us, truly."[14]

On Friday, April 30, 1999, the Sirnics went to bed and looked forward to the weekend's busy church activities. That Sunday was also the Reverend Sirnic's birthday. Their red pickup truck was parked outside the parsonage, located about fifty yards from the Southern Pacific train tracks that crossed the town. Resendiz broke into the rear of the couple's home as they slept, and grabbed a twelve-pound sledgehammer from a garage closet. He struck the Reverend Sirnic twice as he slept, killing him instantly. His wife sustained a vicious blow to the face, and was raped. Resendiz wrapped her dead body in sheets. He leaned the bloody sledgehammer against a wall inside the house, then took off with the couple's VCR, some household items, and their truck. A worried church member discovered the horrific scene on May 2, when the couple failed to show up for Sunday services. Texas Rangers matched DNA samples from the crime scene to samples from Dr. Benton's home.

More than half of Weimar's two thousand residents attended the Sirnics' memorial service. Local parishioners continue to tend to the Sirnics' church garden, where flowers bloom brightly in memory of the faithful couple.

Josephine Konvicka was a seventy-three-year-old widow who lived alone on the outskirts of Weimar. Konvicka's husband, George, had died in 1986. A retired waitress, she had five grown children. Her yellow frame farmhouse was about a mile from the railroad tracks and less than four miles west of the Sirnics' home. Konvicka grew vegetables and peach trees, raised cattle, made quilts for her grandchildren, played bingo with her older sister, and liked to watch television at night. "She was the sweetest, dearest little old lady," one of her neighbors told the *Texas Monthly*. "She would not have hurt a fly." [15]

At the beginning of June 1999, Konvicka hosted an annual family reunion. There was concerned talk of the Sirnics' murder, which had already been linked to Resendiz, but the family could have never imagined how the horror would touch their own lives. [16]

On the night of June 3, Konvicka spoke with one of her daughters, Linda Vacek, by phone. The next evening, Vacek and her husband drove to visit Konvicka and feed her cows. While her husband tended to the animals, Vacek opened the door to her mother's house and witnessed an unspeakable scene. Resendiz had climbed into an unlocked rear window and beaten Konvicka to death in her bedroom with a grubbing hoe. The pick-axe-like tool was found lodged in Konvicka's forehead. Resendiz then turned the house upside down, apparently looking for car keys that were later found in a drawer. He left fingerprints that were matched to the other crime scenes. He also took out a toy train set that had probably been in one of Konvicka's closets and put it on display to taunt investigators.[17]

Konvicka's family, shocked and numb, gathered to mourn her death just days after they had celebrated their annual family reunion. They planted flowers in her memory outside the Catholic church in her hometown of Dubina, Texas.[18]

Noemi Dominguez, twenty-six, was an elementary schoolteacher who dreamed of a writing career. She came from a large, tight-knit family of eight brothers and sisters. A graduate of Rice University, she taught at a Catholic school in Fort Worth, sang in a local church choir, and moved to Houston to teach first grade. At the end of the 1998–1999 school year, she resigned to pursue a master's degree in education at the University of Houston—and to write children's books. Former colleagues say she was quiet, spiritual, and at peace. "Sweet and wide-eye innocent," said a former Rice University classmate.[19]

Dominguez lived in a neat apartment near rail tracks on the south side of town. On June 3, her sister Brenda spoke to her by phone about the family's plans to meet at an animated cartoon convention in Dallas.[20] Alarmed when she did not show up, her brother Alejandro went to his sister's apartment on June 5 to check on her. He entered Noemi's bedroom and described his terrible discovery to the jury at Resendiz's capital murder trial: "I lifted this quilt my mother made for her, and a few articles of clothing. Honestly, I jumped back and I think I shrieked."[21] Resendiz had raped and clubbed Noemi Dominguez to death sometime between the evening of June 3 and June 4. Her head was mangled, and her blood was later found on the weapon used to murder Josephine Konvicka. Noemi's stolen Honda Accord was found a week later in Del Rio, near the Mexican border. Police lifted Resendiz's latent fingerprints from the car. They also later recovered Dominguez's jewelry from Resendiz's home in Mexico.

In July 1999, Noemi Dominguez's students at Franklin Elementary in Houston planted an oak tree in the school's foyer garden in her honor. Nearly nine feet tall, it stands there today, near the first-grade classroom where she once shaped and inspired young minds.

George Morber Sr., eighty, was a retired prison guard in the tiny farming community of Gorham, Illinois (population: 290). He lived in a trailer home on the outskirts of town, less than one hundred yards from the Union Pacific rail line. His daughter, fifty-two-year-old **Carolyn Frederick**, lived next door with her husband. She had three grown children of her own.

On June 14, 1999, Morber took his ailing wife to a local hospital. Sometime the next day, Mrs. Frederick headed over to her father's house, where she did the cleaning every week. Her husband stopped by in the early afternoon, and discovered his wife near the front door. She was dead on the floor, covered with a blanket.

His father-in-law was farther inside the house, tied to a chair with a telephone cord. He had been shot through the back of the head with his own shotgun—which Resendiz then used to bludgeon Carolyn Frederick.

Resendiz left his fingerprints in the home, and drove off with Morber's truck. "Our community has just been stunned by this senseless act," said Morber's son, Bill.[22] The father and daughter were memorialized by the National Organization of Parents of Murdered Children, Inc.

Fannie Whitner Byers was an eighty-one-year-old widow who lived with her dog, Puppy, in rural Carl, Georgia. Her home was so close to the CSX freight railroad tracks that the windows rattled constantly. She didn't mind. Byers liked the sound, and she kept busy enough with her gardening and housework. She lived simply—her isolated home didn't even have a bathroom. But her outhouse suited her just fine.[23]

On December 10, 1998, Resendiz staked out Byers as she finished her yard work. She was bludgeoned to death with a pickaxe. Local authorities had charged another man with the murder, but dismissed the case in August 2000 after Resendiz confessed following his conviction for Dr. Benton's murder. He gave detailed information about the crime scene, including a missing Bible he had stolen from Byers's home. Byers left no survivors.

Jessie Howell, nineteen, and **Wendy Von Huben**, sixteen, had been dating for three months. Jessie had a record of trouble-making, but was described as a quiet, typical teenager. Wendy's dad believed his brown-haired, green-eyed daughter took off "because she just turned 16 and felt like she could conquer the world."[24] She had argued with her parents about grades and dating.[25]

In late February 1997, the free-spirited youths ran away together from their home in Woodstock, Illinois, and headed south to Florida. The pair was spotted in various cities across the state, including Tampa, Lakeland, Sarasota, and Bradenton. But on March 23, 1997, Jessie was found beaten to death alongside train tracks in Marion County, Florida, more than an hour northwest of Orlando. A frantic search for Wendy ensued. She had last been heard from on March 18, when she phoned her parents asking for money and indicating she wanted to come home. They wired her money immediately for a bus ticket, but she never returned. The case sat unsolved for three years.

In July 2000, two months after his conviction in the Benton case, Resendiz came clean on his role in the young couple's fate. He drew a map that led Florida investigators to Wendy's skeletal remains. She had been strangled in the woods and wrapped in a blanket about fifteen miles south of where Jessie had died.

Resendiz said that he had met Jessie and Wendy at a switching station near Jacksonville, and that they joined him in a freight train car to find work picking oranges. During a pit stop, he clubbed Jessie to death with a three-foot length of rubber hose; Wendy was killed eight hours later.[26]

Family and friends said the couple had become engaged before they embarked on their final journey together.

Criminal Neglect

Never before has there been a more graphic illustration of how border insecurity and bureaucratic incompetence threaten the American public. Time and again, Angel Resendiz broke the law getting into our country; broke more laws while in the country; and then broke the law repeatedly and brazenly after being released, deported, and allowed to return. By the time Resendiz met up with young Jessie Howell and Wendy Von Huben (his earliest known murder victims to date) in the early spring of 1997, he had already amassed a mile-long rap sheet.

Born in Mexico in 1959, Resendiz first entered the country illegally as a teenager and settled in Florida. Federal authorities admit that the following criminal history of Resendiz's encounters with the INS probably omits even more incidents, because paper records of such encounters often are destroyed after two years:

Before Killing a Dozen Americans: Resendiz's Brushes with the Law[27]

August 1976	First reported attempt to enter the United States ended with his arrest by United States Immigration and Naturalization Service agents at the port of entry in Brownsville, Texas. He was returned to Mexico.
September 11, 1976	Arrested for trespassing at a car lot in Sterling Heights, Michigan. Turned over to INS and granted voluntary departure.
October 2, 1976	Arrested by Border Patrol trying to cross the border in McAllen, Texas, and returned to Mexico.
September 1977	Convicted and jailed for destroying private property and leaving the scene of a crime in Corinth, Mississippi; voluntarily returned to Mexico on October 13, 1977.
June 1979	Broke into a home in Miami, Florida, beat the eighty-eight-year-old owner until he was semiconscious, ransacked the home, and stole a car.
July 13, 1979	Arrested and charged with burglary in Clark County, Kentucky; extradited to Miami for June 1979 crimes.
May 23, 1980	Received twenty-year prison sentence for Miami burglary, auto theft, and aggravated assault charges.
September 13, 1985	After serving less than six years of twenty-year sentence, paroled, and then deported to Mexico from Brownsville.
December 10, 1985	Less than three months after deportation, back in the United States and charged with falsely claiming United States citizenship in El Reno, Oklahoma. Received eighteen-month sentence. Did not serve full term. Unknown if he was deported after release.

June 1, 1986 Apprehended in Laredo, Texas, for illegal reentry into the United States, and possession of fraudulent United States voter registration card, and birth certificate. Received an eighteen-month sentence for false representation of United States citizenship. Served fifteen months.

October 2, 1987 Released to INS and deported to Mexico through Brownsville.

January 19, 1988 Arrested in New Orleans on charges of defrauding an innkeeper and possessing a concealed weapon. Charges dismissed for lack of evidence.

November 30, 1988 Arrested by INS agents in St. Louis for fraudulently applying for Social Security cards with false information, possessing a firearm, and illegal entry.

March 29, 1989 Convicted in federal court for lying to federal officials, being a convicted felon in possession of a firearm, and illegal reentry after deportation. Received thirty-month prison sentence.

May 13, 1991 Deported from El Paso, Texas, to Mexico after release from prison.

March 3, 1992 Back in the United States, arrested for residential burglary in Las Cruces, New Mexico. Sentenced in August 1992 to three years' imprisonment (eighteen months suspended).

April 1993 Paroled from New Mexico; unknown if INS deported him.

June 9, 1993 Arrested by a Texas Department of Public Safety trooper in Carson County for driving a stolen vehicle and evading arrest. Sentenced to twenty-nine days.

December 7, 1994 Arrested by Albuquerque, New Mexico, police for driving stolen vehicle. Released on bond.

May 28, 1995 Indicted in Albuquerque for receiving stolen vehicle and resisting arrest; bench warrant issued for his arrest and placed in FBI criminal database.

August 19, 1995 Arrested by Santa Fe railroad police for trespassing and possessing a firearm, in a rail yard in San Bernardino, California. Convicted on all charges and sentenced to thirty days' imprisonment.

September 6, 1995 Voluntarily returned by INS to Mexico.

Resendiz's Brushes with the Law (cont'd)

August 4, 1996	Issued a warning for trespassing at a railroad yard in Macon, Georgia.
August 6, 1996	Arrested for trespassing at a railroad yard in Kentucky; pled guilty, sentenced to three days' imprisonment, and released.

The Revolving Door

Voluntary departure is the wink-and-nudge practice of releasing illegal aliens on their own volition and trusting them to return to their home country—and stay there. The option exists in order to cut detention, hearing, and transportation costs related to the formal deportation process. But this supposedly taxpayer-friendly policy is a far better deal for illegal border-crossers than it is for law-abiding Americans.

Illegal aliens who are granted voluntary departure get to bypass tough sanctions that would otherwise legally bar them from the country for ten years and jeopardize future applications for permanent residence status. This no-consequences policy is an open invitation for illegal immigrants to boomerang right back into the country.

The law supposedly prohibits illegal aliens who have been convicted of aggravated felonies[28] from receiving voluntary departure. The Border Patrol can also detain any alien who attempts to enter illegally after reaching a "threshold" number of apprehensions. (The threshold varies by patrol sector.) But these safeguards are tougher on paper than in practice.

According to federal watchdogs, the INS has an abysmal record of tracking voluntary departures, updating records to reflect an alien's true number of prior apprehensions, and making sure that dangerous criminal aliens do not benefit from the program. When the Inspector General's Office examined a sample of INS-granted voluntary departures from fall 1996 to winter 1997, nearly 70 percent of the cases revealed no evidence that criminal background checks had been done prior to the aliens' releases.[29] Even when checks are done, outdated and incomplete records still often result in aggravated felons receiving voluntary departure.

As the inspector general had discovered in 1998 — before the Resendiz case came to light — the INS was failing to take full advantage of the IDENT lookout database to check the criminal records and past deportations of illegal aliens caught at the border. In 1996, the agency had entered the fingerprints of only 41 percent of aliens deported and excluded from the country; only 24 percent of fingerprint records were accompanied by aliens' photographs. Less than two-thirds of all aliens apprehended along the United States–Mexico border had been enrolled into the IDENT system. The report concluded ominously: "We believe this results in previously deported aliens (including aggravated felons) being released from INS custody when subsequently apprehended because the INS is unaware of their immigration or criminal histories."[30]

On June 1, 1999, Resendiz walked into this criminal alien revolving door for the eighth time in fewer than eighteen months. At approximately 9:00 P.M. that evening, he tripped on a seismic sensor planted in a desert-like area about seven miles east of the Santa Teresa Border Patrol Station in New Mexico.

After a brief helicopter chase, agents tracked down Resendiz hiding in brush near some railroad tracks. He gave them one of his dozens of aliases. When they asked the usual questions: Had Resendiz ever been arrested or deported? The convicted criminal alien gave his usual answers: no and no.

Back at the station, an agent took his fingerprints and photo and checked them in the IDENT system. The program reported five prior apprehensions of Resendiz. His prints matched a few other entries, and the system offered the border agent some scanned photographs for comparison with Resendiz's face. But the agent in charge didn't bother looking at them because, as he later told investigators, "his supervisors encouraged agents to return to the field as soon as possible and not spend excessive time in the office."[31]

Two days after he was voluntarily released, Resendiz found his way across the border. First, he traveled to Houston, Texas, where he bludgeoned Noemi Dominguez in her bed; then to Weimar, where he beat Josephine Konvicka to death; then up to Gorham, Illinois, where he killed George Morber Sr., and his daughter, Carolyn.

When the Border Patrol let him go on June 1, 1999, Resendiz was the subject of three outstanding warrants for his arrest: one issued on January 5, 1999, by Houston-area law enforcement authorities related to the Benton burglary and murder; another issued by the FBI on May 27, 1999, charging Resendiz with being an unlawful fugitive from justice and describing his connection to the murders of Benton, the Sirnics, and Christopher Maier; and the old 1995 bench warrant related to burglary charges in New Mexico. In addition, he had three past deportations and nine criminal convictions on his record, including several aggravated felony convictions that should have disqualified him for voluntary departure.

How did the INS let this monster slip out of its fingers? Initially, the INS blamed a "computer glitch." But Resendiz's fatal release was neither a failure of software nor of hardware.

The computers did not tell the Border Patrol agents that Resendiz was a wanted fugitive, suspected murderer, and career criminal because INS employees (many of whom later complained that they didn't know how to use their high-tech equipment) repeatedly failed to input the information.

This was not a technology problem. It was human error compounded by apathy compounded by ignorance.

INS's Bloody Blunders

When news of Resendiz's June 1, 1999, release by Border Patrol agents in New Mexico became public, the INS sought vainly to pin the blame on everyone and everything but itself. Some complained there hadn't been enough money to link the IDENT system to other criminal databases. INS spokesman Russ Bergeron and others pointed the finger at police and investigators for not asking the agency to put Resendiz's warrant information in its system. The killer's data were missing, Bergeron explained, because "nothing has been input into IDENT at the request of the outside agencies."[32]

Aside from the pass-the-buck pusillanimity, there was one other problem with that statement. It was patently false.

In the six months leading up to Resendiz's encounter with the Border Patrol on June 1, 1999, the INS had received numerous requests from local and state investigators to put internal alerts about the fugitive serial killer in the INS's tracking system.

"Border Lookout" Ignored

After Claudia Benton's body was discovered at the end of 1998, West University Place police officer Kenneth Macha, who worked in the slain doctor's suburban neighborhood, contacted INS Special Agent Kelly Dozier in Houston. Macha inquired about putting a "border lookout" into the agency's system. Such an alert would notify border officers and other INS officials that Resendiz was a wanted man and should not be released. Dozier referred him to the Customs Service, which has a limited database called TECS (Treasury Enforcement Communications System) for checking aliens at ports of entry. She never once mentioned to Macha the existence of the IDENT lookout database, which red-flags criminal alien border-crossers such as Resendiz, because she didn't know about it. She also told federal investigators that "she did not normally use IDENT because it was not usually working."[33]

Macha followed Dozier's advice and contacted a Customs Service agent to request that a lookout be placed in the TECS system. But that agent never did so and later could not recall what he told Macha about the matter.

Never Followed Up on Call

Also in early January 1999, a Houston police analyst contacted another INS special agent, Marco Saltarelli, who specialized in apprehending and deporting criminal aliens and was assigned the Resendiz case. The police analyst asked for Resendiz's "A-file"—the INS cache of records that includes jail records, prior indictments, photographs, and other documents that could help track Resendiz down. Saltarelli agreed to order the file.

The Houston cop informed the West University Place investigators that Saltarelli would have the file available. Macha and a colleague met with Saltarelli in February and took photos from the file. Once again, Macha inquired about putting a border lookout on Resendiz. Saltarelli phoned a Customs agent to check whether a lookout had been placed in the TECS system—but never mentioned the existence of IDENT to the officers. The Customs agent later acknowledged to federal investigators that he never followed up on Saltarelli's call.[34]

Federal investigators later learned that the TECS lookout was not placed until June 21, 1999 — after Resendiz had been placed on the FBI's Ten Most Wanted list.[35] Another missed opportunity arose when Saltarelli contacted the INS Houston District's intelligence officer, Michael Juliano, at the end of February 1999. Juliano authored a weekly intelligence report highlighting information about investigative cases; it was distributed throughout the Houston district and the agency's Central Region Intelligence Office. Saltarelli supplied data about the Resendiz case for the report, which appeared during the week of February 22–28, 1999. Two senior intelligence officers in the Central Region read the report and offered to make an electronic wanted poster for Resendiz to be distributed nationwide by e-mail to all INS border stations and other enforcement sites.

Juliano sent them a photo for the poster — and never heard from them again. Nor did the high-ranking intelligence officers ever suggest that IDENT be used to flag Resendiz at the border.[36]

Too "Busy" to Remember

On March 1, 1999, Texas ranger Drew Carter contacted yet another INS special agent in Houston, Albert Plasket, to obtain Resendiz's A-file. The West University Place investigators accompanied Carter to the INS office. Plasket and other special agents discussed the case with the cops, but none ever mentioned the existence of IDENT's lookout capabilities. Nine days later, Carter phoned Plasket to make sure there was an "internal hold" on Resendiz — so that if the INS came into contact with him, the agency would keep him in custody. Plasket took no action to place Resendiz in the IDENT lookout system — and later claimed not to remember taking Carter's call.[37]

Small wonder. Plasket was apparently busy with other matters. Barely a month after meeting with the cops, Agent Plasket
was indicted in a separate matter for extortion and theft of government funds and later sentenced to one year's probation after
resigning from the agency.[38]

"IDENT Who?"

During the second week of June 1999, the FBI formed a multi-
agency task force to coordinate the Resendiz manhunt. An FBI
special agent sent a request to INS headquarters in Washington
for a lookout to be placed in the agency's "NAILS" system—
another database used primarily by inspectors at ports of entry
to check incoming travelers. The NAILS lookout on Resendiz
was placed on June 28, 1999. But no one at INS headquarters
thought to place a lookout in the five-year-old IDENT system,
even though the agency regularly touted the costly program's
success in nabbing criminal aliens.

In the meantime, another FBI agent contacted an INS senior
special agent in Houston requesting any INS files in addition to
Resendiz's A-file that might assist the task force. The INS agent,
Thomas Cason, queried several databases—but did not review
IDENT or even mention it to the FBI.[39]

Despite wide publicity about the IDENT system (much of
which came from the agency itself), INS special agents, their
supervisors, and senior intelligence officers claimed ignorance
of its ability to place border lookouts on dangerous criminal
aliens. Yet most of these officials admitted that they had received
training in the system.

To make matters worse, managers of the INS's Alien and
Criminal Apprehension Unit in Houston said the machines in
their office didn't work. Cason, the INS senior special agent in
Houston, didn't even know his district office had an IDENT

workstation. The top two managers in the district's investigations office—who had been responsible for distributing a memo informing their subordinates about the IDENT lookout system and related policies in August 1998—had no clue themselves about how IDENT worked. No one used IDENT, sniffed another high-ranking Houston INS official.[40]

Not until it was too late, anyway.

A Glimmer of Competence

David Estevis was the lead INS intelligence officer in the Del Rio Border Patrol Sector along the Texas border with Mexico. On June 10, 1999, after receiving a warning package about Resendiz from the multi-agency task force, Estevis acted immediately to ensure that all of his colleagues along the border were alerted to the dangerous suspected killer. Unlike the know-nothings and do-nothings back in Houston, Estevis was aware of IDENT's lookout function—even though he had never himself been trained on the system and had never used it before. He took personal responsibility for finding out how to use it, and made several phone calls to Cason—the senior special agent back in Houston—requesting Resendiz's fingerprints. Cason never got back to him.[41] Instead of giving up on Cason's unreturned calls, Estevis turned elsewhere.

He obtained the prints from an FBI agent and sent them to the INS's Biometric Support Center in Washington with a note stating that it was "important for the safety of our agents" (let alone the American public) for Resendiz to be enrolled in IDENT's lookout database. On June 22, 1999, Resendiz was finally added to the IDENT lookout database. It was Estevis who, after reviewing a printout of IDENT information, discovered that Resendiz had been apprehended and released eight times since January 1998—including the fateful June 1, 1999, release that freed Resendiz to continue his killing spree.

Estevis had taken the initiative that so many of his superiors—who don't deserve to be called "intelligence" officers—had failed to take. Unfortunately, Estevis's rare display of competence didn't come soon enough for Christopher Maier, Leafie Mason, Claudia Benton, Norman and Karen Sirnic, Josephine Konvicka, Noemi Dominguez, George Morber Sr., Carolyn Frederick, Fannie Byers, Jessie Howell, and Wendy Von Huben.

Promises, Promises

On July 13, 1999, Angel Maturino Resendiz surrendered to Texas ranger Drew Carter and federal authorities at a port of entry near El Paso, Texas. Resendiz sits today on Death Row, eating chocolate cream pies, watching Spanish-language television, whining about depression, and selling locks of his hair on Internet auction sites.[42]

After his conviction, the INS and the Justice Department vowed publicly to reform the IDENT training program and integrate the immigration databases with other law enforcement criminal tracking programs—chief among them, the FBI's National Crime Information Center database, which contains comprehensive data on individuals with outstanding federal warrants and significant criminal histories.

In March 2000, the INS said it would proceed "as expeditiously as possible" to merge the two systems. By December 2001, however, the inspector general reported that the integration of the databases "is proceeding slowly. Even after the Resendiz case spurred increased attention in 1999 to the need for such integration, the process has not gone quickly and an integrated system may still be many years away."[43]

The databases are unlinked today, and it remains INS policy *not* to use the $65 million IDENT system to check the criminal backgrounds and fingerprints of every illegal alien apprehended at our borders and ports of entry. Doing so, says the agency, would be too time-consuming and administratively impossible— especially at the border, where officials note that the INS apprehends some 1.5 million illegal aliens every year.

And yet, as Representative Lamar Smith of Texas has pointed out, the feds are able to subject each and every law-abiding American buying a gun from a federally licensed dealer in the United States to instant background checks—using a much cheaper and more efficient computer system. (The $37 million National Instant Criminal Background Check System contains more than 38 million criminal history records, over half a million wanted-persons records, and over four hundred thousand records of restraining and protective orders.[44] In its first two years alone, the system processed more than 18.5 million criminal background checks on Americans.)

The message is clear: Our government is far more committed to cracking down on gun-owning Americans who want to protect themselves than it is to protecting those citizens from criminal illegal aliens.

Chapter 5

In Cold Blood

Foreign Cop-Killers on the Loose

For every lazy bureaucrat who shirks the serious job of protecting American lives from alien menaces, there is a heroic figure like David Estevis.

But the men and women who put their lives on the line to save Americans are no safer than civilians when dangerous elements such as Angel Resendiz and the September 11 terrorists are allowed to roam the United States.

Seventy-two law enforcement officers died on September 11 because of foreign terrorists, and countless more around the country have been killed by alien criminals who shouldn't even be in the United States in the first place. Here are the stories of just a few:

A Man's Man

Los Angeles Police detective Russell Kuster's life and character are the stuff of Hollywood movies. Born in Kentucky, raised in Indiana, and living in southern California, Kuster was the strong and silent type. He had a quirky habit of calling every young newbie under his wing in the LAPD homicide unit "Roy." He dearly loved his wife Sue, a former Fresno beauty queen.

Kuster's friends and colleagues told the *Los Angeles Times,* he "was the kind of guy who got mad if people bad-mouthed President Bush.... The kind of guy who had pictures of Ronald Reagan, Clint Eastwood and John Wayne behind his desk and who liked to listen to the Marine Corps hymn. The kind of guy who joked around."

A "man's man, a cop's cop and a Marine's Marine," another friend said.[1]

A grizzled twenty-five-year veteran, Kuster had handled some of the most high-profile cases in the city, including the drug overdose death of comedian John Belushi. On October 9, 1990, Kuster witnessed one last tragic case of a preventable death: his own.

While dining off-duty at a Hungarian restaurant in his Hollywood precinct, the fifty-year-old Kuster overheard a hostile customer arguing with management and terrorizing patrons. Kuster identified himself as a cop and tried to calm the pistol-waving man. His intervention cost him his life.

The gunman turned the red laser sight of his nine-millimeter pistol on Kuster and fired four rounds. As he lay mortally wounded with a bullet near his heart, Kuster returned fire and killed the assailant with a shot to the head. Kuster was a year shy of retirement.

In a strange twist of fate, the two had crossed paths before. Kuster's murderer was Bela Istvan Marko, an illegal alien from Hungary with an extensive rap sheet. In his homeland, he had been arrested for robbery, blackmail, rape, and theft. He entered the U.S. illegally outside of San Diego in 1981. A year later, Hollywood detectives arrested him in the fatal shooting of his roommate. Kuster handled the paperwork. The district attorney eventually dropped the case after Marko claimed self-defense. But he was convicted on drug-peddling charges later in 1982.

When the INS finally moved to deport him after the drug offense, Marko applied for political asylum. The liberal asylum laws allowed this criminal alien to leave custody and disappear back into the American landscape. He bided his time for a few years before committing sexual assault in Nevada. While Marko served time in a Nevada prison in 1985, the INS secured a deportation order.

But Hungary wouldn't take him back and no one else would accept him. Marko was freed in 1989 under a custodial program that required him to check in with INS authorities periodically. The twice-convicted criminal alien continued his rotten lifestyle undeterred. "We couldn't put him adrift in a boat," an INS official lamented.[2]

Had Marko been set adrift in a boat, Detective Kuster's violent death might have been prevented.

Where's Mommy?

Officer Tina F. Kerbrat was a vivacious rookie Los Angeles Police Department officer, the devoted wife of a city firefighter, and the loving mom of three-year-old Nicole and six-year-old Craig. On February 11, 1991, barely a day after her thirty-fourth birthday, Kerbrat was shot to death while attempting to question two men drinking on a public sidewalk in the industrial strip of Sun Valley.

One of the suspects was Jose Amaya, an illegal alien from El Salvador who had been ordered by the INS to leave the country.

Before Kerbrat was able to step out of her police cruiser, Amaya fired four times at her at nearly point-blank range with a .357 magnum revolver. She was fatally struck once in the face. Kerbrat's partner returned fire, killing Amaya.

According to his family, Amaya first entered the country illegally in 1988. He traveled back and forth illegally between El Salvador and California, filing a request for political asylum soon after arriving in the United States. In the fall of 1988, the INS denied the request. But Amaya again remained in the country. After waiving his right to appeal the denial, he agreed to abide by an order to leave the United States voluntarily. Amaya left, but shortly returned. In August 1990, he was arrested at a Border Patrol checkpoint while trying to cross into California illegally. But Amaya remained in the country.

Then–Los Angeles police chief Daryl Gates blasted the laxity of the deportation process. In characteristically blunt language, he assailed Amaya as "an El Salvadoran drunk—a drunk who doesn't belong here" and noted that Kerbrat's death was "another failure of our immigration service [which] doesn't pay much attention to those who are here, who ought not to be here." The INS came up with procedural alibis and poorhouse rhetoric for the failure to kick Amaya out of the country for violating his voluntary departure order and for breaking the law again when he attempted illegal reentry. "Our people are absolutely working their fingers to the bone," whined Ben Davidian, INS western regional commissioner. "When you're faced with that immensity of a problem and the short numbers of staff we have, one begins to understand how difficult our job is to do."[3]

Meanwhile, Hispanic activists demanded an apology from Gates for speaking the truth and protested in front of police headquarters as Officer Kerbrat's colleagues mourned. Gates responded to the race-card-playing critics in a letter to the editor published by the *Los Angeles Times*:

[Tina Kerbrat] died while trying to protect the people of Los Angeles by making their streets safe. She died while serving all the people of Los Angeles without regard for their race, nationality, creed, religion, age, sex or their status of residency in this country. She died without warning; without reason. The shame of the United States' immigration system failure continues. Instead of addressing the problem, too many demand apologies from the too few who dare allude to the criminal element among our undocumented residents as being undesirables who should be deported.[4]

Nearly four thousand people turned out for Officer Kerbrat's funeral. The North Hollywood police station where Kerbrat worked built a shadow box memorial for her. An award for police rookies was named in her honor. But for Kerbrat's husband and children, three-year-old Nicole and six-year-old Craig, no memento can replace her loss. Self-pitying INS officials should be shamed by the continuing deadly legacy of the deportation morass, and the words of Tina Kerbrat's young daughter should never cease to haunt them:

"Where's Mommy?" the child asked as her slain mother's casket was carried into church. "Are we going to go see Mommy die now?"[5]

Robbed of a Life

James Eric Saunders Jr. was born into this world without a father—and the INS is partly to blame.

On October 7, 1999, James Eric Saunders Sr., a seven-year veteran of the Washington State Patrol, was gunned down in cold blood by an illegal alien from Mexico during a routine traffic stop. Trooper Saunders, thirty-one, died four months before the birth of his second child. He also left behind wife Billie Jean and two-year-old daughter Megan.

Saunders's murderer, Nicolas Solorio Vasquez, had a long criminal history. He was a convicted drug offender and violent criminal who had been released or deported three times by the INS. After each release, he reentered the country illegally and headed back up to the Pacific Northwest to commit more crimes. During one of these trips, Vasquez was charged with attempted murder involving another illegal alien—but the alleged victim was deported before the case could be prosecuted. Vasquez was booted out of the United States soon after, but quickly resurfaced in southeastern Washington. On July 26, 1999, police booked him into a Franklin County jail for unlawful delivery of cocaine and heroin. The INS should have taken Vasquez into custody immediately upon his release. Federal law mandates that immigration authorities detain criminal aliens with extensive rap sheets such as Vasquez's until their deportation outside the United States.[6] Local jail officials notified the Border Patrol of his presence by fax the day following his arrest; agents visited the Franklin County Corrections Center numerous times during the period of Vasquez's confinement. But they just plain forgot to pick him up.[7]

INS agents initially claimed not to have received the faxed booking sheet. They later acknowledged having received it, but were either "unaware" of it or had "no memory" of seeing it. "The INS's mission should be 'detect, detain, and deport,' " says Saunders's attorney, Diehl Rettig of Kennewick, Washington. "Yet, they have no formal policy for detecting illegals in jail. It's hit or miss."[8]

Indeed, the General Accounting Office reports that in the last half of 1995 alone, nearly two thousand deportable criminal aliens walked out of jail and disappeared into the American mainstream without any INS intervention. A GAO follow-up report on the post-release criminal activities of 635 of these criminal aliens found that 23 percent had been rearrested.[9]

Two months and two days after Vasquez walked out of jail, Saunders kissed his pregnant wife and toddler daughter, left for work, and never came back. At 8:59 P.M., he pulled over a green Mazda pickup in the town of Pasco. He radioed dispatchers to let them know of the routine stop. A minute later, Saunders was shot multiple times in the head and neck. A passerby used Saunders's radio to call for help, but it was too late. The truck owner who was later tracked down and found in possession of the murder weapon—a nine-millimeter gun—was Vasquez.

This illegal alien was charged with aggravated murder and sentenced to life without the possibility of parole in the summer of 2001.[10] At the hearing, Billie Saunders spoke of the devastating impact of her husband's death on her young family: "Every day I am faced with the sinking realization that my husband will never be coming home.... My whole world was shattered," she said. "There are so many things our children will never have in their lives," she said. "Our children have been robbed of a life that should have included both their mom and their dad."

First Words Never Heard: "Da-da"

Just twenty-two days after Nicolas Vasquez gunned down James Saunders in Washington State, yet another foreign cop-killer struck. The tragedy turned another young officer's pregnant wife into a widow and single mother.

On October 29, 1999, Sergeant Ricky Timbrook of Winchester, Virginia, was on patrol in the small town of 24,000. That night, the thirty-two-year-old police officer joined colleagues in a street chase. Minutes before midnight, Timbrook was shot point-blank in the head while in pursuit of a suspect. He died about half an hour later at a local hospital, leaving behind pregnant wife Kelly. She gave birth to their only child, Ricky Lee Timbrook Jr., two months later. More than three thousand mourners attended Timbrook's funeral; the entire city paused to observe thirty-one seconds of silence in honor of his badge number.

The man eventually arrested, convicted, and sentenced to death in May 2001 for Timbrook's murder was Edward Nathaniel Bell. He was a resident alien from Jamaica with a history of trouble with the law. In 1997, Bell had been arrested by Sergeant Timbrook and convicted for illegal possession of a concealed and loaded handgun.

INS agents arrested and detained Bell on $6,500 bail nearly a year later in an effort to deport him. But Bell knew how to play the game. He went to an immigration judge in Arlington, Virginia, and requested a bond reduction. Judge Joan V. Churchill, who began work as an INS lawyer in 1967 and has sat on her perennially backlogged bench since 1980, agreed to reduce Bell's bail to $3,500. He posted the amount and was released on October 9, 1998.

Over the next year, Bell won numerous delays in his deportation proceedings. Acquaintances testified at Bell's capital murder trial that in his spare time, he talked of shooting his arresting officer and showed off a gun. Sometime after being charged with Sergeant Timbrook's murder, Bell actually had the gall to apply for American citizenship. His final hearing in Immigration Court had been scheduled just days after Timbrook's death.

In testimony before Congress in December 2001, former Winchester city attorney Paul Thomson, who prosecuted the Bell case, noted:

Obviously, tougher... pre-trial detention and release requirements would have seriously impaired Bell's ability to greatly
harm law enforcement officers and the community. However,
detention eliminates all the risk of harm and would save precious INS resources. For example, releasing a defendant on
bond pending removal presents INS agents with the difficult
task of tracking down potentially dangerous criminals who
are motivated to kill government agents associated with
their deportation proceedings. Also, the Immigration pre-
trial supervision of Bell was non-existent. There was no
home electronic monitoring or other meaningful intensive
reporting requirements or curfew.[11]

That remains the case today for most aliens released on bond
pending deportation.

In June 2002, the Virginia Supreme Court unanimously upheld
Bell's conviction and sentence. He remains on death row as of
July 2002. Ricky Lee Timbrook Jr. is now almost three years old.
His first words were "Da-da"—for a father who did not live long
enough to hear his name spoken by his first and only child. Little Ricky Lee "will never know the joy of waking up to his daddy
every day," his mother notes.[12]

A Great Protector

Los Angeles County Sheriff's Deputy David March was a widely
respected officer and seven-year veteran of law enforcement. A
loving husband and stepfather, he grew peppers in his garden
and enjoyed deep-sea fishing. In an e-mail to his boss following
an evaluation earlier this spring, he wrote: "My goals are simple.
I will always be painfully honest, work as hard as I can, learn as
much as I can and hopefully make a difference in people's

lives."[13] He was scheduled to be transferred to a station closer to his hometown of Saugus in April 2002.

But on the morning of March 29, 2002, Deputy David March's life was cut short after he pulled over a man for a routine traffic stop in a San Gabriel Valley suburb. The driver stepped out of the car, walked toward March, pulled out a nine-millimeter semiautomatic pistol, and fired at close range several times before fleeing. March, thirty-three, died later that day of gunshot wounds to the head at a nearby hospital.

His suspected killer, Armando Garcia, is an illegal alien from Mexico who had been deported three times—in 1992, 1994, and 2001—and convicted of two felonies while in America. As of July 19, 2002, he remained a fugitive in the slaying of Deputy March.

Garcia has an extensive criminal history, from drug dealing and weapons violations to suspected murder. Despite a federal law requiring criminal prosecution for illegal reentry into the United States, neither the INS nor the U.S. Attorney's Office in Los Angeles took any measures to keep Garcia off the streets.[14]

"We've lost a great protector," Los Angeles County sheriff Lee Baca told thousands of mourners at March's funeral. "A protector of life. A protector of human spirit."

Yet another cop buried, another illegal immigrant on the loose, and another family robbed because of the failure simply to enforce the law. Such are the hidden, tragic consequences of interminable "due process" and tolerance for criminal aliens.

Chapter 6

The Torturers Next Door

"I had always hoped that this land might become a safe and agreeable asylum to the virtuous and persecuted part of mankind, to whatever nation they might belong."[1]

—George Washington, 1788

America has always welcomed those fleeing political persecution abroad. But Lady Liberty would have a heart attack if she knew who was exploiting her generosity now. The land of the free has become the new home of some of the world's most depraved thugs. Among them—living among us—are known or suspected warlords, women-beaters, psychological torturers, butchers, and other violent war criminals.

It's horrifying enough when immigration authorities inadvertently allow the likes of the September 11 hijackers, illegal alien serial killer Angel Resendiz, and alien cop-killers to roam our country. But our government officials make matters even worse when they *deliberately* allow such wretched refuse to enjoy the good life here as tourists, refugees, businessmen, legal permanent residents, and even naturalized American citizens.

Neither the INS nor any other federal agency formally tracks convicted or suspected human rights persecutors. Foreign war criminals are not included in border watch lists. But according to various human rights groups and newspaper investigations, there may be anywhere between one hundred and seven thousand foreign nationals living in the United States who have committed human rights atrocities around the globe.[2] The *Miami Herald* estimated that at least eighty live in South Florida alone.[3]

Many have taken advantage of compassionate asylum and refugee policies intended for the victims of their abuse. Others obtained (and then illegally overstayed) visas with the aid of United States military and intelligence officials, who argue that their presence abroad is "destabilizing" to their home countries.

Richard Krieger, a former State Department official based in Florida who has single-handedly and relentlessly hunted down many of these alien brutes and war criminals, says: "It is time our government acted on behalf of our interest and not the interest of foreign countries. Otherwise, whom do we welcome next?"[4]

Here are just ten of the shadiest characters who were allowed into our backyards by our nation's consular, immigration, and intelligence officials, and remain here today.

Call them America's *Least* Wanted.

Eriberto Mederos

Country of origin: Cuba

Status: Naturalized American citizen

Whereabouts: Free on bond in Miami

Eriberto Mederos is one of the most infamous suspected war criminals to wash up on our shores. A former intern at a Havana psychiatric hospital who allegedly tortured political prisoners on behalf of the Cuban Security Services, he was known as "El Enfermero" or "the nurse." Mederos hitched a ride to the United States on a Cuban boatlift in 1984 and found work as a nurse in Miami at a home for the elderly.

It was there Eugenio de Sosa Chabau recognized him as his torturer in their native Cuba. Editor of the dissident newspaper, *Diario de la Marina* and vocal critic of Castro's rise to power in the late 1950s, de Sosa Chabau spent two decades as a political prisoner in Cuba. He recalled being hooked up to wet electrical prods by Mederos at Cuba's Mazorra Psychiatric Hospital. Mederos, he said, delivered electric shocks to his temples and testicles during fourteen brutal sessions of so-called therapy. "You feel like an explosion in your head, and you lose consciousness," de Sosa Chabau recalled. When he awoke, after losing control of his bodily functions, he would usually be lying in his own filth.[5]

Numerous published accounts in mainstream news outlets documented Mederos's atrocities after his arrival in the United States. Former Cuban prisoner Amaro Gomez Boix recalled in the *Miami Herald* in 1989 how Mederos came to him every morning:

> Almost every day, his various assistants call out loudly the names of the unfortunate chosen who will be asked to lay [*sic*] down on the wet cement so that the electrical current will travel better. Mederos then fastens the electrodes and the entire process is performed with routine skill, which often entails overlooking the placement of a rubber bit in the prisoner's mouth. It is no surprise then, that when that first jolt of power zaps the prisoner's body, his teeth grind down on his tongue, turning his mouth into a bloodied foam.[6]

Other inmates described similar treatment. Guards chained down Jose Ros, hosed him down while naked, and shocked him three times a week. Jorge Ferrer recalled men breaking their teeth as electric currents ran through their bodies.[7] In 1991, Mederos's brutality was described in a booklet called *The Politics of Psychiatry in Revolutionary Cuba,* published by the widely respected Freedom House. Authors Charles J. Brown and Armando Lago exposed the plight of twenty-seven political dissidents who were diagnosed with "mental illness" and "treated" by Mederos with electroshock torture. The *Miami Herald* followed up with another series on El Enfermero in 1992. Despite the media reports, vocal protest from Florida's Cuban community, and dogged whistle-blowing by Krieger, the INS inexplicably rewarded Mederos with United States citizenship in the spring of 1993.

Krieger, who runs a watchdog humanitarian group called International Educational Missions, spearheaded the drive to denaturalize Mederos. He urged the INS to strip foreign criminals of their citizenship for lying on their application form. One question asks applicants: "Have [you] ever persecuted (either directly or indirectly) any person because of race, national origin, membership in a particular social group, or political opinion?" Another asks, "Have [you] ever been a member of or in any way associated (either directly or indirectly) with the Communist party?"

In September 2001, the INS heeded Krieger's advice and arrested Mederos for illegally obtaining citizenship by lying about his moral character and his association with the Communist Party in Cuba.[8] His trial began in mid-July 2002, as this book went to press.

Fourteen of Mederos's victims agreed to provide depositions and testimony. But de Sosa Chabau will not be among them. He died of cancer on New Year's Day 2002. His fifty-two-page action against Fidel Castro for crimes against humanity, co-signed by a group of eight other Cuban exiles last fall under a Belgian war crimes law, will proceed. In the meantime, Mederos is free on $500,000 bail in Miami.

Asked to explain how the agency granted citizenship to one of the most notoriously accused electroshock torturers of the Castro regime, James Goldman, chief of investigations for the INS, responded: "There is not a lot of evidence in the file."[9]

Kelbessa Negewo

Country of origin: Ethiopia

Status: Naturalized American citizen

Whereabouts: Atlanta

Another monster in our midst is Kelbessa Negewo. A former senior government official and head of the secret police in Ethiopia, Negewo oversaw the torture and execution of political prisoners in the late 1970s. A decade later, Negewo obtained a visitor visa and moved to the United States, where he found work as a bellhop at the Colony Square Hotel in Atlanta. He immedi-ately filed a political asylum claim, which was granted in 1988.

A female Ethiopian refugee who worked as a waitress recog-nized Negewo in 1989 as the man who led the "Red Terror" tor-ture campaign. The waitress, Edgegayehu Taye, joined two other female Ethiopian refugees, Elizabeth Demissie and Hirute Abebe-Jira, in suing Negewo for human rights abuses under an obscure law called the Alien Tort Claims Act. It allows foreign residents to take to United States courts those who break the law of nations or a treaty of the United States.[10]

The women, who were all teenagers at the time of their tor-ture, gave graphic testimony of being stripped, bound, hung upside down from poles, beaten for hours, and jailed under Negewo's personal supervision. Guards poured water in Taye's wounds to increase the pain; she was held for three years without charges. They whipped Abebe-Jira's legs and back with wire; her mouth was stuffed with a stocking soaked with blood and vomit. Demissie was tied to a wooden pole, lifted in the air, and beaten severely. Her fifteen-year-old sister, who had been imprisoned with her, was taken away by Negewo's guards and never seen again.[11]

In 1993, a federal court awarded the plaintiffs compensatory and punitive damages in the amount of $1.5 million. United States district court judge G. Ernest Tidwell, who presided over the nonjury trial, said each woman "clearly established her claims of torture" and "chilling" abuses by Negewo.[12] The judgment was upheld on appeal.

But despite the damning testimony of three of his emotionally and physically scarred victims, Negewo received United States citizenship from the INS in 1995. It was an "unconscionable snafu," says Atlanta attorney Michael Tyler, who helped represent the three torture victims pro bono. "How the INS could grant citizenship [to Negewo] after the trial befuddles us all."[13]

Over the past nine years, the torture victims have urged the INS to right its egregious wrong and strip Negewo of the privileges of United States citizenship. When Negewo declared bankruptcy to escape paying the 1993 judgment against him, the women gave up that pursuit in order to concentrate on denaturalization efforts. "Their ultimate goal is to deny him sanctuary in this country," said Tyler. "He doesn't deserve to be here. It is anathema to our concept of asylum."[14]

Negewo lives in Atlanta at an unlisted residence. The INS currently has no plans to initiate denaturalization or deportation proceedings against him.

Emmanuel "Toto" Constant

Country of origin: Haiti

Status: Holds expired tourist visa

Whereabouts: Queens, New York

Before coming to this country, Emmanuel Constant created and led the Front for the Advancement and Progress of Haiti (FRAPH). Don't let the name fool you. FRAPH was a savage paramilitary organization linked to the murders of some three thousand prodemocracy activists since the 1991 ouster of United States–backed Haitian president Jean-Bertrand Aristide. Constant was known and feared by his countrymen as "The Devil."

FRAPH's torture methods, such as "facial scalping" (using machetes to peel the skin from a person's face from ear to ear), have been widely documented by human rights watchdogs.[15] During his illegal junta's three-year reign of terror, Constant called for his followers to kill American soldiers and advocated the use of biological weapons. In the fall of 1993, Constant helped lead a raid against a U.S. Navy ship, the *Harlan County*, which was prepared to dock at Port-au-Prince with American and Canadian troops to help rebuild Haiti.[16] The ship's withdrawal, broadcast live on CNN, humiliated international dignitaries. "That was the day FRAPH was actually born," Constant bragged.[17]

Despite his top-ranking position as a violent coup leader and death squad terrorist, Constant obtained a special, six-month United States tourist visa often issued to foreign government officials. (He later admitted to being on the payroll of the CIA.[18]) After the junta collapsed, The Devil quietly entered the United States through Puerto Rico at the end of 1994. He landed in a neighborhood in Queens, New York, where he lived unobtrusively in an apartment with his aunt and conducted real-estate and computer businesses on the side. After an outcry from shocked

Haitian refugees who encountered Constant at the local Block-buster, discos, galleries, and food markets, an immigration judge issued a deportation order against Constant in 1995. It was withdrawn when the Clinton State Department objected.

After eleven months in detention, Constant was released from INS custody under a confidential agreement. The feds claimed that he did not present a threat to public safety in the United States.[19]

In December 2000, a Haitian court handed down a life sentence to Constant in absentia for the 1994 murders of civilian Aristide supporters in the shantytown of Raboteau. The United States has refused to meet Haiti's extradition request. State Department officials say Constant has an outstanding deportation order against him, but that it will not be executed for the foreseeable future.[20]

Despite his blood-splattered legacy, Constant remains free to earn a comfortable living and haunt the streets of Queens unencumbered.

Carl Dorelien

Country of origin: Haiti

Status: Holds expired tourist's visa

Whereabouts: Detained in Miami

The Devil's former countryman and fellow coup conspirator, Colonel Carl Dorelien, has had a strange journey of his own to our country. In Haiti, Dorelien served as head of personnel for the national army that seized power from President Aristide in 1991. Dorelien directed a seven-thousand-man force linked to a three-year campaign of murder, rape, kidnapping, and torture that resulted in the deaths of some five thousand Haitian civilians.

In 1997, Dorelien made headlines in America—not for his dubious past, but for winning a $3.2 million lottery prize in

Florida. Dorelien had somehow reinvented himself and attained the ultimate American fantasy. An official LOTTO press release described him as "a native of the Caribbean region" who had lived in the Port St. Lucie area for the past two years.[21] An aunt told the *Palm Beach Post* that he had been down on his luck, "at the end of his rope," and out of work—even as he sported a Ralph Lauren shirt and a gold bracelet.[22] How did he get here? He entered on a six-month tourist visa, overstayed, and filed a political asylum claim.

After news of his lottery win alerted outraged human rights activists to his presence in Florida, immigration officials belatedly got on the ball. In the summer of 2001, the INS finally took Dorelien into custody. When agents knocked on the door of his suburban home, his wife lied and told them he was not home. He was trying to escape out a rear window. He retreated back into the house and, after a five-minute standoff, turned himself over to authorities.[23]

Dorelien, like Constant, was convicted in absentia in a Haitian court for his alleged role in the 1994 Robateau massacre that left as many as thirty people dead after they were tortured, shot, and dumped into the sea. He denies any culpability in the matter, and has appealed his rejected asylum claim. Dorelien currently bides his time at Miami's Krome Detention Center awaiting deportation that could, one INS official admits, "take quite a long time."[24] If ever.

Thi Dinh Bui

Country of origin: Vietnam

Status: Legal permanent resident

Whereabouts: Orange County, California

Thi Dinh Bui's current life appears to be the epitome of the American Dream. He's a hardworking immigrant who delivers newspapers in Westminster, California, for a living and has nine children. Like thousands of other refugees, Bui fled Vietnam and emigrated to the United States in 1994. But according to many of his native countrymen, the former South Vietnamese army captain hid dark secrets about his history from immigration authorities.

From 1975 to 1981, Bui served as a trusty in the Thanh Cam Communist reeducation camp near Hanoi after the end of the Vietnam War. In a signed affidavit filed with the INS, a fellow refugee alleged that Bui beat his fellow prisoners and killed another inmate by stomping on his stomach until he died. "Bui dragged me by my legs up the stairs to the solitary confinement room, banging my head against the steps," the surviving camp inmate wrote. "He threw me into a room and left me there; he thought I was dead. He then proceeded to beat Major Tiep Van Dang to death. I personally witnessed this brutal murder."[25]

The whistleblower was Father Le Huu Nguyen, a Roman Catholic priest, who has forgiven Bui for the beatings he received but says he felt compelled to tell the truth about Bui's responsibility for murder when he discovered Bui was living in the United States. "This man was used by the Communists, but he is innately evil," Nguyen said. "I saw what I saw."[26] At least nine other witnesses came forward with tales of abuse by Bui, and the INS launched an investigation in 2000.

The probe is shrouded in secrecy; federal officials won't say when the matter will be resolved. Even if the agency prevails in a deportation hearing, Bui may still remain in this country indefinitely because Vietnam does not have an extradition treaty with the United States.

The sister of the man Bui allegedly killed is furious. "He is a cruel animal, not a human being," said Nham Dang of Arlington, Virginia. "Like with World War II, if those who killed Jews came to the United States, you wouldn't accept them. I think [Bui] has done a similar crime."[27]

Yusuf Abdi Ali

Country of origin: Somalia

Status: Legal permanent resident

Whereabouts: Last known residence was Arlington, Virginia

In his home country, they had a nickname for Yusuf Abdi Ali: "Tokeh" ("The Crow"). He was a colonel in the Somalian army under the country's dictatorial president, Mohammed Siad Barre. Witnesses accused him of executing hundreds of civilians who belonged to a minority ethnic clan, the Issak, during the 1980s. When Barre's regime collapsed in 1990, Ali was in the United States receiving military training from our government. After his training ended, he headed up to Canada, found work as a municipal security guard, and filed for refugee status.

In 1992, a Canadian public television documentary aired accusations from Somali villagers who said Ali had massacred unarmed people and burned them alive.[28] After the broadcast, Canada belatedly acted on a year-old warrant for the colonel's deportation and dumped him on the United States. Despite another media exposé of his alleged crimes, this time by CBS News, Ali settled down here, left the country briefly, reentered under an alias, and blended in uneventfully until 1998. He once again found work as a security guard.

Responding to pressure from angry Somali refugees, the INS arrested Ali in February 1998 outside Washington, D.C., and charged him with lying on his application forms. INS spokesman Russ Bergeron told the *New York Times*: "The information that we obtained indicates that this person was directly involved in the incidents that led to the deaths of thousands of people."[29]

Investigators had lined up a dozen witnesses against Ali. But the agency's bid for deportation was foiled on a technicality and thrown out by an immigration judge.[30]

Ali disappeared into the American population. His last known residence was northern Virginia. Perhaps he is back in uniform, working as a security guard, for people who have absolutely no clue about the allegations of genocidal atrocities lodged against him by his former countrymen—and by our own government.

Zijad Music

Country of origin: Bosnia

Status: Refugee

Whereabouts: Burlington, Vermont

Vermont is famous for maple syrup, teddy bears, Ben & Jerry's ice cream, and picturesque snowfalls. It is also known around the world as one of America's safe havens for war refugees. Among them is a man named Zijad Music who appears to be the model refugee—a cheerful laborer working two jobs as a furniture mover and a baker, raising two children, and enjoying American freedom.

But there is another portrait of Music painted by those who knew him in his home country: a gun-toting, drunken Serbian nationalist who belonged to a paramilitary unit known as "El Manijakos" ("The Maniacs"). The armed gang was known for waging alcohol-driven raids, terrorizing and murdering Muslims and Croats in the northwestern city of Prijedor, Bosnia. Tens of thousands of non-Serbian residents were purged systematically from the city or placed in detention camps and killed.

In an investigative series by former *Boston Globe* reporter Steve Fainaru, close relatives, former members of El Manijakos, and alleged victims all identified Music as a participant in the death squad. Family members say Music's father died of grief over his son's involvement with Muslim persecutors. A Serb military official called Music a good soldier who, while Muslim, was "more of a Serb than half of the people in Manijakos.... He performed his assignments very well. Of course he did some small bad things, but everybody did a few bad things."[31]

Music denies involvement with El Manijakos, but he appeared in a video obtained by the *Globe* wearing the paramilitary group's distinctive badge, holding a gun, and carousing with other uniformed members.

The INS acknowledged that it never bothered to verify Music's claim of persecution before granting him refugee status and admitting him to the United States. After the newspaper report airing allegations against Music was published in 1999, INS officials expressed dismay. The field office in St. Albans, Vermont, launched a cursory investigation. But despite the fear of Music expressed by other Bosnian refugees living in Burlington, nothing has come of the probe. El Manijako is home free.

Carlos Eugenio Vides Casanova and Jose Guillermo Garcia

Country of origin: El Salvador

Status:
    Vides Casanova: legal permanent resident
    Garcia: legal permanent resident

Whereabouts: south Florida

Vides Casanova and Garcia are old colleagues and countrymen happily living out their twilight years in south Florida retirement communities. In their native land, they served as top-ranking El Salvadoran military generals who — backed by the

United States—oversaw a bloody twelve-year civil war against Marxist insurgents. From 1979 to 1983, Garcia headed the Defense Ministry and Vides Casanova led the National Guard.

Among the 75,000 casualties of the chaotic war were four innocent American churchwomen who were kidnapped, raped, and executed by Salvadoran National Guardsmen. Dorothy Kazel was a nun with the Ursuline Sisters of Cleveland. Ita Ford and Maura Clarke were Maryknoll nuns from New York. Jean Donovan was a lay missionary from the Cleveland Mission. They were shot in the head at close range, and their battered bodies were discovered in a shallow grave in December 1980.

Although five rank-and-file soldiers were convicted of the murders in 1984, questions remained about who ordered or sanctioned the killings at the top of the military hierarchy. A 1983 report commissioned by the Reagan administration and prepared by retired United States district court judge Harold Tyler found that the El Salvadoran government had initially sought to cover up the military's role in the women's murders. Tyler determined that the National Guard had known the identities of the killers within days of the murder, but that the official response to the information had ranged "from indifference to active cover-up."[32]

Judge Tyler specifically described Vides Casanova as "evasive" when questioned about early efforts by National Guard officers to conceal the crime, and he concluded that "it is quite possible that [Vides Casanova] was aware of, and for a time acquiesced in, the cover-up."[33] A decade later, a United Nations report concluded that there was substantial evidence that Vides Casanova did indeed know of a cover-up and facilitated the obstruction of justice, and that Garcia refused to thoroughly investigate the murders.[34]

In the ten years between the publication of these two reports, the State Department issued United States visas to both Garcia

and Vides Casanova. According to former State Department official Richard Boucher, both received B-2 nonimmigrant tourist
visas—Garcia in 1984, Vides Casanova in 1989.[35] Garcia applied
for, and received, political asylum in 1990. Vides Casanova
obtained legal permanent resident status.

Angered by their presence here, the victims' families filed a
civil lawsuit against the El Salvadoran generals in 1999 under
the Torture Victim Protection Act, which allows the families of
persecuted victims to use United States courts to hold high government officials accountable for subordinates' actions. A West
Palm Beach jury, while sympathetic to the plaintiffs, acquitted
the two military leaders in November 2000 because they believed
the defense argument—echoing the defense of Nazi war criminals like Field Marshal Hermann Goering—that the men did not
have effective control over their troops.

The case is on appeal, and another case against the generals
brought by El Salvadoran torture victims now living in the
United States went to trial in June 2002. One of them, Catholic
lay worker Neris Gonzales, was kidnapped, brutally beaten, and
raped at the hands of the National Guard in December 1979,
when she was eight months pregnant. Her infant child later died
of injuries related to the assault.[36]

Another of the plaintiffs, surgeon Juan Romagoza Arce, was
shot while working at a Catholic church clinic. Abducted by
National Guardsmen, he says he was stripped, beaten, sodomized,
chained to an iron rod, tortured with electroshock, and kept in a
"coffin-like box." His hands were permanently disfigured to prevent him from working as a surgeon. Arce says Vides Casanova
was physically present during his detention on two occasions.[37]

While Vides Casanova and Garcia enjoyed their grandchildren
and soaked up the Florida sun, the families of the murdered
churchwomen continue to push for the expulsion of the generals.

"I am very upset that the United States is becoming a retirement community of choice for butchers," said William Ford, brother of Maryknoll nun Ita Ford.[38]

Richard Krieger agrees. He is pushing the INS to investigate whether Vides Casanova and Garcia lied on their INS application forms. Garcia, for example, was granted asylum based on fear that he would be assassinated if he returned to his home country. But Garcia has since gone to El Salvador for a visit and returned safely.

"The United States, with our tradition of freedom, should not be letting these people in," says Krieger. "My maxim is that of the Holocaust: never again. That means in any country. We should not betray that legacy."[39]

Juan Evangelista Lopez Grijalba

Country of origin: Honduras

Status: Entered on tourist visa, gained "temporary protected status,"
   arrested in April 2002

Whereabouts: Krome Detention Center, Miami

Like many of his counterparts in the Honduran army, Juan Evangelista Lopez Grijalba was trained by the United States military. He became a senior intelligence officer and head of the Honduran secret police, and is widely believed to have cofounded a clandestine military unit called Battalion 316. This terrorist outfit was trained and equipped by the CIA, which later acknowledged that the Honduran military "committed hundreds of human rights abuses since 1980, many of which were politically motivated and officially sanctioned" and were linked to "death squad activities."[40]

Human Rights Watch reported that Battalion 316 was responsible for the torture and disappearances of many as 184 suspected leftists in the early 1980s, including an American Jesuit priest.[41]

After the Honduran National Commissioner for the Protection of Human Rights, Leo Valladares Lanza, published his own report implicating Lopez Grijalba and others in human rights atrocities, a judge in Honduras ordered Lopez Grijalba's arrest in 1996 to face two charges of murdering university students.

By that time, Lopez Grijalba had secured a tourist visa from the United States Embassy in Tegucigalpa and arrived safely in the United States. The *Miami Herald* reported that the former army colonel flew in and out of our country several times between 1995 and 1998.[42] He overstayed his original visa, but received temporary protected status under a special program for Hondurans living in the country after Hurricane Mitch hit Honduras in the summer of 1999. The special status allowed him to work and live here while his native country recovered from the natural disaster.

Public records reviewed by the *Herald* showed Lopez Grijalba living in a gated condominium community in west Miami. But neither journalists nor INS agents were able (or willing) to track the retired colonel down until April 2002. After seven years of sunny comfort in Sweetwater, Florida, Lopez Grijalba was finally arrested without incident in his home. The INS had allowed him to retain his temporary protected status until his arrest, when the privilege was finally revoked. As of July 2002, Lopez Grijalba remained in INS custody pending deportation.

"We are delighted that the INS and the United States Attorney's Office have acted on information that we provided them," the International Education Mission's Richard Krieger said. "We have a heck of a lot more of them out there to go after."[43]

Debasing a Sacred Privilege?

Although the INS has taken cursory steps to detain a small group of suspected human rights abusers in Florida, not a single case has been prosecuted successfully by the agency over the past eight years.

Moreover, there is no statutory mechanism for keeping such abusers out in the first place. Congress has twice considered and twice failed to pass a measure, called the Anti-Atrocity Alien Deportation Act, that would formally bar foreign torturers from entering the United States. It would provide a speedier process for stripping United States citizenship from naturalized residents found guilty of human rights crimes. And it would broaden the mandate of the Justice Department's Office of Special Investigations (which currently probes and prosecutes Nazi-era war criminals) so that it can investigate, denaturalize, and prosecute any modern-day war criminal who has participated in torture or genocide abroad.[44]

Representative Mark Foley of Florida, a sponsor of the bill, is not giving up. "We must locate and take action against these criminals," he says. "After all, statutes like Megan's Law allow communities to find out if known sex offenders move into the area. These same communities, however, could be oblivious to the fact that a brutal thug—who went on a rampage in a place like Haiti or Kosovo—is living anonymously among them."[45]

The American public may not be at risk of physical harm from many of these persecutors, especially those who are elderly retirees. But their mere presence here is irreconcilable with fundamental immigration principles. We want people who cherish freedom, not those who worked in other countries to smother it. We want people who respect the law, not those who once engaged in bloody lawlessness. We want people who embrace the American Dream, not those who caused nightmares abroad. The bestowal of United States citizenship on such persecutors is a slap in the face to every law-abiding immigrant who is required to show "good moral character" and "attachment to the principles of the United States Constitution" before becoming a naturalized American.

But in November 2001, Attorney General John Ashcroft dangled the promise of American citizenship before any foreigners, including criminal illegal aliens, who come forward with information that would aid the investigation of the September 11 terrorist attacks. Under the "responsible cooperators program," informants need only provide tips that are "useful and relevant." The information does not even need to lead to an arrest or conviction of a suspected terrorist. In exchange, foreigners will receive extended American visas, as well as permission to work here and apply for permanent residency leading to eventual naturalization. Those in violation of their current visas will be offered parole or deferred prosecution.

Said Ashcroft: "For many people, a visa that opens the pathway to American citizenship is worth its weight in gold."[46] The program is being publicized around the world.

Offering incentives to procure criminal evidence from informants is nothing new, of course. Our law enforcement officials shouldn't be denied creative means of gathering intelligence. But bribing foreign thugs with our most precious gift—United States citizenship—is fraught with moral (if not physical) peril. How many more ruthless torturers and callous generals can we tolerate in our neighborhoods, puttering around in their rose gardens while their victims' families mourn aghast? How many more Nurses and Devils and Crows and Maniacs?

Entry into this country must remain a fiercely guarded privilege, not a cheap bargaining chip to be tossed like a crumb to any willing scavenger.

Part III: Our Own Worst Enemies

Chapter 7

House of Horrors

The INS Mess

"What's happened in the INS is enough to drive a man to drink."[1]

So fumed Attorney General John Ashcroft in the spring of 2002, reacting to news that four Pakistani crewmen had illegally jumped ship in Norfolk, Virginia. They had been granted special visa waivers by an INS inspector who hadn't been told of tightened security rules governing temporary shore leaves.

This snafu came on the heels of Dead Hijacker Visa-gate, the INS's boneheaded mailing of student visa approval notices to the Florida flight school of dead September 11 hijackers Mohamed Atta and Marwan Al Shehhi. The school got the paperwork exactly six months after the hijackers' suicidal terrorist attacks on America. "I could barely get my coffee down," President Bush said after that miniscandal. "I was stunned and not happy. Let me put it another way: I was plenty hot."[2]

It's reassuring to see our leaders in Washington get hot and bothered over the laughingstock agency whose initials have come to stand for the "Incompetent and Negligent Service." And

145

"Information Not Sought." And more recently: "Ignoring National Security."[3]

But in the grand scheme of the INS's crimes and misdemeanors, these two incidents barely register a blip. Lawmakers should save their unmitigated fury for immigration officials who have deliberately and consciously undermined our safety by

— smuggling illegal aliens

— aiding foreign drug dealers

— accepting bribes from deported felons

— peddling fraudulent documents

— arranging fake marriages

— selling out citizenship

— trading sex, money, and Oriental rugs for visas, green cards, border crossing cards, and work authorization papers

Sound too horrific to be true? Read on.

Climate for Abuse

According to former Justice Department inspector general Michael Bromwich, the INS routinely outpaces the Federal Bureau of Investigation, Drug Enforcement Administration, Bureau of Prisons, and Marshals Service in terms of criminal activity by its agents. The current inspector general, Glenn Fine, has repeatedly "found that the INS has not sufficiently demanded accountability either of individual INS employees or from the organization as a whole."[4]

Immigration officials emphasize that a minority of the agency's 32,000 employees turn to crime. Yet, as former INS commissioner Doris Meissner admitted (and she knows firsthand), there is a "climate for abuse" at the INS that "doesn't exist in those other agencies."[5]

Leaving no doubt that it was business as usual at the INS, inspectors, examiners, and special agents continued to rack up corruption charges in 2001–2002. Here's just a partial list of INS criminals uncovered in my research:

A High-Priced Setup

INS agent Jesse Gardona, a fifteen-year veteran, worked for the Anti-Smuggling Unit in Los Angeles. But he apparently didn't understand the meaning of "anti" in "antismuggling."

According to court documents, in the summer of 1998, Gardona led a team of antismuggling agents to a Los Angeles drop house in which eleven illegal immigrants from El Salvador were being held. Four days later, according to an FBI agent's affidavit, Gardona arranged for the release of those eleven smuggled aliens. They were turned over to an associate of Gardona's — convicted drug dealer Jose Jesus Quintanilla — who ransomed them to relatives for up to $1,800 each.[6] Gardona allegedly took a cut of up to $300 a head.

At the time of his arrest, Gardona was in the process of moving from Los Angeles to Fresno as part of an INS *promotion*.[7] Gardona's lawyer argued that Gardona broke the law because he "was very moved by the plight" of smuggled aliens.[8] Investigators said he was paying off a debt he owed Quintanilla for help in setting up side businesses.

In January 2001, Gardona received an eighteen-month federal prison term for conspiring to accept bribes and harboring and transporting illegal immigrants — a small price to pay for betraying the public trust. Ever ready with the agency's defensive spin, Los Angeles INS district director Thomas Schiltgen insisted: "We look at this as an isolated situation." He stated that he was not inclined to review or revise his standard practices. "We continue to have a great deal of trust in our officers."[9]

Mr. and Mrs. Ethics

In March 2001, INS employee Rosemary LaGuardia Slattery was arrested while on official work assignment in Charlestown, North Carolina. She was teaching a course called Professionalism and Ethics. Local authorities charged her with getting fraudulent refunds from a department store by buying a garment and returning a cheaper substitute altered by using a device that made fake manufacturer-quality labels.

In August 2001, she pleaded no contest and was sentenced to one hundred hours of community service. Detective Paul Hernandez of the Charlestown police department told me that Mrs. Slattery "was not very cooperative. I don't think she was remorseful. I think she was just sorry that she got caught. If she could have gotten away with it, I believe she would still be at it today."[10] Slattery remains on unpaid leave from the INS's Federal Law Enforcement Training Center in Glynco, Georgia.[11]

Before taking on the role of ethics instructor, Slattery worked in INS internal affairs. She is married to William Slattery, who was former INS district director in New York City from 1990 to 1994 and later served as executive associate commissioner for field operations—the third-highest-ranking INS position in the nation.

After golfing and sharing a sauna with ex–South Korean spy and convicted felon Yung-Soo Yoo, Mr. Slattery reportedly directed investigators to halt INS raids of Korean-owned garment factories. He was also accused of giving unjustified bonuses and promotions to his future wife, Rosemary, while she was a trainee special agent in New York. An internal investigation cleared Mr. Slattery of any wrongdoing in 1996, but he resigned two years later amid continued complaints of malfeasance and cronyism from fed-up field managers.[12]

Selling Stamps

Jerry Floratos, a twenty-year INS employee, was an information officer at the agency's New York headquarters. He spent his mornings behind a window, answering questions and issuing visa stamps to customers who waited patiently in long lines. On his lunch breaks, Floratos secretly provided cheap shortcuts to dozens of illegal aliens. A contract security guard who worked in the same building would meet him with passports to be stamped by Floratos for between $75 and $200 each. After a year, Floratos had reaped more than $10,000 in bribe money. In March 2001, he received a three-month jail term, two years of supervised release, and a $10,000 fine.[13]

Sex with Detainees

At the long-troubled Krome Detention Center in Miami, two INS guards ignored the laws they were sworn to uphold. In May 2001, detention officer Lemar Smith pleaded guilty to having sex with a transsexual detainee at Krome. (Federal rules forbid federal prison officers from engaging in sex with persons under their custody.) He was allowed to cop a plea to avoid more serious felony rape charges. But Smith received an eight-month prison term.[14]

In October 2001, Clarence Parker, a contract employee who also worked as an INS guard at Krome, pleaded guilty to engaging in a sexual act with a female detainee awaiting deportation. He received three years' probation.

At sentencing, U.S. district judge Federico A. Moreno revealed even more outrageous INS neglect: Soon after Parker was let go by the INS in the summer of 2001 for his sexual misconduct, he had been hired by a private company to work at a Florida state facility for juvenile male sex offenders. Parker's former INS supervisor at Krome failed to disclose the sex allegations against him and rated him "very good" in a referral.

Judge Moreno, exercising the public responsibility that no other federal official had shown, ordered Parker to resign from the job immediately.[15]

Cheryl Little, a lawyer who represents female detainees abused at Krome, wasn't surprised by the endorsement of Parker. INS officials, she says, "would rather die than admit to mistakes. They can act with impunity. They protect each other. That's how it's always been."[16]

Cocaine and Heroin Smuggling

In September of 2001, immigration inspector Clark Anthony Miller was arrested on charges that he had conspired to help smuggle more than one thousand pounds of cocaine into the United States. Investigators said Miller was part of a conspiracy to wave a vehicle loaded with cocaine through his inspection lane without proper inspection. Miller resigned from INS shortly after his arrest.[17]

Also in September 2001, inspector Luis Abreu was arrested on conspiracy charges for his alleged role in a heroin-trafficking ring at Miami International Airport. A two-year investigation by several local, state, and federal agencies uncovered an elaborate drug-smuggling operation using "mules" who ingested pellets of heroin and flew from Colombia into Miami. Abreu is accused of allowing the mules to pass through airport security without interference and cooperating with the Suarez international heroin-trafficking and money-laundering operation. Following Abreu's arrest, John Shewairy, chief of staff for the Florida District of the INS in Miami, issued a statement noting: "We hold our employees to the highest standards of conduct."[18]

Go to the Head of the Class

In October 2001, INS officer Ricardo Scott, another Miami International Airport inspector, pled guilty to demanding and accepting bribes from four applicants for citizenship. He charged $200 to $500 to the four aliens, who had previously failed their citizenship tests.[19]

Life in the Fast Lane

José Flores Lopez, Eduardo Rodriguez, and Juan José Rodriguez (no relation) were all veterans of the INS who worked the international bridges in Brownsville, Texas. They sold INS documents to Mexican and Central American nationals for $300 to $500 apiece. The aliens would then use the documents to speed through the inspectors' stations at the Brownsville port of entry.

Over a period of two years, federal investigators watched hundreds of illegal aliens drive through the fast lane aided by Lopez, Rodriguez, and Rodriguez. Surveillance cameras caught Lopez collecting cash payoffs from smugglers at a nearby convenience store. "During his stops at the convenience stores, he would pop open his trunk," said assistant United States attorney Oscar Ponce. "The smugglers would then load his car with groceries and drinks while he sat inside, accepting payment."[20]

In November 2001, Lopez received a thirty-four-month sentence and a $20,000 fine. Juan José Rodriguez was sentenced to twenty-two months' imprisonment. Eduardo Rodriguez received a twenty-month sentence and a $6,000 fine.[21]

Six G's for a Visa

Fredy Barragan was a ten-year veteran of the INS at Miami International Airport. With the help of his wife and sister-in-law, he charged foreign nationals between $2,000 and $6,000 each for illegally stamping their visas. Investigators determined that the family smuggling conspiracy netted that much on at least thirty occasions.

While his ring was in business, the INS promoted Barragan, putting him in charge of secondary screenings of tourists, business people, and asylum applicants. The women, who were Barragan's sales agents, pleaded guilty to conspiracy bribery charges and admitted they helped Barragan solicit and collect cash. Barragan resigned from the INS and was sentenced to ten months in prison. The women were sentenced to home detention and five years of probation.[22]

Gay Sex for Residency

In Chicago, immigration examiner Russell Mendez was a four-year veteran of the INS responsible for detecting fraud and misrepresentation while reviewing requests for green cards and citizenship. But when this watchdog wasn't policing misconduct, he was committing it.[23]

In January 2002, Mendez pleaded guilty in federal court to obtaining sexual favors from two male immigrants in return for approving applications for permanent residency. After admitting that he demanded sex from one of the men in 1997 and the other in 1998, he pleaded guilty to two counts of soliciting gratuities.

Mendez retired from the INS in October 2000, while the criminal investigation was under way.[24] Chicago INS spokeswoman Gail Montenegro confirmed to me that Mendez will be able to collect his government retirement funds from jail.[25]

High-Level INS Fraud

In the aftermath of September 11, federal watchdogs released several reports on the agency's continued neglect of basic law enforcement functions. Investigators found that INS inspectors at international airports were still failing to check passports of foreign tourists traveling on the Visa Waiver program. The agency continued to drag its feet on integrating its central criminal database with other law enforcement systems. And in a February 2002 report on unchecked immigration benefit fraud, the

General Accounting Office called the agency "fragmented and unfocused."[26]

But warning signs were evident long before September 11. A 1996 General Accounting Office report warned of a "small cottage industry" in counterfeiting and selling fake INS documentation, and warned of "a second, smaller, but more egregious form of corruption in which an INS employee is sought out to sell a legitimate INS document or benefit in return for a bribe or favor. . . ." The report continued:

> The temptations and rewards for selling these official documents are great. For example, while it has been estimated that an employment authorization card may sell for as little as $50, a border crossing card might sell for as much as $325, a temporary resident permit for $2,300, and a Green Card for roughly $5,500. Thus, a corrupt official could gain hundreds or thousands of dollars per transaction depending on the type of document or nature of the fraud.[27]

The INS, investigators concluded, made little effort to punish the alien customers and beneficiaries of document fraud schemes.

> "INS's failure to take action against these aliens undermines the credibility of INS' enforcement," the report said. "It must be made clear throughout the immigrant communities that aliens engaged in fraudulent schemes to obtain benefits to which they are not entitled will risk official penalties. If other aliens see that there are no penalties, more aliens may be tempted to circumvent the system."[28]

Just as the INS has failed to deter fraud from the outside, it has made little headway in preventing fraud from the inside despite a stream of embarrassing reports. Every year, the agency points to the few who are caught and claims that these apprehensions show that "the system works."

But light sentences, bureaucratic reshuffling, and under-the-rug settlements have proven to be weak deterrents. Meanwhile, law-abiding immigrants continue to face unprecedented backlogs on the processing of petitions and applications for naturalization. And law-breaking crooks within the agency continue to sell for profit everything from passport stamps to tourist visas to green cards to citizenship.

Anyone who claims INS officers are prone to bribery because they are poorly financed by the government is misinformed. During the last eight years, Congress has tripled the agency's budget from $1.5 billion in 1993 to nearly $5 billion in 2001. That figure is expected to rise to $6.1 billion in fiscal 2003. Spending on both enforcement and service has skyrocketed steadily over the years, but neither function has improved.

Lack of resources doesn't explain why veteran INS managers in district offices across the country and overseas repeatedly engage in brazen and treacherous schemes to undermine the laws they are sworn to uphold. Nor does it explain why INS leaders fail consistently to root out fraud.

"Destroy Everything!"

In 1994, INS deputy assistant district director for adjudications William Tait was convicted on charges of selling green cards for greenbacks in San Francisco. A twenty-two-year agency veteran, Tait oversaw tens of thousands of applications as the number two official in charge of applications and petitions for permanent U.S. residence in the Bay Area. Tait also had authority to bypass the standard review process when issuing green cards.

Tait's coconspirator, Hubert Eric Jung-San Hunt, told immigration authorities that Tait gave him blank forms authorizing green cards and told him how to put on his clients' fingerprints and signatures. In a secretly taped conversation, Tait reportedly told Hunt to cover up their scheme, ordering him to "Destroy everything. All your computer records, destroy it all. . . . The only thing we can do is damage control."[30]

Despite his gross abuse of power, treacherous behavior, and apparent attempt to obstruct justice, Tait received a mild sentence of thirty months' incarceration, three years' probation, and a fine of $10,100.

Trips to Aruba, Oriental Carpets, Etc.

John Lonergan, assistant district director for examinations, was the third-highest-ranking INS officer in New Jersey from 1988 to 1995. A career bureaucrat with a total of twenty-four years' experience, Lonergan oversaw the flow of aliens into Newark International Airport.

In need of a new roof on his home, Lonergan accepted a $5,000 bribe from alien middleman Nagy Khairallah in exchange for supplying Khairallah with fraudulent forms allowing two Iraqi men to enter the country illegally. Khairallah specialized in obtaining false immigration documents, and he later admitted to federal officials that he had made several payments to Lonergan in exchange for assistance in procuring false immigration documents.[31]

For four years, Lonergan continued to dole out immigration favors to Khairallah in exchange for providing papers that allowed illegal aliens to enter and work in the United States. Among the gifts totaling $10,000 that Lonergan received: a trip to Aruba, two Oriental carpets, a cell phone, and a big-screen television.[32]

A federal jury convicted Lonergan of taking bribes, helping aliens enter the country illegally, and lying to FBI investigators. He received a forty-one-month prison term, a $20,000 fine, and three years of supervised release. Assistant United States Attorney Stuart J. Rabner, the lead prosecutor in the case, said after the trial: "If ever there was a case where deterrence mattered, it is this one."[33]

But if the Lonergan conviction was supposed to send a strong message of accountability to his fellow employees, it seems few—from the lowest rungs to the highest echelons of power at the INS—were listening.

Arranged Sham Marriages

Two years after Lonergan's widely publicized conviction, a federal jury convicted Boston's INS assistant district director for management, Adrian Federico, on charges of making false statements on immigration documents. Prosecutors alleged that the twenty-three-year INS veteran collaborated with her brother, restaurant owner Oscar DeStefano, in an elaborate marriage-fraud scheme involving DeStefano's illegal alien employees.

DeStefano admitted arranging sham marriages for his workers, received a light ten-month home detention sentence and a $20,000 fine, and testified against his sister at trial. Despite abusing her high-ranking position at the INS, Federico received a less severe sentence than her brother: nine months of home detention and a $10,000 fine.[34]

From Red to Green on His Computer Screen

John Shandorf was a supervisory asylum officer at the INS's New York City office in Queens. Second in command at the asylum office, he was responsible for ensuring that his subordinates processed applications fairly and accurately. After hours, investigators found, Shandorf made mincemeat of the laws he was sworn to uphold.

Between 1996 and 1998, according to prosecutors, Shandorf directed three separate bribery schemes. Accomplices would identify aliens with pending asylum requests or would lure Albanian and Yugoslavian nationals as recruits, who paid a fee of between $3,000 and $4,000 to guarantee asylum approvals. Officials said Shandorf would then use his access to INS computer systems to change his subordinates' asylum assessments from disapproval to approval.

In February 2000, Shandorf received a twenty-one-month prison term and three years' supervised release for bribery.[35]

The Aldrich Ames of Immigration

Jerry Wolf Stuchiner was a top INS official overseas, first as the agency's chief officer in Hong Kong and later as the senior official in Honduras. In both posts, the nineteen-year veteran was responsible for enforcing laws against human trafficking. But this watchdog became lapdog for a foreign criminal enterprise — and got away with it.

Stuchiner was arrested in 1996 on possession of five fraudulent Honduran passports, which he admitted he intended to sell to Chinese alien smuggling groups in Hong Kong at $30,000 to $40,000 each. He pleaded guilty to forgery and was sentenced to three and a half years in prison. The sentence was later revoked because of a legal technicality,[36] and Stuchiner was resentenced on a lesser charge to three months in jail. The government of Hong Kong granted him early release in the summer of 1997 before the colony's rule reverted to China.

Despite myriad other allegations of shady activity, which earned him a reputation as the "Aldrich Ames of the immigration world" among some INS officials, the Justice Department failed to file its own charges against Stuchiner.[37]

Where is he now? Stuchiner is an active member of the California bar and practices immigration law in Las Vegas. On the
Web site of his law practice, Paladin International Incorporated,
Stuchiner touts his "25 years experience with US Immigration
Service and US Embassies" and his certified expertise in "immigration defense, appeals, labor certifications, refugee and asylum law." No mention of his intimate familiarity with document
fraud and people smuggling. But Stuchiner lets his potential
clients know that his professional motto, which scrolls promi-
nently across the top of site, is: "Play to Win." [38]

To Russia, With Love

In April 1997, then–Attorney General Janet Reno assigned one
of her top Justice Department lieutenants, Robert K. Bratt, to
"improve the integrity" and "solve the systemic problems" of the
nation's naturalization system. [39] Too bad he was busy ruining
the integrity of that system by securing a visa for his Russian sex
partner.

A Justice Department press release touted Bratt as "an experienced management troubleshooter, who has overseen sensitive
and complex departmental efforts." Bratt had won numerous
awards, including the President's Distinguished Executive Rank
Award, and the Attorney General's Award for Excellence in
Management, the highest management award given within the
Justice Department. [40] Behind this smokescreen of accolades for
his "innovative and dynamic leadership," Bratt was cutting corners, risking international blackmail, and putting his own pruri-
ent interests ahead of America's interests.

Before and after his assignment to the INS, Bratt used his
"innovative" management skills in a scheme to get visas for two
Russian women he had met through a matchmaker. According to
a lengthy Department of Justice Inspector General's report, Bratt
flew to Moscow on four occasions between November 1996 and

June 1997. During his travels, he met up with a woman who had worked for a Russian dating service called Scanners. Through the matchmaker, Bratt met Ludmilla Bolgak and Yelena Koreneva – and developed a sexual relationship with the latter. After extensive socializing, he promised his Muscovite gal pals that he would supply them with visas, plane tickets, and lodging in his Washington, D.C., home and Delaware beach house.[41]

Upon discussing the matter with several State Department employees and embassy officials, Bratt determined that the women would not be granted visas through the standard procedure. (Koreneva, Bratt's girlfriend, had previously been denied a tourist visa by the Moscow embassy because officials determined she would not likely return to her home country.) So Bratt arranged for one of his assistants, Joseph R. Lake, to obtain visas for the women through a special embassy program that bypassed the normal interview, approval process, and long lines endured by other Russian citizens. This special referral program is reserved for visitors whom the United States deems it is in its best governmental or humanitarian interest to allow into our country.[42]

On Bratt's behalf, Lake asserted falsely on visa referral documents that the women worked for the Justice Department's Criminal Division in Moscow. Lake identified Bolgak as an "interpretor [sic]/translator" and Koreneva as an "administrative secretary." Lake wrote on the application that if the women were permitted to visit the U.S., it would "acquaint them with [our] Govt. institutions, economy, culture and lifestyle. Such experience and familiarization can only have positive impact on their return."[43]

Both women were granted the special visas, but they said they ended up not using the travel permits because of work schedule conflicts. "Regardless of the reason for it," federal investigators wrote, "the women's failure to use the visas does not mitigate the misconduct associated with knowingly submitting false statements" on the visa forms.[44] The inspector general noted that Bratt repeatedly lied to investigators and was "recklessly indifferent to the security interests of the government."[45]

Moreover, the office concluded, Bratt—who had one of the highest levels of security clearance—violated government regulations with respect to contact with foreign nationals.[46] He knew little about Bolgak and Koreneva's backgrounds and associations, making him vulnerable to blackmail, extortion, and pressure from Russian intelligence sources and the Russian mafia. That vulnerability was only heightened when he informed the women of his promotion to INS and later tried to hide the true nature of his relationship with Koreneva.

By day, Bratt advised his employees on how to avoid foreign threats to American intelligence; one brochure he distributed warned against bringing foreign nationals into easily bugged hotel rooms and divulging personal information to them. By night, Bratt ignored all the cautious counsel he gave to others and carelessly opened himself up while wining and dining with Koreneva (whom he allowed into his hotel room) and Bolgak (whom he invited to tour his office in D.C. and stay at his home along with Koreneva).[47]

How were Bratt and Lake punished for putting the U.S. government at risk? While the inspector general normally would have recommended significant discipline for what it concluded was "egregious misconduct" by Bratt and Lake, they suffered no consequences because both conveniently left the department before the investigation was completed.[48] In March 1997, Lake retired early from the Department of Justice Criminal Division and received a $25,000 severance bonus.[49] The very next day, he violated the buyout program rules by returning to work as a paid consultant for the department under Bratt.[50]

The next month, Lake followed Bratt to INS to "advise and assist" on the "re-engineering" of naturalization programs—again in violation of buyout program rules.[51] In March 1998, Bratt was removed from his INS post and transferred to the DOJ's management division. In August 2000, he took early retirement.[52] Both Bratt and Lake continue to collect their tax-subsidized pensions, leaving behind subordinates who learned well from their award-winning boss and his right-hand man that rules are for suckers—and that immigration laws are meant to be exploited, not enforced.

Suffer the Whistleblowers

Only one group of INS employees can count on receiving harsh and speedy discipline for their actions: whistleblowers who expose the failures and misconduct of their colleagues.

Tangling with Reno

Martin Edward Andersen worked in Janet Reno's Justice Department as a senior policy planning advisor for international law enforcement training programs. In 1997, he blew the whistle on numerous instances of gross security failures, favoritism, and ethical lapses by top officials under Reno's command, including the international skirt-chaser at the INS, Robert K. Bratt.

Andersen's reward for alerting his superiors to rampant corruption? He was immediately stripped of his security clearance, work duties, and regular office and sent to an administrative cubbyhole to do nothing. For a while Andersen passed the time reading history books. But then he fought back.

Andersen charged Reno's office with retaliating against him for his whistleblowing activities. He was backed by the United States Office of Special Counsel, which guards federal civil servants against whistleblower reprisals and other merit system violations. The Office of Special Counsel bestowed a public service award to Anderson for placing himself "at a substantial risk" in the national interest.[53]

Martin Edward Andersen later left the Justice Department and now works as media director of the Government Accountability Project, a Washington, D.C.–based whistleblower protection organization.

Citizenship USA

The Office of Special Counsel also protected Neil Jacobs, one of several intrepid whistleblowers who stepped forward to expose the Clinton-Gore administration's shameful Citizenship USA scam.

A nearly three-decade veteran of the INS and assistant director for investigations at its Dallas office, Jacobs testified before a United States House of Representatives panel in 1996 that his office alone had bestowed citizenship on more than ten thousand immigrants without the necessary background checks. "Enforcement," Jacobs said, "was basically left out of the entire citizenship process."

Citizenship USA had become a "sacred cow" into which his office supervisors pumped limitless resources and manpower— while ignoring thousands of criminal aliens "that are running around on the street mugging people, raping people, [and] stealing."[54]

Auditors from the firm KPMG conducted an independent review and confirmed the veracity of Jacobs's allegations: more than 90 percent of all Citizenship USA cases were handled improperly, and more than 70 percent of cases had defective or nonexistent fingerprints. The study estimated that some 115,000 new citizens had "unclassifiable" fingerprints that were never resubmitted for criminal checks, and that an additional 61,000 received citizenship without submitting any fingerprints at all.

The auditors also discovered that 369 people were naturalized despite having been convicted of a felony or a crime involving "moral turpitude." Of an additional 5,954 cases that failed to support naturalization, 5,634 involved individuals who failed to reveal that they had been arrested for a felony or crime involving moral turpitude. An additional five thousand or so had misdemeanor records, or failed to disclose arrests for misdemeanors. And thirty-eight others had final deportation orders against them or were currently in deportation proceedings at the time they were granted citizenship.[55]

Former chief counsel for the House Judiciary Committee David Schippers reported in his book *Sellout* that at least one criminal "was actually in jail at the time he was naturalized."[56]

As always, INS promised to fix its ways in the wake of the scandal, but it was business as usual. KPMG auditors reported that five months after reforms were ordered, only one of twenty-four INS sites that handled 85 percent of all naturalization applicants had put tighter screening mechanisms in place. Several INS service centers were found to be sending fingerprint cards to the wrong FBI address.[57]

Meanwhile, instead of applauding Jacobs for his brave testimony about the corrupting effects of Citizenship USA, the INS began an internal inquisition into Jacobs' conduct. He was suspended from his job for twenty-one days and reassigned to a nonsupervisory position, despite an exemplary service record and accomplishments. The independent Office of Special Counsel backed Jacobs and concluded that the INS had retaliated against him.

Last year, Jacobs settled his case in return for a new job in Hawaii and a $30,000 lump sum payment. But as part of the settlement, he will not be allowed to serve in a supervisory role.[58]

Some other INS employees who complained about the abuses of the Citizenship USA program didn't fare as well as Jacobs.

Among them was Joyce Woods. The Chicago District adjudications officer, who processed citizenship applications, told Congress in September 1996 that she had discovered ten boxes of paperwork in her office showing that many Citizenship USA beneficiaries had been naturalized despite records indicating alleged past crimes, including rape, aggravated felonies, gang activity, and drug trafficking.

The inspector general's office confirmed many of her allegations. When she expressed concern to her superiors, they sent a strong message to her that proper screening was "not a priority."[59] After her testimony, when she was turned down for a position as a criminal investigator at INS despite a perfect score of 100 on a competitive test for the job, Woods lodged a retaliation complaint.

The inspector general generously acknowledged that her claim was "not spurious," but concluded there was "insufficient evidence" to support her.[60]

Exposing Our Northern Exposure

Even after September 11, the INS continued to punish internal critics. Consider the outrageous plight of Border Patrol officers Mark Hall and Robert Lindemann. Both are veteran agents who work in the Detroit sector, which covers more than eight hundred miles of watery boundaries with Canada.

The pair had testified before Congress on several occasions, dating back to 1999, about their employer's inadequate attention to our northern borders. They offered prescient warnings about the threat of terrorists and other criminal aliens exploiting lax immigration enforcement. Hall said in 1999:

> During the Gulf War, the Detroit Border Patrol was in a high state of security. We received intelligence almost daily of potential terrorist smuggling efforts from Canada in our area of operation. The intelligence indicated that smuggling of terrorists across the border to transit to "safe houses" in our area was a very real probability. Due to extremely low staffing levels, vigilance on the border was minimal to none. This was the best we could do with the dismal manpower we had at that time. Our staffing today is less than it was then.[61]

Lindemann cautioned in February 2000: "The longer it takes to increase officers and support personnel, modernize and augment technology, and provide adequate detention and removal funding on the northern border and Southeast, the more attractive these areas will be for alien and drug smugglers."[62]

After the terrorist attacks in 2001, Hall and Lindemann spoke to the press about their longstanding concerns. On NBC's *Today Show*, Hall remarked: "I believe the border is so far out of control that we don't even have an idea how far out of control it is."[63] Lindemann told the *Detroit Free Press* that agents in Michigan remained ill-equipped to protect the United States–Canadian border. Twenty-eight field agents were sharing one working boat and a remote surveillance camera that had been out of service for six months.

"The stuff is falling apart," Lindemann said. "We're putting it together with duct tape."

Hall added: "The northern border has been basically abandoned by the government."[64]

The agents' candor, dedication, and alertness ought to have been greeted with cheers by INS management. Instead, their managers lambasted them for "insubordination" and "treason."[65] The agency acted quickly to stifle "dissent" and initially considered *firing* the pair.

Instead, Hall and Lindemann, partners for fourteen years, were separated, their schedules were changed, and their pay was reduced. In late September 2001, Hall got a letter from an INS supervisor notifying him of a proposal to suspend him for ninety days without pay and demote him for a year for "embarrassing Border Patrol, and jeopardizing national security" by speaking publicly. Signed by Deputy Chief Patrol Agent John France, the letter lectured Hall: "It is likely that your comments will, at a minimum, cause ill will amongst the public and possibly unnecessary paranoia in the country at a time when it is our job to protect the borders and instill confidence in the public that they are safe from terrorists."[66] Lindemann received the same letter.

Senators Charles Grassley of Iowa and Carl Levin of Michigan came to Lindemann and Hall's defense. So did the Office of Special Counsel and the Inspector General's office, which stated in a memo to INS: "We seriously question the decision to propose discipline against Hall and Lindemann and believe it would not be upheld."[67] After a public uproar, the INS reversed course and promised to provide both agents back pay plus interest for the loss of special pay.

"Any federal employee who knows about homeland-security problems that aren't being addressed and brings them up is providing an invaluable service to the public," Senator Grassley said. "They deserve praise and support, not pay cuts and demotions."[68]

Despite its reversal in the Hall and Lindemann case, the INS remains hostile territory for whistleblowers. The agency refused to order whistleblower-protection classes for the Detroit office.

None of the managers involved in retaliating against the agents were themselves subject to discipline. Disabling alarm bells continues to be more important to INS managers than heeding them. And that is why the agency's heroic Paul Reveres are vastly outnumbered by its dastardly Benedict Arnolds.

Once Hired, Never Fired

The reason for the INS's intractable lack of discipline—and apathy toward both internal and external fraud, mismanagement, and corruption—is obvious. Too many of the agency's corrupt-o-crats suffer little or no consequences.

For most INS workers who are caught misbehaving under color of authority, punishment is neither swift nor stiff. The civil service safety net shields fallen employees from effective discipline. Penalties for INS employees guilty of misconduct are "spotty and uneven," the Inspector General's office told Congress in the aftermath of the September 11 attacks.[69]

Although the attorney general has the power to fire employees of the FBI and CIA at will, he does not have the same authority to summarily terminate INS employees who willfully deceive Congress or the Justice Department. A measure authored by Republican representative Darrell Issa of California to subject INS employees to at-will termination was defeated in April 2002.

To fix the INS, a bipartisan consensus in Washington pushed for splitting the agency into two parts after September 11. INS chief James Ziglar tried to stave off such legislative attempts with his own internal plan to streamline the managerial chain of command, reform field operations, and hire a "chief financial officer" and "chief information officer."

The Bush administration ended up joining the abolition bandwagon in late April, when the White House endorsed the

Barbara Jordan Immigration Reform and Accountability Act, authored by Republican congressman James Sensenbrenner of Wisconsin. In April 2002, the House passed Sensenbrenner's bill by an overwhelming margin. One office would deal with law enforcement, the other with naturalization services. Two months later, the Bush administration announced plans to fold the INS into a new homeland security agency.

But none of these cosmetic restructuring plans is likely to change the immigration bureaucracy's core culture of corruption. Without a law allowing career INS civil servants to be fired at will for misconduct or deception—and without sweeping personnel changes—the new framework for the old INS will continue to shelter scofflaws, snakes, sellouts, and sexual abusers who compromise homeland security.

Chapter 8

Welcome to Miami

"**Potemkin village:** an impressive facade or show designed to hide an undesirable fact or condition."

—Merriam-Webster's Collegiate Dictionary

Grigory Potemkin was a flamboyant eighteenth-century prince, soldier, and paramour of Catherine the Great. After conquering Crimea and Ukraine, he conducted a grand tour of new, clean, safe, and well-run villages for the czarina and other foreign dignitaries. A jealous diplomat later weaved a tall tale accusing Potemkin of having constructed false facades of prosperity along the tour route to deceive the royal entourage. These propped-up towns, the diplomat claimed, were populated by role-playing peasants and decorated with bogus warehouses filled with bags of sand instead of grain.

In 1995, a gang of Potemkins at the INS engineered one of the most appalling bureaucratic ruses in recent American political history. Senior-ranking immigration officials, eager to leave a good impression with a visiting delegation of congressional representatives, orchestrated the reckless release of scores of illegal aliens from the INS's Krome Detention Center in Miami. These guardians of the public interest deliberately let free fifty-eight aliens—nearly half of whom had criminal histories or unknown criminal backgrounds, and more than half of whom had no medical clearance as required before their release. A majority had not been screened as required by law for communicable diseases such as AIDS and tuberculosis.

At Miami International Airport (MIA), the INS schemers created the illusion of efficiency by evacuating detention cells, moving jailed detainees to unsecured areas, and hiring extra immigration inspectors temporarily to eliminate long lines. They also instructed underlings to lie to congressional representatives about detention area procedures.

Next, these modern-day Potemkins stonewalled federal watchdogs and obstructed investigation of their scheme. The agency's "response to document requests was abysmal," noted Inspector General Michael Bromwich a year after the scandal took place. "Many witnesses became overtly hostile when confronted with documents that suggested the truth of some of the allegations. Ultimately, some senior INS district and regional managers refused to be interviewed." Others refused to sign affidavits that they acknowledged were accurate; smoking-gun e-mails were deleted; and top managers created an "extremely difficult and hostile environment" for investigators trying to get to the bottom of things.[1]

What happened at INS's Krome Detention Center and Miami International Airport symbolizes the ultimate corruption of our immigration system—the abuse of laws, privileges, and people for professional aggrandizement and political gain. As the inspector general noted: "It is one thing to instruct personnel to comport themselves professionally because of the arrival of VIPs and to 'scrub the decks' to present a clean and tidy workplace. It is entirely different to give instructions that increase the risk of a public safety incident and that run counter to the very mission of the agency."

What happened afterward to the agency's architects of deception—in a word, *nothing*—shows just how indifferent our immigration authorities remain to the integrity of our laws and the safety of our citizens. Of thirteen officials implicated in the Miami/Krome scandal, *eleven remain employed* by the INS.[2] Despite their actions to mislead Congress and endanger the public, these true-life Potemkins currently hold some of the most important and highly sensitive positions of trust in the post-September 11 world.

Setting the Stage

Long before Mohamed Atta touched down at MIA, dark clouds had descended over the Sunshine State's busiest international port of entry. Overwhelmed and understaffed, the INS's airport inspection and detention facilities in Miami were plagued with crime, corruption, medical crises, low morale, and increasing tensions between managers and union leaders. Frustrated immigration inspectors contended with long lines and pressure from supervisors to hustle foreign visitors through their swamped stations.

At the Krome Detention Center, a converted missile base twenty-three miles from downtown Miami, allegations of abuse by INS employees dated back to 1985. The detainee population, made up mostly of Haitian and Cuban refugees, exploded in the late 1980s and early 1990s. As INS's top official in Miami described it, Krome was "bursting at the seams" by the spring of 1995. The camp's medical director warned of potential health epidemics if overcrowding continued.

In Washington, D.C., meanwhile, momentum was building for Congress to reduce illegal immigration. Then–Speaker of the House Newt Gingrich created a House Immigration Reform Task Force, which was assigned to develop policy recommendations by June 30, 1995.[3] Representative Elton Gallegly, a California Republican, chaired the fifty-four-member panel. Several of the panelists volunteered to participate in fact-finding missions at the borders and at major ports of entry to investigate how the INS handled the influx of immigrants.

The task force toured San Diego and New York. On June 10, 1995, a seven-member delegation of congressional representatives headed to Miami. Also traveling with the group were INS commissioner Doris Meissner, director of congressional affairs Pamela Barry, and INS eastern regional office director Carol Chasse. Awaiting the delegation in Miami were INS's Miami District director Walter Cadman, deputy district director Valerie Blake, Krome camp administrator Kathy Weiss, and subordinates from both the airport and detention facilities.

On the afternoon of June 10, 1995, the delegation arrived at MIA. Local officials escorted the group to Terminal E, the primary international arrivals area. The primary inspection area of the terminal contains thirty-six booths. The secondary inspection area includes a "soft secondary" section (with rows of seats and a counter manned by immigration inspectors) and a "hard secondary" section (with similar seating, a manned counter, and a corridor leading to two holding cells for detained immigrants deemed to be flight risks or public dangers).

The delegation observed twenty-nine of thirty-six manned primary inspection booths, easy-flowing lines, light crowds, and just two detainees being held in the hard secondary cells. The VIPs were whisked through a second terminal, attended briefings, held a press conference, and moved on to the Krome Detention Center. At Krome, the delegation observed a neatly run facility holding some 286 aliens—which was well within its optimum capacity. The tour was brief and uneventful. The delegation flew home, satisfied.

The INS directors had pulled off a grand and flawless production. Almost.

Choreographing Deceit

Rehearsal for this high-stakes visit began weeks before the congressional delegation arrived. Commissioner Meissner summoned Miami District Director Cadman to her Washington, D.C., office three weeks before the tour.

Cadman, like Meissner, was an upwardly mobile, career bureaucrat. He joined INS in 1976, worked his way up the ranks, and scored the plum job of Miami district director in 1992.[4]

After the meeting, Cadman sent an e-mail to his local deputies and Eastern Regional Director Carol Chasse (based in Burlington, Vermont) to relay his marching orders from headquarters. The visit, Cadman told his colleagues, was considered "EXTREMELY important" to Meissner. Cadman related that Meissner was concerned that employees might be pulled aside to give the Beltway visitors "the real story"—as had happened when task force members visited the San Diego border. "This, of course, carries with it some real risks," Cadman fretted.

For the Miami visit, Meissner wanted "a sharp-looking, heads-up group of employees doing their jobs visible to this influential group." According to Cadman's e-mail, she wanted the visitors to come away "with the clear impression of competent, dedicated people doing the best they can with what they are given, and the ability to do significantly more if provided the resources by Congress to do so."

Presenting the appearance of competence was a tall order for the Miami crew. "Maybe we need to brainstorm this," Cadman advised in his e-mail to coworkers. He suggested a special staff meeting to discuss the impending visit, and signed off.

From Vermont, Chasse sprang into action. She advised Cadman in an e-mail reply that "[e]mployees complaining that they can't do their jobs due to lack of resources" would look bad. She offered to "do anything to help you prepare." In a follow-up telephone discussion, Chasse cautioned that rank-and-file union members "would be a little unbalanced in their presentation" to the task force members if given the opportunity to address them.

Chasse's concerns were echoed by Pamela Barry, the INS's chief congressional liaison in D.C. Once an aide to former California governor Edmund G. (Jerry) Brown Jr., Barry was Meissner's right-hand woman and was instrumental in arranging the delegation's trip and doing advance work before the big day. At a Miami planning meeting on May 25, 1995, investigators say, Barry ordered officials not to discuss staffing problems with the task force and told them not to "whine" about the lack of resources.

On June 2, 1995, Meissner held a teleconference with Chasse, Cadman, Barry, and others to reiterate the importance of INS "putting its best foot forward" during the visit—without, of course, distorting reality. (Wink, wink.)

Meanwhile, Cadman denied a request from union representatives to present their views at MIA. And Chasse later admitted to investigators that in the days before the visit, she ordered her deputy, Michael Devine, to "do whatever it takes to get the population down at Krome."

A Change of Scenery

On June 9, 1995—one day before the task force's arrival—Krome was a mess. The alien population numbered more than four hundred, nearly double the facility's optimum capacity. Female detainees slept on cots crammed in the lobby of the facility's medical clinic. Violent criminals bunked with noncriminals, minors with adults.

Krome camp administrator Kathy Weiss acted essentially as a set designer—carrying out the order to do whatever it took to clean up the scenery in time for the delegation's visit. She reported to Deputy District Director Valerie Blake and Assistant District Director for Detention and Deportation Kenneth Powers, who was responsible for management of Krome. Weiss's deputy, Vincent Intenzo, supervised day-to-day operations at the detention facility.

After a flurry of communications among senior managers in the Miami district, at Krome, and in the eastern region office, the conspirators embarked on a mission to reduce the population from a high of 429 (as of June 9, 1995) to fewer than 300 detainees. Most problematic were the center's 107 female detainees, 55 of whom had been packed into the medical center.

Weiss wrote in an e-mail describing her plan of action: "We intend to move 40–50 aliens to non-INS facilities upstate. The group will include a subgroup destined for New Orleans and another group to be stashed out of sight for cosmetic purposes."

Blake cheered her on in an e-mail reply and made light of the Herculean effort: "Great work so far.... Should I stop by Krome at midnight for a drink, or will you guys still be working?"

But there was no time to spare for small talk or late-night toasts. The Krome gang was on the move. They arranged for forty-five detainees to be transported north to Tampa for temporary storage at a county jail; a subgroup of Chinese nationals headed from there to New Orleans.

An additional thirty-six aliens were packed on a bus with bag lunches and shipped to a county jail in Key West—a three-and-a-half-hour drive from Miami.

Lastly, Krome officials began releasing detainees (mostly women and Cubans) into the community in violation of medical clearance guidelines and contrary to advice from an INS intelligence analyst.

On June 9, twenty-two detainees went free. Early the next morning, another thirty-four walked out the door. Two more left before lunch. A total of fifty-eight were sprung over two days—including nine with criminal records, eighteen with unknown criminal histories, and thirty-five without medical clearance. Fourteen of them had actually been denied parole just days before their hasty release.

All told, 139 detainees were reshuffled, removed, and released from Krome—swept off the stage just in time for the delegation's visit.

Casting Calls, Costume Changes

Over at the airport, INS officials were readying props and players, too. Deputy District Director Blake told MIA managers that she wanted things to run "smoothly"—no passenger backups, no lines, and full staffing at all costs. Airport managers brought in an additional four immigration inspectors for the visit.

The supervisor for the Terrorist, Drug, and Fraud Unit was told to have his five immigration inspectors prepared to be pulled away from their main duties and returned to the primary inspection area if needed. An additional thirteen inspectors on their morning shift were authorized to work overtime to cover the afternoon visit by the Beltway entourage.

In the hard secondary area, where criminal aliens, aliens without documents, and aliens with suspected fraudulent documents were normally detained in two small holding cells, Blake effectively ordered an evacuation. She wanted the cells "clean" (emptied out). Approximately one hour before the delegation arrived, supervisors moved eight detainees from the cells into an unsecured seating area. A guard was assigned to watch them while the delegation inspected the cells.

Two criminal aliens with multiple convictions were returned to the cells before the visit; the group in the seating area included four detainees who had attempted to enter the country with fraudulent documents. Managers and frontline inspectors were instructed to provide false information about which aliens were detained in hard secondary cells.

As a final costume touch, District Director Cadman ordered immigration inspectors to remove their leather gear belts (which held handguns and handcuffs) during the visit to create a "kinder, gentler" appearance of professionalism. Never mind that such an order exposed inspectors—and the public—to potential harm from dangerous aliens. The show was about to begin.

Lights, Camera, Action

Michael Wixted and Michael Boze, president and treasurer of the local union that represented INS workers, were uninvited walk-ons on the afternoon of June 10, 1995. They met at the airport and posted handwritten signs in an employee lounge urging inspectors: "Don't Lie to Congress" and "Tell the Congress the Truth!" Wixted and Boze headed for the inspection booths, whereupon INS assistant district director for external affairs George Waldroup grabbed Wixted by the arm and attempted to drag him from the area. "It got to the point where it was basically assault and battery, and I left my booth to help Michael [Wixted]," said INS inspector Alfonso Galafa."[5]

The scuffle ended just before the task force members arrived to observe the inspection floor. Despite a lull in passenger traffic that early Saturday afternoon, managers made sure to shift personnel to fully staff the primary inspection booths. When one immigration inspector noted that emptying the airport of passengers would cause the delegation to conclude that inspectors had nothing to do, Waldroup responded: "SHHHHHHH."

Wixted and Boze, meanwhile, attached themselves to the delegation, and Eastern Regional Director Carol Chasse allowed them to attend a briefing in the soft secondary area.

The group moved on to hard secondary, where the politicians observed clean and orderly detention cells occupied by two criminal aliens. But as fellow inspector Leonardo Reyes later told federal investigators, "the area was *not* normal. The detention cells were clean and open and there were aliens sitting in the back of the room waiting to be processed. The detention cells are usually filthy, smelly and packed with aliens waiting for processing."

One of the visitors asked inspector Jose Leon: "What type or class of aliens get detained in the cell?"

Reciting the lines he was given by his supervisor, Assistant Port Director Paul Candemeres, Leon gave answers he knew were false: "Only criminal aliens."

When asked whether there were any other reasons that aliens would be detained in cells, Leon answered, "No." Several of Leon's supervisors, who heard the false information and knew that the cells routinely held a wide range of aliens, including children, did nothing to correct it.

When the delegation proceeded to another briefing, District Director Cadman ordered Wixted and Boze off the premises. After a heated argument, he threatened to have Dade County police arrest the pair. "Arrested for what?" Wixted asked. "This is not private property. I am not breaking any laws by being here." Cadman prevailed. Before the cops arrived, Wixted and Boze departed without ever having had a chance to address the task force.

It was smooth sailing from there. The delegation moved on to Krome for a brief visit, and then headed home. The task force filed a perfunctory report after the trip, with no mention of anything unusual or remarkable in Miami. Wrapping up the tour, Commissioner Meissner crowed to the press that the task force members were "extremely impressed with the quality of our personnel, and they have been amazed with the volumes we've been handling."[6]

The Curtain Falls

A few days after the delegation's departure, Wixted, Boze, and other union leaders from Local 1458 of the American Federation of Government Employees convened. Three inspectors—George Nadeau, Kerry Kauffman, and Doug Pierce—were picked to write a letter to the task force detailing the grand deception by INS management. Despite well-grounded fears of retaliation, a total of forty-seven workers signed the four-page memo outlining how they were forced to "purposely and actively" lie to Congress and endanger the public and themselves. The whistle-blowing letter reached Washington on June 27.

Reaction was swift. Congressman Gallegly forwarded the union's complaint to Attorney General Janet Reno, bristling: "We came to Miami in search of the truth. After reading the attached memo, we are increasingly skeptical that we were able to find it." The controversy broke publicly in mid-July 1995. "INS Accused of Misleading Hill Task Force," the *Washington Post* announced.[7] Naturally, agency officials expressed shock and dismay. Meissner said she was "deeply concerned."

District Director Cadman claimed he was "deeply disturbed." He asserted that the tour was "completely straightforward and factual." In a response to a *Miami Herald* editorial, Cadman wrote: "I can assure you, unambiguously, that the congressional delegation was not shown a Potemkin Village."

Reno ordered the Office of the Inspector General to conduct an investigation. The probe opened on July 14. After eleven months, 450 interviews, and a review of some four thousand e-mails, the OIG confirmed nearly all of the union workers' charges. In the course of the investigation, the OIG exposed even more deception and mismanagement. Meissner's office failed to produce requested documents. So did the Eastern Regional Office.

The OIG fingered Valerie Blake "as the single person most responsible for orchestrating the effort to present a false picture" to Congress. She continued to engender "cynicism and dishonesty in her subordinates" by being "primarily responsible for attempting to mislead and impede the OIG investigation." Investigators said she "repeatedly contradicted her own testimony and consistently sought to deny allegations, the truth of which she ultimately admitted."

Subordinates followed her lead. "From the beginning," investigators charged, "senior management officials in the Miami District appeared to dismiss the allegations and not take them seriously." Information provided to the office "proved to be incomplete, inaccurate, and misleading. Key evidence contained in electronic mail files of various INS managers was, at best, not properly preserved and produced or, at worst, intentionally deleted." Indeed, the investigators were forced to hire retrieval specialists from Lotus Development Corporation to reconstruct electronic records. George Waldroup refused to supply his computer password; Kathy Weiss deleted and purged e-mails from her directory. Walter Cadman refused to allow investigators access to the district's servers, and investigators found that "virtually all of [his] incoming and outgoing electronic mail messages appeared to have been deleted." Investigators eventually unearthed more than sixty messages related to the MIA/Krome scandal that were sent or received by Cadman.

The OIG also noted that top-ranking officials in the eastern regional office provided testimony that investigators found incredible, unreliable, and doubtful. "During her approximately six-and-one-half-hour long testimony, Chasse responded that she did not know the answer, could not recall, or could not remember at least 245 times," the OIG report said. During his six-hour interview, Chasse's deputy Michael Devine made similar assertions "at least 171 times."

In the halls of Congress and editorial boards across the country, the call for immediate accountability and swift discipline of thirteen officials implicated in the MIA/Krome scheme was universal. "Be sure INS deception at Krome results in termination of con artist," the *Fort Lauderdale Sun Sentinel* urged in an editorial blasting Blake and others.[8]

Gallegly scheduled a hearing for the fall of 1996, in which Inspector General Michael Bromwich testified: "The message must be sent that such misconduct will be discovered and the perpetrators strongly dealt with in order to ensure that such conduct does not recur." The consensus seemed to spell curtains for the Potemkin players.

Exit, Stage Left . . .

In June 1996, the INS called Eastern Regional Director Carol Chasse and Miami District Director Walter Cadman to Washington, D.C., and assigned them to nonsupervisory positions. Chasse's deputy Michael Devine was moved to a nonsupervisory position in Vermont and Cadman's deputy Valerie Blake was shifted to a nonsupervisory role in Dallas. In February 1997, twenty months after the Miami/Krome extravaganza, the Justice Department announced the punishment for the principals involved. The following was reported:[9]

—Blake, whom the OIG had portrayed as the executive producer of the initial deception of Congress, was fired. During the investigation, and prior to her dismissal, she had been promoted to district director in St. Paul, Minnesota, and received a $5,000 Exceptional Service Award from Commissioner Meissner. At the time of her termination, she earned between $70,000 and $90,000 a year.

—Cadman, whom federal investigators described as a "willing participant in efforts to mislead INS headquarters and then to mislead and delay the investigation," accepted a voluntary "demotion" and reassignment to Washington, D.C., as a criminal investigator at INS headquarters. His annual salary upon reassignment was $113,000.

—Carol Chasse, who ordered her underlings to "do whatever it takes" to clean up Krome before the delegation's visit, was reassigned to a regional administration center in Vermont at a salary of $111,000 a year.

—Krome administrator Kathy Weiss, who oversaw the stashing away of detainees "for cosmetic purposes," was moved to the Miami District as a special assistant to Deputy District Director John Bolger. Her salary range upon reassignment was in the mid $60,000s to upper $70,000s.

Michael Devine, Chasse's deputy, was shifted to the INS Service Center in St. Albans, Vermont. Others—including Miami assistant district director for detention and deportation Kenneth Powers; Krome supervisory deportation officer Vincent Intenzo; Assistant District Director for Inspections Aris Kellner; Roger Miller, who was director of INS operations at the Miami Airport but was since transferred to the Tampa Airport as officer-in-charge; Paul Candemeres, the acting assistant port director at the airport; Miami Airport supervisory immigration inspector Jose Leon; and George Waldroup, assistant district director for external affairs—were recommended for suspensions ranging from a few days to less than a month.

Pamela Barry, the INS congressional liaison who was key in arranging the trip and warned airport staffers to remain silent about staffing problems, was exonerated despite admitting efforts to mislead Congress. She was moved to another office within the INS. According to INS spokesman Russ Bergeron, Barry was terminated on June 30, 1998—the only one of the Miami/Krome Thirteen to suffer such a permanent fate.

Commissioner Meissner, despite her intimacy with Barry, her office's failure to produce requested documents to investigators, and her direct involvement in preparations leading up to the MIA/Krome visit, escaped without a scratch.

Criminal charges were considered by the Justice Department's Office of Public Integrity, but were never filed. The administrative penalties, said INS spokeswoman Carole Florman, were "nothing to sneeze at."[10]

Meanwhile, back at Krome, a follow-up investigation by the OIG found that "[d]angerous, convicted felons and other types of criminals continue to be released" into the community. Criminal history checks were not properly documented. Confusion existed over medical background checks. And the movement of aliens was not accurately recorded and tracked in INS record systems.[11]

...Reenter, Stage Right

Out of the spotlight, several of the top punished workers stubbornly fought their disciplinary actions. After winning an appeal from the federal Merit Systems Protection Board, Valerie Blake's termination was overturned. Instead of being fired, Blake received a scant forty-five-day suspension and a single pay-grade demotion. A judge downplayed Blake's conduct as an "overzealous effort" that broke no rules or laws. She later resigned from the INS, in 1999.

Weiss was exonerated by the same board because she was just "following orders." She returned to her old job and was awarded back pay and attorney's fees.[12]

Michael Devine was also exonerated. He was restored to the eastern region office and was promoted to his boss's old position. As acting director for the region, he made headlines again in February 1999 when he disseminated a memo outlining a familiar-sounding proposal to release more than fifteen hundred criminal aliens into the general public in order to free up detention space.[13]

After six months, Devine was demoted because of a separate push to expedite citizenship applications. He has since been relocated to the San Diego office as director of investigations.[14]

Weiss, Powers, and Candemeres remain in supervisory positions in Miami; Intenzo, a deportation officer, and Waldroup, now a "special assistant," also remain in Miami. Kellner is an inspector in Washington, D.C. Miller is an adjudications officer in Tampa. Leon is an inspector in Puerto Rico.[15]

Gallegly and House Immigration Subcommittee Chairman Lamar Smith (R-Texas) lambasted the "imbecilic rulings" that let Blake, Devine, and Weiss off the hook.

Inspector General Michael Bromwich concurred: "The absence of accountability and common sense permeates these decisions," he wrote in an October 1998 letter to the congressmen. The merit board "excused managers because they were merely subordinates who could not be held responsible for following orders of supervisors, while at the same time excusing other managers on the theory that they could not be expected to know what their subordinates are doing."[16]

And for Their Next Roles ...

Two of the managers intimately involved in releasing the Krome criminal aliens into the public have now been entrusted to help the government collar terrorists and other foreign criminals on the loose. Yet, few in Washington have questioned their credibility and crime-fighting credentials.

Carol Chasse landed a job as director of the INS Law Enforcement Support Center in South Burlington, Vermont, where she now oversees a new criminal database facility that assists local, state, and federal authorities in tracking down foreign law-breakers. "Aliens tend to be very mobile and go where the wind blows them," Chasse said at a ground-breaking ceremony for the center in 1999. "We need as much information as possible so nobody slips through the cracks."[17] Chasse certainly knows about cracks.

As for Walter Cadman, he seemed at first to disappear into the bureaucratic ether. In March 1997, Representative Harold Rogers of Kentucky revisited the MIA/Krome debacle. In a hearing with Attorney General Janet Reno, Rogers asked what happened to the people who misled Congress. Reno noted that Cadman had chosen a voluntary demotion at INS headquarters. "Where is he now?" Rogers demanded.

"I cannot tell you precisely," Reno answered.[18]

A year later, his precise location was revealed. Cadman had been quietly named head of the INS's National Security Unit, where he coordinates the agency's counterterrorism efforts. That's right. This deceptive bureaucrat who condoned the reckless release of alien criminals, endangered the public, and misled Congress is now in charge of helping law enforcement agents round up alien terrorists. In February 1998, Cadman testified before a Senate Judiciary subcommittee on the "crucial role" that the INS plays in preventing terrorists' activities inside the U.S. Putting on his best tough-guy, law-and-order act, Cadman touted his agency's abilities:

> Although not nearly as obvious to the public as our border enforcement role, we are playing an increasingly significant role in efforts to identify, detain, and remove individuals once they are already here. As you know, the bombing of the World Trade Center was a wake-up call to the law enforcement and intelligence community. INS moved from working in an ad-hoc manner with other members of the law enforcement and intelligence communities to a more formalized partnership. INS is invaluable to the government's efforts against international terrorism and foreign terrorists who attempt to cross or are found within our borders. INS is the government agency responsible for controlling the entry of aliens into the United States, and detaining and removing aliens who have entered contrary to our laws.[19]

Not a word was mentioned of Cadman's own culpability in releasing criminal aliens into the general public and helping to cover it up. But as Congressman Gallegly asks: "If a person can't be trusted, how can he be given a job dealing with terrorism with the INS? There is something seriously wrong with a system that protects employees who have committed such grievous acts."[20]

To this day, INS spokeswoman Nancy Cohen says the agency remains "very supportive" of Cadman—a deceptive bureaucrat who now holds one of the most important public positions at the

INS in the post–September 11 era, but who refuses to answer press inquiries about his shady past.[21]

The Potemkin village production that took place in Miami in 1995 led to a year-long investigation, hearings, media recriminations, and repeated promises of reform. Yet, the main cast of characters kept their jobs and their generous salaries. They won bonuses and promotions. They thumbed their noses at Congress and federal watchdogs. And they set the stage for the rest of the agency's actors, illusionists, and scam artists to continue doing treacherous business as usual.

Chapter 9

Fatal Errors

The Technology Boondoggle

"GIGO [G(arbage) I(n,) G(arbage) O(ut).]

"An informal rule holding that the integrity of output is dependent on the integrity of input."[1]

—American Heritage Dictionary

Three months after the September 11 terrorist attacks, the inspector general found that INS inspectors in four major international airports—Dulles in Washington, D.C., Honolulu International Airport, JFK Airport in New York, and Miami International Airport—didn't bother to use the comprehensive, interagency database, IBIS, to identify national security threats intending to exploit the Visa Waiver program with stolen passports.[2] (IBIS contains lookout records for stolen passports.)

Six months after the attacks, INS inspector Stanley Mungaray, a ten-year veteran at Miami International Airport, told CBS's *60 Minutes* that NAILS (the agency's main repository for information about suspicious aliens) broke down at least once or twice a week—and that his supervisors encouraged him and his colleagues to keep processing travelers without checking the system. "We don't know who we're admitting and they're getting admitted. We don't know if the person is a criminal, we don't know if he's on the watch list, we don't know anything."[3]

Eight months after the attacks, the *Washington Post* reported that INS offices were still failing to check the names of applicants seeking green cards, naturalization, and other immigration documents against the IBIS lookout system because workers lacked equipment and training to do so. The New York City office had one IBIS computer to handle more than one thousand new applications a day. The Hartford, Connecticut, office had no IBIS computers. Janis Sposato, assistant deputy executive associate commissioner for immigration services, declined to say exactly how many INS workers have not been trained to use the system or how many offices lack IBIS access.[4]

And nearly nine months after the attacks, the *Los Angeles Times* reported that a computer "malfunction" caused the names of 3,500 people identified as suspected criminals and potential terrorists to be dropped from lookout databases used at Los Angeles International Airport for nearly two months during the spring of 2002. One person known to have slipped through without detailed inspection is a naturalized American citizen from Iran who was under FBI investigation for suspected links to terrorism. No other details about the case have been made public.[5]

Why the Breakdown?

Billions of dollars in information technology. More than a dozen tracking databases and automated programs. The most advanced biometric technology in the world. All this and more belongs to the INS, and still we hear the scariest message one could think of coming from frontline immigration officials in the post–September 11 world: *We don't know anything.*

How much more time, how much more money, and how many more dead bodies will it take to push the agency into the twenty-first century?

Piles of government audits and inspections over the past decade have documented the INS's maddening inability to plan, build, monitor, and use information technology to secure our borders. The agency has more than eighty separate computer systems with little ability to share information within the INS or with other federal agencies; access to sophisticated finger-print machines that gather dust and dirt; "smart" visa cards, but no machines to read them; multiple tracking databases from which records have been deliberately deleted; and automated lookout systems that go unused. The agency has twice ordered field offices across the country to close in order to count an estimated five million backlogged INS applications *by hand* because computers were not functioning in time to meet the agency's annual audit deadline.[6]

In August 2000, the GAO reported that the agency had no management controls in place "to fully ensure that the hundreds of millions of dollars it spends each year on new and existing information systems will optimally support mission needs."[7] More than a year later, the GAO reported that the agency was still in no position to know whether its technology investments were "the right things to do" or whether they "are being done the right way."[8]

The confusion persists despite the assistance of more than one thousand private computer consultants and technicians from Texas-based EDS Corporation, which received nearly $300 million in 1994 to provide support services for the INS and was part of a trio of firms that won more than $750 million in additional technology contracts.

While the feds have managed to foul up every major immigration-related computer system that involves keeping people out of the country, the INS has somehow pulled off notable successes in managing technology programs that rush hordes of travelers through the gates. Using palm-print readers or swipe cards, the agency's "passenger accelerated service system" programs at airports and along the borders have gone off swimmingly. Customer service before security, as usual.

Ignoring the agency's abysmal record of technology mismanagement, politicians in both parties issued calls after the September 11 attacks for upgrading, expanding, and acquiring new technology for the INS. The agency's commissioner, James Ziglar, begged repeatedly for more money to fix the agency's "stovepipe" problem of multiple computer systems that don't communicate with each other. But the INS has already invested hundreds of millions of dollars on systems integration without results—and without safeguards to ensure that the data being uploaded are accurate or complete.[9]

Other INS officials blame border security failures on the reluctance of other law enforcement agencies to share their data. The turf wars must end—and in fact, some improvements in this area were made almost immediately after the September 11 terrorist attacks. The USA Patriot Act mandated the sharing of data from the FBI's National Crime Information Center with the State Department and the INS, and the creation of an interoperable electronic data system, called "Chimera," to provide real-time access to law enforcement and intelligence information concerning aliens. Meanwhile, the State Department sped up plans to grant the INS full access to its nonimmigrant visa and photo database. By January 2002, the information was available at all ports of entry.

But remaining vestiges of bureaucratic territorialism do not fully account for the INS's abysmal record of sloppy, inaccurate, and incomplete data entry; lack of training; and culture of technological cluelessness and apathy. As long as the agency work-force continues to treat its high-tech tools as ornamental office furniture, the old computing motto applies: Garbage in, garbage out.

Fouling Up Fingerprints

In June 2002, Attorney General John Ashcroft announced plans to fingerprint hundreds of thousands of Middle Eastern visitors who pose national security concerns, and check the prints against criminal and terrorist databases. Prints will be taken at ports of entry using the Windows-based IDENT computer system.

But as we saw in the Angel Resendiz case, high-ranking INS employees working in intelligence and investigations had no clue how to use the five-year-old, $65 million system to track dangerous criminal aliens—even after receiving training. Managers weren't merely ignorant of the system's lifesaving lookout capability. They were indifferent to its existence.

More than $2 million in IDENT equipment piled up in inventory by early 1997; more than $500,000 worth of hardware awaited delivery for more than one year; and nearly two hundred of the system's computer video cameras sat in warehouses, racking up costly storage charges instead of photographing criminal aliens on the border.[10]

No matter how dummy-proof the hardware and software, the INS still can't compute effectively. From 1995 to 1999, for example, the agency purchased nearly two hundred machines that allow users to electronically send full sets of scanned fingerprints of known and suspected criminal aliens to Washington for input in the IDENT system's lookout database.

Under the old time-consuming system, fingerprints are rolled and inked on paper cards, then sent to headquarters via regular mail. The agency forked over $3.5 million for the purchase, installation, and training for sixty of the high-tech units—called IDENTIX machines—that were earmarked specifically for enforcement operations. The funding package included technical assistance from a private contractor, but INS officials told the computer specialists to bug off and let local district directors handle the installation process.

The result? During its investigation of the INS's deadly Resendiz disaster, the Office of the Inspector General found that the IDENTIX fingerprint machines were placed in illogical places for the processing of apprehended aliens. In some cases, detention and deportation officials said they were not informed of the purpose of the machines and never used them.

The contractor with primary responsibility for servicing the IDENTIX machines noted that the majority of units had not been used to transmit fingerprints to Washington. He told the inspector general that two-thirds of the sites that he visited in 1998 were not using the hardware because it was broken, believed to be broken, or not connected to the central system in Washington; that employees did not understand the machines' basic transmittal functions; and that no one at INS headquarters was directing them to use the machines.[11]

Border Patrol agent Keith Olson exposed persistent IDENT-related flaws in testimony before the Senate in November 2001. The system, he said, "is not always online, making it impossible to input data for all arrested aliens. It also sometimes yields unreliable results. I have personally seen it issue two different record numbers for the same person when in theory there should only be one arrest history number based on the same set of two fingerprints."

But perhaps the biggest flaw, Olson noted, is "its limited amount of storage. Once it reaches its maximum memory, it deletes the oldest records in order to make room for newer entries. Obviously, all fingerprint data should be retained indefinitely."[12]

The storage problem is not the fault of the system. It's the result of the INS's putting efficiency above safety. To keep search times down, the agency chooses to save space and archive old prints every few years—rendering them inaccessible to IDENT users.

And the IDENT fiasco is only the tip of the iceberg.

Biometric Bungling

"Biometrics"—the use of unique physical traits such as fin-gerprints, iris or retinal scans, handprints, and facial or voice recognition to verify identities—remains a big buzz word in post-September 11 Washington as lawmakers search for high-visibility, high-tech measures to prevent the next attack. But much of this technology is already available to immigration authorities. As the IDENT fiasco demonstrates, it simply isn't being used properly.

Since 1998, as legislated by the Illegal Immigration Reform and Immigrant Responsibility Act, the INS has issued some 5 million biometric border-crossing cards for Mexican citizens making short trips to the United States. In October 2001, the Mexican border-crossing cards were combined with visitor visas. The agency also mandated that certain groups of Cana-dian border-crossers, who had been generally exempt from entry documentation requirements, obtain the biometric laser visa cards.

The tamper-proof cards, manufactured by Drexler Technology Corporation of Silicon Valley, use holograms and other secure technology to embed personal data, including fingerprints. But this state-of-the-art feature has been useless to immigration inspectors on the border for the past four years, because they haven't had automatic card readers to access the encoded bio-metric data. That means they can't check the fingerprints on the cards against the fingerprints stored in those IDENT machines gathering dust. Instead, agents continue to rely on low-tech secu-rity methods—matching photos to faces.

That is, if they bother to check at all.

The digital fingerprints have also been embedded on approx-imately 5 million U.S. green cards issued to legal permanent res-idents since 1998. But to date, not a single one of those digitized fingerprints has been accessed by immigration authorities, employers, or anyone else because of the lack of readers. "The 'smart' cards have been effectively rendered 'dumb' cards," Sen-ator Dianne Feinstein of California declared last fall.[13]

More to the point, it is questionable why this technology was incorporated into green card documentation at all, since green cards are rarely used as a primary form of identification. Some of these smart cards, in other words, were dumb ideas to begin with.

Nevertheless, the INS and the State Department (which jointly administer the smart green card program) ordered up one million new cards in January 2002 at a cost of $3 million. Drexler has a five-year contract totaling $81 million to produce up to 24 million more cards. The Enhanced Border Security Act provided no authorized funding for card readers.

Tracking Troubles

The INS's inability to monitor foreign arrivals and departures was infamous well before the September 11 attacks. In Septem-ber 1997, the inspector general reported that the agency had no idea how many foreign tourists, businesspeople, students, and temporary workers in the United States were overstaying their visas. The agency's current estimate is 5 million, or about 40 percent of all illegal immigrants.

But the main recordkeeping system for monitoring visa overstayers, the Nonimmigrant Information System (NIIS), does not produce reliable numbers, because departure records are incomplete, data processing is riddled with errors, and the system only captures a small portion of nonimmigrant visitors (mostly those entering through airports and seaports, as opposed to those entering through a border station).

Here's how it's supposed to work.

Upon arrival, foreigners traveling to the United States from abroad receive a Form I-94 to record their arrival and departure. It's a little white postcard divided in two parts that requires entrants to list their name, date and place of birth, date of entry into the United States, and where they will stay during their visit.

At a primary inspection booth, an INS agent breezes through perfunctory questions (what is the purpose of the traveler's trip, destination, etc.) before writing in an expiration date for the traveler's stay and stamping both sections of the form. The inspector detaches and retains the entry portion, which is sent to a government contractor for simple, key-in processing. A contractor performs quality control and uploads the information into the NIIS database.

The foreign visitor keeps the departure portion of the I-94 form until he leaves the country, at which time he returns it to the airline, which then submits it to the INS, which then submits it to the contractor. In theory, mountains of I-94 cards get stamped, collected, boxed, sent, keyed in, and uploaded in a timely manner so that the INS can match arrival and departure records and determine who has overstayed illegally.

We're not talking rocket science here. FedEx Corporation manages to keep track of the arrival and delivery of approximately 3 million packages every day in more than two hundred countries at the touch of a button. Yet, the INS's NIIS system has not produced reliable data on nonimmigrant arrivals/departures in years. One recent inspector general audit reported that seven INS district offices did not bother to review I-94 forms for accuracy or completeness. Errors included omission of alien's addresses, gender, and/or date of birth; data entered on the wrong line of the form; and data written in the alien's native language instead of English.[14]

Another compounding problem: the agency's reluctance to punish airlines for failing to collect the I-94 forms. "Although there have been some past efforts to correct problems with NIIS," the inspector general's report concluded, "there has been a general lack of follow-through."[15]

As detailed in the first part of this book, a wide-ranging group of profiteers—the travel industry, pro–illegal alien groups, the governments of Canada and Mexico, and business lobbyists—helped sabotage efforts to improve the old manual system and install the comprehensive entry-exit system mandated by federal law. In its place, the INS erected a small pilot program: the Automated I-94 system. But even this limited effort has been a failure.

Instead of the old I-94 forms, the system uses boarding pass–sized cards with personal information and travel data encoded on magnetic strips. The data are uploaded directly to the NIIS system, eliminating the paper logjams and ensuring more accurate and timely recordkeeping. Or at least, that's what the agency had hoped. In practice, only four airports—in Philadelphia, Pittsburgh, St. Louis, and Charlotte, North Carolina—currently use the system. Only two airlines—U.S. Airways and

TWA — contributed automated data to INS for flights arriving from just seven cities: Munich, Frankfurt, London, Amsterdam, Madrid, Rome, and Paris. The inspector general concluded in an August 2001 audit that "despite having spent $31.2 million on the system from 1996 to 2000, the INS does not have clear evidence that the system meets its intended goals."[16]

After September 11, INS commissioner James Ziglar vowed to have a fully automated entry-exit data collection system in airports and seaports by the end of 2003; at the nation's fifty largest land ports of entry by the end of 2004; and all other ports by 2005. Yet, by mid-2002, the agency still had no clear plan how exactly the $380 million system would work. Ziglar's timeline isn't only optimistic, it's sheer fantasy.

There is a deeper problem. Even if all the I-94 data were uploaded, the system would still be of little practical use, since the INS has no specific enforcement program to identify, catch, or deport nonimmigrant overstayers. A "successful" automated I-94 system, in other words, would merely allow the INS to report with greater accuracy and efficiency the number of visa overstayers whose whereabouts are unknown and whom authorities are ill-equipped to hunt down and remove from the country.

Free Rein for Foreign Students

Twenty-three years. That's how long the nation dallied before getting serious about tracking the nation's 550,000 international students — including thousands from terrorism-sponsoring and terrorism-supporting countries.

The first wake-up call came in 1979, during the hostage crisis in Iran, when the INS admitted it couldn't identify the location of some nine thousand Iranian students in the United States. Congress directed the agency to collect vital information for a foreign scholar database. As ordered, the INS acquired mounds of international student paperwork from universities and colleges—but allowed the valuable data (including student arrival dates, passport numbers, course loads, and expected graduation dates) to accumulate in unseen immigration files.

A second wake-up call came in 1993. That's when the feds revealed that one of the World Trade Center bombers, Jordanian Eyad Ismoil, had entered on a student visa and then dropped out of sight before driving an explosive-laden truck into the towers. In response, the INS launched a pilot monitoring program dubbed CIPRIS—the Coordinated Interagency Partnership Regulating International Students—in twenty-one southeastern schools. CIPRIS was a technological success, but politics and funding disputes tripped up further deployment of the program.

Expansion plans lay dormant until the nation's third and bloodiest wake-up on September 11, 2001.

Within weeks, Congress authorized $33 million for the long-delayed creation of a comprehensive centralized database for foreign student enrollment, biographical, and visa information. The INS rolled out two new acronyms for the tracking system: SEVP (the Student and Exchange Visitor Program) and its Internet-based counterpart, SEVIS (the Student and Exchange Visitor Information System). Using an automated enrollment system and bar-coded student visa application forms, SEVIS will replace the molasses-slow, paper-based system that led to the embarrassing issuance of student visa approval notices for dead hijackers Mohamed Atta and Marwan Al Shehhi six months after their terrorist attacks on America.

In theory, the new program will immediately alert immigration authorities to visa status change requests such as Atta and Al Shehhi's, and to student no-shows, such as September 11 hijacker Hani Hanjour. SEVIS also promises to provide instant, real-time information on disciplinary problems, criminal activity, and unusual clustering of students from terrorism-friendly countries in our schools and vocational training programs.

INS officials claim the system will be fully operational no later than January 1, 2003. But even as they rolled out the ambitious program in Boston and other test markets, doubts arose over the timeliness and accuracy of the data to be collected and uploaded into the glitzy new system.

"Real-time" reporting, for example, will depend on the meaning of "real-time." Colleges and universities—which long opposed the tracking system—have already begun complaining about the burden such reporting will place on them during peak enrollment periods. When asked how soon after a "reportable event" (e.g., any information that a school is required by law to report—such as a change in academic status or termination of program) a designated school official must relate that incident on SEVIS, the agency replied: "The INS is unable to provide a definitive answer to this question."[17] Unable—or unwilling.

The *Chicago Tribune* exposed another troubling shortcoming that will undermine the integrity of SEVIS: the INS's failure to keep track of the schools authorized to issue student visa application forms. These forms, known as I-20s, contain the information about foreign students that will be uploaded electronically to the new system. Only federally authorized educational institutions can issue the documents, which must then be approved by the INS and presented upon entry into the country.

The *Tribune* found that dozens of Chicago-area schools authorized to issue the forms had not been reviewed in years. Several no longer existed. One of the approved schools, the Lou Conte Dance Studio, had no idea where the authorization came from. "We really don't have any knowledge about it and don't understand why we are on the list in the first place," studio spokeswoman Jill Chuckerman told the paper. The agency admitted that the problem is rampant and that it is not unique to Chicago.

Indeed, as Harvard University economist George Borjas has noted:

> In the San Diego area alone, the INS grants its seal of approval to nearly 400 institutions, ranging from the University of California at San Diego to Avance Beauty College, the College of English Language (where new courses start every Monday), the Asian American Acupuncture University, and the San Diego Golf Academy. Because there are so many INS-approved institutions, anyone with the money can buy a student visa to enter the U.S. America has effectively delegated the task of selecting immigrants to thousands of privately run entities whose incentives need not coincide with the national interest."[18]

By May 2002, the agency had no plan in place to scrub the list for obsolete schools, fly-by-nights, and fraudulent operators issuing I-20 forms.

Congressman Pete Hoekstra of Michigan, who chaired congressional hearings on foreign student tracking, remains skeptical of those with unbridled faith in SEVIS: "I have a lot of respect for INS employees, but I think that over the last few years we have been promised a number of improvements and they really haven't delivered."[19]

The Justice Department's inspector general echoed those doubts in a May 2002 special report. In addition to finding that Huffman Aviation, the school where Atta and Al Shehhi trained, failed to meet the INS's own authorization requirements, investigators concluded:

SEVIS alone will not solve the problems of the INS's tracking of foreign students. For example, the INS must review
and properly re-certify the thousands of schools that are currently certified to enroll foreign students, must ensure that
its employees and schools timely and accurately enter information into SEVIS, and must ensure that the information
from SEVIS is analyzed and used adequately. We also believe
that it is unlikely that the INS will be able to meet the January 30, 2003, deadline for full implementation of SEVIS.[20]

The report noted that INS officials had no training program in
place for administrators in charge of collecting data, and that
INS officials themselves lacked understanding of regulations for
certifying schools and had no proposal for assigning someone,
anyone, to examine the data once they were collected. Even if
they did, the inspector general wrote, "it is not clear that the INS
will use this information any more fully than in the past."[21]

And that is precisely the peril of shoveling millions of dollars
into new systems, workstations, and other technological equipment to fight the War on Terror. The data are only as good as the
people entrusted to collect, process, and *use* them for the common defense.

Chapter 10

"It Ain't Over 'Til the Alien Wins"

"People who should get in, get in; people who should not enter are kept out; and people who are deportable should be required to leave."[1]

Credibility in immigration policy rests on these three simple principles, laid out by the late Texas congresswoman Barbara Jordan.

What America giveth, it must also be able to taketh away. When the State Department and INS grant entry and citizenship privileges to foreign torturers, terrorists, criminal aliens, and other unworthy foreigners, they must be allowed to fix their grave mistakes quickly and efficiently.

After September 11, the speedy detention and deportation of some twelve hundred aliens suspected of terrorist ties gave the illusion of competence in this last crucial area of immigration enforcement. Although civil liberties advocates and Arab-American activists immediately attacked the swift ruthlessness of the INS and the Justice Department,[2] the obstacles to actually getting rid of unwanted guests are myriad. The system is clogged by conflicting statutes, incomprehensible administrative regulations, bureaucratic and judicial fiefdoms, selective enforcement, and a feeding frenzy of obstructionist immigration lawyers. It continues to favor aliens' rights over citizens' safety.

The Corruption of Citizenship

To become an American citizen, as my parents did, an immigrant must be a legal permanent resident for five years, pass English and civics tests, and demonstrate "good moral character." Immigrants are also supposed to demonstrate an "attachment to the principles of the U.S. Constitution" and show "favorable disposition toward the United States." The INS is supposed to withhold citizenship from aliens who have committed crimes, have engaged in fraud, or are otherwise unworthy.

As usual, however, theory and practice are a galaxy apart.

Among those who call themselves American citizens today are six al Qaeda terrorists convicted or implicated in conspiracies against Americans: Nidal Ayyad, El Sayyid Nosair, Ali Mohammed, Khalid Abu al Dahab, Wadih el Hage, and Essam al Ridi. (For more information, see Appendix A.) According to the INS, not a single one has had the privilege of citizenship stripped away since his role in plotting against America was revealed.[3]

While federal law specifically provides for a denaturalization process for Nazi war criminals,[4] it does not allow the INS to take American citizenship away from naturalized Americans convicted of terrorist acts against the land that embraced them.

Countless others obtained citizenship by cheating on their citizenship tests or by bribing corrupt INS officials. An untold number may even have obtained citizenship because of the agency's sloppy handling of office supplies. Tens of thousands more obtained citizenship despite having criminal records that should have disqualified them.

As far back as 1988, federal auditors had discovered that the INS was not routinely implementing criminal background checks. The agency is supposed to submit applicants' fingerprints to the FBI, which sends back criminal histories to the INS within sixty days. But the auditors found that nearly half of applications for green cards (which promise an almost inevitable path toward citizenship) contained no record that the INS had performed fingerprint and background checks.[5] A year later, in 1989, a second federal audit "found virtually a complete absence of evidence that background investigations and fingerprint checks were conducted."[6]

In 1994, investigators revisited the issue. In a single year, 1993, the auditors found 90,000 applicants who did not get fingerprint checks because their print cards were unreadable and nobody at the INS followed up to rectify the poor-quality prints. When fingerprints were readable, the auditors had little confidence that they actually belonged to the applicants, because the INS had outsourced fingerprint services to shady nonprofits, liquor stores, hairstylists, photographers, bridal shops, and immigrant "advocates" working out of the trunks of their cars, all of whom could easily falsify fingerprints for customers.[7] Applicants could have been submitting the fingerprints of dead people or monkeys; the INS would have never known and continued not to care.

After promising to correct these gross security failures, the INS failed to pass muster with General Accounting Office reviewers, who reported in late 1994 that INS field offices *still* were not checking applicants' criminal histories—and that they rarely corrected unreadable fingerprint cards before approving applications.[8] Meanwhile, the agency took its sweet time fixing its broken system of outsourcing fingerprint services. (Not until 1997 did it place new controls over designated fingerprint service providers.[9])

The Clinton-Gore Legacy

As bad as these systematic failures were, however, they were merely a prelude to the biggest citizenship scandal in our nation's immigration history: the $95 million, taxpayer-funded Citizenship USA program under the Clinton-Gore administration. In that infamous episode, Vice President Al Gore pushed the INS to reduce the wait time between application and naturalization from two years down to six months in key states before the 1996 elections, presumably because he thought most of the aliens granted citizenship would vote for Democrats.

The only way the INS could meet the expedited schedule was by forgoing criminal background checks.[10] The Clinton-Gore administration's wholesale giveaway of our precious birthright of citizenship resulted in the naturalization of thousands of criminal aliens. Of the 1.3 million immigrants who benefited from Clinton-Gore's Citizenship USA push, an estimated 180,000 did not undergo any fingerprint checks for criminal records. In addition, Justice Department investigators found that more than 80,000 aliens had fingerprint checks that generated criminal records—but were naturalized anyway.

Of the Citizenship USA beneficiaries with confirmed criminal records, the Justice Department selected about 6,300 of the worst felons to be denaturalized by the INS. You might think it only natural that the agency with the power to confer citizenship on aliens would also retain the power to take it away. Not so.[11]

The Ninth Circuit Court of Appeals ruled against the INS, stating, "There is no general principle that what one can do, one can undo."[12] In other words, although the INS had erroneously granted citizenship to 6,300 felons, it did not necessarily follow that the INS could revoke their citizenship.

The judges added: "For the Attorney General to gain the terrible power to take citizenship away without going to court, she needs Congress to say so."[13]

Congress never has. An attempt by Congressman Lamar Smith to give the INS express administrative authority to denaturalize individuals who lied on their citizenship applications died in 1998. The bill would have also extended the statute of limitations for administrative denaturalizations from two years to five years, a commonsense proposal given the INS's perennial processing backlog.[14]

Meanwhile, in 1998, the Justice Department indicted twenty people for their role in falsifying the naturalization examinations of more than thirteen thousand immigrants in twenty-two states over a period of two years. Among those indicted were Daud Mohammad Amiri and Khalilullah Raouf, both involved in recruiting immigrants from Afghanistan. The ring raked in more than $3 million; testers would supply the answers or hand out passing grades to immigrants who had not even taken the tests. The agency promised to track down, retest, and deport if necessary the thirteen thousand immigrants who forked over the bribes. But to this day, the INS cannot say how many were ever reexamined, stripped of their citizenship, or kicked out of the country.[15]

How many of these fellow Americans were assisted by Amiri and Raouf? Are any of these cheating citizens—so much for their "good moral character"—part of terrorist sleeper cells? Have they expanded their network by using their citizenship status to sponsor other "family members" for legal permanent residence and eventual naturalization?

We'll never know. And until Congress passes a naturalization reform bill giving the INS the explicit power to take back what it so often recklessly gives away, such citizenship-related snafus will continue to be written with indelible ink.

Can't Return to Sender

Thousands of foreign nationals convicted of crimes in the United States cannot be deported because their home countries will not take them back. Among them are cop-killers such as Hungarian national Bela Marko; nearly one thousand hardened criminals from Cuba dumped here by Fidel Castro in 1980 as part of the Mariel boatlift; and fifteen hundred criminal aliens from Central America who were scheduled for deportation but detained here at the request of their native governments after Hurricane Mitch ravaged the region.[16] The Central Americans' "temporary" stays have dragged on for four years.[17] Also eligible for "temporary" protected status are criminal aliens from terrorist-friendly havens Somalia and Sudan who have already received final orders of deportation.[18]

To make matters worse, the United States Supreme Court ruled in June 2001 that the INS could not detain such criminals indefinitely.[19] Attorney General John Ashcroft was forced to order the agency to release about 3,400 criminal aliens who were housed in detention facilities in all fifty states. Nearly one-third had been jailed for serious crimes, including murder, rape, and child molestation. All were required to "report to authorities periodically" after their release, but there is no tracking system to monitor them.[20]

At the same time that many countries refuse to take their criminals back, acquiescent America continues to welcome tens of thousands of their compatriots every year. Ashcroft threatened to ask Secretary of State Colin Powell to stop granting visas to citizens of countries that do not cooperate with our deportation efforts.[21] But so far, only Guyana and Cambodia have suffered any consequences.[22]

And as if we didn't have enough criminal aliens crowding our shores, Democratic congressman Barney Frank of Massachusetts pushed for passage of a mind-boggling bill that would allow already deported foreign convicts—including some arsonists, robbers, and child pornographers—back into the country to appeal their deportations.[23] The name of this criminal alien reentry program: The Family Reunification Act of 2001.

Cons and Absconders

Government watchdogs have found the INS to be habitually lax in its efforts to track down and help boot out the worst criminal offenders among the alien population. A number of federal laws require the agency to initiate deportation actions against aliens convicted of aggravated felonies as quickly as possible and before they are released from federal or state prisons.[24]

Congress increased funding and staffing for a Justice Department program to speed up this process. Yet, thousands of criminal aliens have been released into the public after serving their sentences because of INS's failure to screen and send them into deportation hearings. This failure is both costly and dangerous to the public. If the INS had completed proceedings for all deportable criminal aliens released from federal and state prisons in 1995 before their release, it could have avoided nearly $63 million in detention costs.[25]

Meanwhile, untold hundreds of thousands of "absconders" are roaming the country—illegal alien fugitives who have been ordered deported by immigration judges, but who continue to evade the law. In December 2001, INS commissioner James Ziglar revealed for the first time under oath that the INS did not know the whereabouts of "about 314,000" fugitive deportees. Only then did Justice Department officials move for the first time—yes, for the first time—to place their names in the FBI's National Crime Information Center database.[26]

The absconder statistics remain in dispute after the agency conceded to reporters from the Washington, D.C.–based *Human Events* newspaper that it could not vouch for the accuracy of the number. Some, including Congressman George Gekas, a Pennsylvania Republican who chairs the House Immigration Subcommittee, believe the actual number could run as high as one million.[27]

This much remains indisputable: All of these fugitives have been ordered out of the country by an immigration judge. They were either deported in absentia, or sentenced in a courtroom and then released on their own recognizance pending final deportation, only to disappear.

In January 2002, the Justice Department unveiled the Absconder Apprehension Initiative. The U.S. government said it would finally begin ejecting fugitive deportees, beginning with about a thousand immigrants from Middle Eastern countries who had been convicted of felonies in the United States. But after announcing the new campaign to round up these alien evaders, the INS admitted it would take at least a year to enter all their names in the FBI criminal database—and that the new system would probably enable the INS to locate just 10 percent of the missing deportees.[28]

Staff shortages also hampered the ambitious absconder apprehension effort. In May 2002, several agents and supervisors told the *New York Times* that the INS office in New York could barely handle the added function. The employees noted "that only 14 federal immigration agents and 9 police investigators are assigned to find and deport roughly 1,200 illegal immigrants who came from countries where Al Qaeda has been active.... After three months, fewer than 150 have been arrested."[29] By the end of May 2002, the Justice Department admitted that only 585 absconders out of 314,000 had been located. Not a single known or alleged terrorist has been caught.[30]

In the meantime, the INS continues to entrust tens of thousands of ordered deportees to leave on an honor system, sending them notices asking them to turn themselves in. The INS notices— the objects of international derision—are known as "run letters" among illegal aliens.[31]

Even if the INS tracked down every last one of the absconders, there would be no place to detain them. Detention space has been sorely misallocated and misused. Nearly $30 million earmarked for building new state-of-the-art detention facilities in San Francisco, for example, was instead diverted to speed up processing of citizenship applications.[32] Currently, the agency has only about 20,000 beds, one-tenth the number of aliens who are ordered deported each year.[33]

It's not all the INS's fault. Some of the blame for the deportation system's inability to prioritize, as usual, lies with Congress. Even as the INS failed to initiate deportation proceedings against the rottenest apples in the criminal alien basket, Congress passed laws in 1996 expanding the list of deportable offenses to include some misdemeanors and retroactive crimes. Before passage of the Illegal Immigration Reform and Immigrant Responsibility Act (IIRIRA)[34] and the Antiterrorism and Effective Death Penalty Act (AEDPA)[35] in 1996, criminal immigrants could be deported only if they committed a crime resulting in a prison sentence of at least five years.

As a result of the new laws, immigrants became subject to deportation after being convicted of selling drugs, committing a crime of moral turpitude, or committing an aggravated felony that resulted in at least a one-year sentence. Aliens who engaged in such crimes before passage of the acts could be subject to deportation.

Some of those swept up by the acts were legal permanent residents with decades-old convictions for shoplifting and other minor offenses, who in many cases were never sentenced to serve jail time for their original crimes. Predictably, the mainstream media and immigrants' rights advocates quickly seized on these "horror stories" as evidence of the INS's terrible authoritarianism. The *New York Times* took up the cause of longtime alien residents whose "only crime was being caught."[36]

In two related cases, the United States Supreme Court struck down key retroactive measures and automatic deportation provisions against legal permanent residents contained in IIRIRA and AEDPA.[37] The rulings essentially allow criminal aliens to keep their green cards and retain permanent legal residence in the United States, against the will of Congress.

Immigrants' rights activists claimed partial victory, but complained that the remaining laws left intact by the high court allowed aliens guilty of nothing more than jumping subway turnstiles to be booted out of the country. Led by the National Immigration Forum, the procriminal alien crowd launched a crusade called "Fix '96" to repeal the 1996 immigration reform laws.

These critics miss the bigger picture. The deportation system is still rigged largely in foreigners' favor. Both the small fries and the big cahunas who get caught in the dragnet take years to exhaust their appeals.

Into the Legal Abyss

While the INS receives much deserved flack for the deportation quagmire, a large portion of the blame lies with the independent agency in charge of the nation's immigration courts, the Executive Office for Immigration Review (EOIR), and its appellate body, the Board of Immigration Appeals (BIA), which thrive on making the deportation process as time-consuming and unwieldy as possible.

Together, these two independent agencies—separate from the INS, but also housed under the Justice Department—hold the ultimate keys to deportation. While the INS has responsibility for apprehending and bringing immigration charges against aliens, it is the obscure EOIR that has jurisdiction over the nationwide Immigration Courts and their companion appeals system. More than two hundred immigration judges preside in fifty-two courts across the country. They oversee removal proceedings, as well as bond redetermination hearings, in which the judges can reduce the bond imposed by the INS for aliens in custody who seek release on their own recognizance before final deportation.[38]

The BIA's twenty-odd members, based in Falls Church, Virginia, are politically appointed bureaucrats who have the power to overturn deportation orders nationwide. The panel—comprised largely of alien-friendly advocates from immigration law circles—receives more than 30,000 appeals every year, and has a backlog of 56,000 cases, of which 34,000 are more than a year old, 10,000 are more than three years old, and some are more than seven years old.[39] There's even a saying among immigration insiders in Washington about the deportation process: "It ain't over 'til the alien wins."[40]

One Justice Department employee who runs an independent Web site on the deportation morass observes:

Between the incompetence of the INS, the complete lack of alien detention center space, and the bureaucracy of the EOIR, our system for deporting known illegal aliens and criminal alien residents is a sad joke. But no one is laughing. If all of the illegal aliens and deportable resident alien criminals were rounded up tomorrow, the system would not be capable of handling them. It would be an absolute disaster. The INS and the EOIR wouldn't have the foggiest idea of what to do with them! The aliens would all be released back out on the street on immigration bonds and go back right where they were as if nothing happened, while their cases would grind on through the system of Immigration Court hearings and endless appeals.[41]

EOIR director Kevin Rooney summarized the plethora of appeal options available to all aliens—even criminal aliens—in his February 2002 testimony to Congress: "Even if an alien is removable, he or she may file an application for relief from removal, such as asylum, voluntary departure, suspension of deportation, cancellation of removal, adjustment of status, registry or a waiver of inadmissibility."[42]

What does all this bureaucratic jargon spell? Delay, delay, delay. Each of the loopholes enumerated by Rooney is written into the Immigration and Nationality Act. If an alien loses a BIA judgment, he can then seek relief in the federal circuit courts of appeal.

While most Americans are unaware of these dirty little secrets, the legal tricks for evading the flimsy immigration dragnet are well known among the alien population. An Internet search of the phrase "how to avoid deportation" yields thousands of hits, including this one from a Web site called GotTrouble.com:

Relief from deportation
There may be a way to avoid deportation, even if a person has a criminal record. The law provides relief for:

1) long term permanent residents who have not been convicted of certain serious felonies;

2) persons who have been in the United States for a long period of time and can show that being forced to leave would cause serious hardship to their family members who are United States citizens or permanent residents;

3) persons who [claim they] would be subject to torture or other physical harm if they were returned to certain countries;

4) persons who [claim they] would be subject to persecution on account of political opinion, race, national origin, or membership in a particular social group; or

5) in some limited situations, persons who are married to United States citizens or can qualify for permanent resident status.

The special circumstances that might allow a person to avoid removal are highly technical. An experienced immigration attorney should be consulted.[43]

The Web site provides a helpful directory of immigration lawyers in all fifty states to assist the troubled alien in need of "relief." These loopholes have been exploited by countless convicted aliens jailed for crimes ranging from drunk driving to baby-killing. Here's just a small sample of the criminal aliens let off the deportation hook:

The Infant Killer

Citing "severe emotional hardship" to her family and American-born children, a three-member panel halted the deportation of Haitian nanny Melanie Beaucejour Jean. She had been convicted in upstate New York of killing an eighteen-month-old baby in her care. "I hit him two or three times with my fist on the top of his head. I did this to stop him from crying. It did not work," she told Monroe County, New York, investigators. "I do not know how long I shook the baby, but I did not stop until he was unconscious," her police statement said.[44]

At the request of the INS, United States immigration judge Phillip J. Montante Jr. ordered her deported back to her native land more than two years ago. But thanks to a trio of pro-alien, Janet Reno–installed bureaucrats, Beaucejour Jean continued to enjoy the sweet life in America.[45]

Cecilia Espenoza, Lory D. Rosenberg, and Gustavo Villageliu—all appointed to the Board of Immigration Appeals by Clinton attorney general Janet Reno—concluded that Jean's crime "does not constitute a crime of violence" and is not an aggravated felony subject to deportation guidelines. Legal analyst Beverley Lumpkin noted in her ABC News online column that Espenoza and Rosenberg are known as "reflexive advocates for aliens who just don't care about the facts of a case." Espenoza's left-wing roots are so deeply ingrained that she named her son after the violent Marxist guerrilla Che Guevara.[46]

In May 2002, Attorney General John Ashcroft announced a rare reversal of the immigration board's decision on Beaucejour Jean, who was deported to Haiti soon after the ruling. "Aliens arriving at our shores must understand that residency in the United States is a privilege, not a right," Ashcroft wrote. "For those aliens . . . who engage in violent criminal acts during their stay here, this country will not offer its embrace."[47] Tough words. But they're not invoked frequently enough.

The Sentence Shaver

Min Song was a Korean national convicted of theft as an eighteen-year-old in 1992. He was sentenced to a year in prison for the aggravated felony, which was a deportable crime. To avoid removal from the country, however, Song persuaded a judge to trim the sentence from a year to 360 days. At less than a year, the suspended sentence was no longer grounds for automatic deportation. The immigration appeals board accepted the sleight of hand and allowed Song to stay in the country.[48]

The decision also paves the way for convicted aggravated felons of all kinds to pressure bleeding-heart judges to modify their sentences in order to avoid deportation.

"It's a great pro-alien, pro-immigrant decision because there's been a lot of setbacks for criminal aliens," crowed John T. Riely, Song's lawyer.[49]

The Serial Drunk Driver

Fernando Alfonso Torres-Varela, a Mexican national, was convicted of drunk driving three times. He knowingly drove while intoxicated and knew that he was driving with a suspended or revoked license. The INS sought to deport him for committing a crime of moral turpitude. He appealed to the BIA.

Despite holding in the past that a crime of moral turpitude involved conduct "that is contrary to the accepted rules of morality and the duties owed between persons or to society in general," the board concluded that Torres-Varela's serial drunk driving did not qualify as such a crime. The INS's request to deport Torres-Varela was denied.[50]

Accomplice to Child Molestation

Stephanie Short, a German national, was convicted of encouraging her three-year-old daughter to submit to sexual assault at the hands of her stepfather. He was convicted of sexual offenses; she was convicted of aiding and abetting the assault of a minor with the intent to commit a felony. She served three years of an eight-year sentence and was released on parole.

The INS sought Short's deportation based on her conviction for a crime of moral turpitude. An immigration judge supported the move. Short appealed to the BIA. In a mind-boggling decision, the board determined that it "was inappropriate to consider the husband's conviction record for purposes of determining the underlying crime of which the respondent was convicted of aiding and abetting."[51]

In other words: It was wrong for the judge to consider the fact that Short's husband raped her toddler with her approval. "As the Board no longer holds that an assault with intent to commit any felony necessarily constitutes a crime involving moral turpitude without regard to the nature of the underlying felony," the convoluted decision stated, "the [Immigration] Service has not established that the respondent was in fact convicted of a crime involving moral turpitude where it failed to establish the underlying felony that was intended."[52]

The late *Chicago Tribune* columnist Mike Royko blasted the ruling: "We actually pay taxes for that kind of gibberish. Here we have a woman who, at one point in the original FBI investigation, confessed to a crime of moral turpitude. She was found guilty of aiding and abetting a crime of moral turpitude. She spent 3 years in prison for joining in on the moral turpitude. My guess is that even creeps like John Gacy, Richard Speck and Jack the Ripper would agree it was a crime of moral turpitude."[53]

Catch and Release

The "voluntary departure" option is the most dangerous loophole exploited by aliens seeking relief from the EOIR and BIA. Intended as a cost-saving measure to streamline the deportation process, voluntary departure allows aliens to enter into an agreement to leave the United States of their own volition and to avoid the consequences of a formal order of removal (such as being barred from reentering the country for ten years). This frees the alien to leave and attempt to reenter legally, leave and enter illegally, or violate the agreement and continue to stay here illegally.

The 1996 Illegal Immigration Reform and Immigrant Responsibility Act passed some new restrictions on the policy, including stricter time limits, increased civil penalties, and added eligibility criteria. Aggravated felons and terrorists are not supposed to be eligible, but in 1999, the Justice Department's inspector general warned: "INS does not know which illegal aliens granted voluntary departure by immigration judges have left the United States because the process for verifying departures is flawed." There is no tracking system.

"Immigration judges and INS trial attorneys are not required to provide information or instructions to aliens about how to verify their departure, nor did we witness them do so in our courtroom observations," the inspector general continued. "In most cases, INS has no further contact with the alien after the immigration judge issues the voluntary departure order."[54]

Therein lies the recipe for absconders run amok.

The inspector general's report also noted that immigration judges "inappropriately grant voluntary departure to some aggravated felons" because both the courts and the INS fail to conduct adequate criminal history checks on illegal aliens before letting them go.[55] In response to persistent charges that criminal checks were not being done on aliens in removal proceedings—even after the September 11 terrorist attacks—INS executive associate commissioner for the field operations office Michael Pearson issued a memo on December 20, 2001, to "clarify" that such checks should be done prior to release from INS custody.[56] How reassuring.

This "catch and release" process continues to frustrate INS agents on the front lines. Senior Border Patrol agent Mark Hall, whose union represents officers who patrol the U.S.– Canadian

border in Michigan and Ohio, told Congress in November 2001:
"When illegal aliens are released, we send a disturbing message.
The aliens quickly pass on the word about how easy it is to enter
this country illegally and remain here. This practice is devastating to our sound border enforcement strategy."[57]

Exploiting Asylum

Claiming asylum is another quick and easy way to buy time in
the immigration bureaucracy. It allows savvy visitors who have
no legitimate claim of political or religious persecution to
extend their stays in the United States while visa applications
are pending—or simply to disappear after gaining entry to the
country. Asylum hearings often take up to a year to be scheduled. Most claimants are on their honor to show up. Unsurpris-
ingly, untold numbers never do.

In 1995 alone, according to Representative Elton Gallegly of
California, 94 percent of asylum seekers allowed into the country at the JFK and Miami international airports were never
heard from again, despite the condition they return for hearings
on their claims.[58]

At least three high-profile Middle Eastern militants (that we
know of) have exploited the asylum system with murderous
intent during the past decade:

— One was Ramzi Yousef. Six months before the 1993 World
   Trade Center attack, Yousef landed at New York City's JFK
   Airport from Pakistan. He showed inspectors an Iraqi passport without a visa. He was briefly detained for illegal entry,
   and fingerprinted, but was allowed to remain in the country
   after claiming political asylum. The INS released him because
   it didn't have space in its detention facility. Yousef headed to

Jersey City to plot the February 26, 1993, bombing. Hours after the bombing, he fled the country from New York City's JFK Airport on a fake Pakistani passport. He was apprehended in Pakistan two years later.[59]

— A second was Gazi Ibrahim Abu Mezer, the Palestinian bomb-builder who entered illegally through Canada in 1996 and 1997.[60] He claimed political asylum based on alleged persecution by Israelis, was released on a reduced $5,000 bond posted by a man who was himself an illegal immigrant, and then skipped his asylum hearing after calling his attorney and lying about his whereabouts. In June 1997, after his lawyer withdrew Mezer's asylum claim, another federal immigration judge issued a sixty-day voluntary departure order for Mezer to leave the country permanently. Instead, Mezer went to Brooklyn, built pipe bombs, and plotted the murder of untold thousands in New York City before being arrested in July 1997 when one of his roommates tipped off police.[61]

— The third was Mir Aimal Kansi, convicted in 1997 of capital murder and nine other charges stemming from his January 1993 shooting spree outside the CIA's headquarters in McLean, Virginia. Despite his history as a known Pakistani militant who had participated in anti-American demonstrations, Kansi arrived in the United States with a business visa in 1991. He invoked the magic words — "political asylum" — based on his status as an ethnic Pakistani minority, and was granted a stay and work authorization. While his asylum application was pending, he found a job as a courier, obtained a driver's license in Virginia, purchased an AK-47, murdered two CIA agents, and wounded seven others. The day after the shooting spree, Kansi fled to Pakistan from Washington, D.C.'s National Airport. He was captured in Pakistan nearly five years later.[62]

After the Mezer and Kansi apprehensions, the INS adopted significant asylum reforms. Asylum seekers were barred from working for six months or until their cases were approved, whichever came first. The number of asylum officers was more than doubled to eliminate the application backlog. In addition, Congress enacted a one-year deadline for asylum applications from the time of arrival. Congress also established an "expedited removal" system and mandatory detention procedures in 1996 to allow INS officers to turn away and bar from admission aliens with fraudulent documents (or no documents) who make dubious asylum claims at land and air ports of entry.

As a result of the new rules, frivolous asylum applications initially plummeted and the backlog shrank.[63] But in 1999, the Justice Department's inspector general found that gaping holes remained. The office reported that INS agents did not do terrorism background checks on more than 90 percent of the 150,000 asylum applications filed annually. Michael Pearson, associate commissioner for INS field operations, asserted that there was a policy to conduct the checks. But it wasn't being followed, especially along the United States–Canada border. Pearson's excuse: "It has to do with our workload and what's going on at the time and the number of people we have on the northern border."[64]

In a separate report on the Brooklyn bomb plotters, the inspector general noted that "there is no single INS entity responsible for assuring that terrorism checks are performed for all aliens or all asylum applicants." Moreover, investigators found:

Not only are aliens normally released pending their deportation hearings, but also it is extremely rare that an alien attempting to enter the United States illegally is prosecuted criminally, even though Entry Without Inspection is a criminal violation... criminal prosecutions are rare even for the felony offense of Reentry After Deportation, which applies when an alien attempts to enter the United States after he has been previously ordered deported or excluded.[65]

The Victims of Our Deportation Disregard

The systemic failure to prosecute illegal aliens—and to vet their criminal backgrounds after they claim asylum—ended in tragedy for at least one family in the United States. In the spring of 1998, twelve-year-old Juan Delgado of La Habra, California, was molested, butchered to death with a meat cleaver, dismembered, and encased in concrete blocks by an Egyptian national who had been granted religious asylum two years earlier.

The killer, John Samuel Ghobrial, had fled Egypt after being arrested on suspicion of molesting his seven-year-old cousin and stabbing him repeatedly with a penknife. Ghobrial escaped to Greece and traveled to Mexico before crossing the border illegally into Texas. He denied having a criminal history on his asylum application, and claimed that he lost an arm after being pushed in the path of a train by Muslims who harassed him for being a Coptic Christian. Immigration officials took his heart-wrenching story at face value, but in April 2002, Ghobrial was sentenced to death for murdering Delgado.[66]

"Immigration should investigate the background of the people they let in this country," said an outraged Maria Asturias, who allowed Ghobrial to live in her backyard shed for three weeks before the murder. "If they had investigated, they wouldn't have allowed him entry, and we could have avoided this horrible tragedy."[67] Immigrant advocates, however, continue to oppose any attempts to conduct criminal background checks for fear of jeopardizing the safety of asylum applicants' families abroad.[68]

Corrupt immigration lawyers make the problem worse. Robert Porges, a Harvard Law School graduate and operator of the nation's largest asylum practice, admitted in February 2002 that he ran an immigration fraud factory whose legal assistants and paralegals cranked out thousands of bogus persecution claims for illegal Chinese. Porges's firm published more fiction than Random House.

"I was aware many of the stories submitted by the aliens were either false, inaccurate or exaggerations," Porges admitted to United States district court Judge Denise Cote. "I deliberately or consciously avoided facts which I knew were not true....I deliberately did not investigate.... In effect I closed my eyes to what I knew were stories created by employees of the Porges law firm," he said. Porges made clear to the judge that he "personally approved every asylum application."[69]

Porges and his wife, Sheery Lu Porges, also admitted tipping off Chinese smugglers ("snakeheads") to the best entry routes in the United States. Porges's firm bailed out detained immigrants and assisted smugglers who kidnapped and held the immigrants for ransom. Fees topped fifty thousand dollars per person; the business allegedly earned as much as $13 million from the scheme, dating to 1993.[70] In plea agreements, the couple stipulated that the firm filed over one thousand fraudulent asylum applications, but federal prosecutors say the total number of cases affected by the conspiracy may be as high as seven thousand.[71]

Porges's lawyer, Larry Bronson, lamented his client's fate. "It's a sad day," Bronson noted, because Porges is "going to jail for conduct which is conducted every day by people in this business."[72]

That claim is backed by former immigration lawyer Matt Hayes of New Jersey, who lambasted his former colleagues for profiting off the scams. The incentives for corruption are strong: "There are over 100,000 new political asylum cases each year,"

Hayes noted. "But this volume also drives down rates and makes the lawyer less than diligent in assessing the credibility of his client's asylum claims. To be too diligent could mean one less fee."[73]

Politically Correct "Persecution"

Even as the government tries to control the flow of these false asylum seekers, it continues to succumb to lobbying from special interest groups to broaden the definition of persecution — which United States law says must be based on "race, religion, nationality, membership in a particular social group, or political opinion." Under pressure from feminist, antiabortion and gay rights groups, government agencies and immigration judges have ruled since 1994 that applicants may qualify for asylum based on declarations of homosexuality, assertions of women's rights, fear of female circumcision, and even spousal abuse in their home countries.[74]

The floodgates have been opened to every aggrieved, politically correct group. Mark Krikorian of the Center for Immigration Studies has noted that the State Department estimates that 110 million women in Africa, the Middle East, and Asia have been subjected to female genital mutilation.[75] Feminists demand streamlined asylum procedures for these women and all others claiming to suffer from "gender-based persecution."

The trend is growing, despite unpunished fraudulent cases such as "Adelaide Abankwah," a celebrated asylum-seeker from Ghana who fabricated a story about being the "queen mother" of the Nkumssa tribe. "Abankwah" claimed she would be subjected to tribal genital mutilation if she were deported from the United States.[76] When the INS challenged her story in 1997, celebrities such as Gloria Steinem, Julia Roberts, and First Lady Hillary Clinton crusaded on her behalf.[77]

But "Abankwah" was actually Regina Norman Danson, a Ghanaian hotel worker who had stolen the real Abankwah's passport. According to I. Jay Fredman, Abankwah's lawyer, Danson has yet to be prosecuted for fraud or ordered deported.[78] "Danson ruined my client's life, embarrassed her family, and ruined the credibility of all bona fide asylum seekers. Everybody—Hillary Clinton, Gloria Steinem, Chuck Schumer—got sucked in. They saw a good story and it didn't matter whether it was true."

Danson is by no means the only alien to fabricate claims of persecution. A GAO report found a 90 percent rate of fraud in five thousand petitions for asylum.[79]

In January 2002, Attorney General John Ashcroft carried on the Clinton legacy of broadening victim status by approving rules for a new visa program (called the T-visa). It covers "victims of human trafficking" brought into the country through smuggling rings who fear "extreme hardship involving unusual and severe harm" if returned to their native countries.[80]

These expanded asylum criteria are an open invitation for renewed fraud and exploitation. The changes have occurred without any serious public debate about who among the world's least fortunate should be shuttled to the front of the immigration line. The need for careful discrimination in our immigration policy is greater than ever since September 11.

The inability to sort out the truly oppressed from rank opportunists, fugitive oppressors, and terrorist plotters poses a continuing threat to all Americans.

What Must America Do?

"I have not yet begun to fight."

—John Paul Jones, 1779

Everything has changed," goes the post–September 11 cliché. Yet, as the loopholes, lapses, corruption, mismanagement, and chaos documented in this book have shown, so much remains the same. This book began with a starter list of nine simple things a terrorist can do to invade America. It ends with a list, by no means comprehensive, of what Americans at home must do to fight back against foreign threats.

Guard the Front Door
Time for a Targeted Visa Moratorium

In May 2002, FBI director Robert Mueller warned that walk-in suicide bombings in America are "inevitable."[1] That doesn't mean we should sit back and make it easy for terrorists—whether strapped with explosives or bearing nuclear, chemical, biological weapons—to obtain visas and first-class tickets to complete their missions. Congress should bar all new travelers and immigrants from al Qaeda breeding grounds until we weed out and track down the infiltrators already here.

The Enhanced Border Security and Visa Entry Reform Act of 2002 placed a ban on temporary visitor visas for individuals from the seven official state sponsors of terrorism (Cuba, Iran, Iraq, Libya, North Korea, Sudan, and Syria).[2] But the law doesn't go far enough. At least eight other al Qaeda–friendly countries belong on a visa moratorium list, including Afghanistan, Algeria, Egypt, Lebanon, Somalia, United Arab Emirates, Yemen,[3] and Saudi Arabia. They may not be designated official sponsors of terrorism, but these governments actively contribute to a culture of anti-American hatred that has no place on our soil.[4]

Until the INS has a comprehensive foreign tracking database up and running, until every consular officer and immigration inspector has access to, training in, and regular use of an up-to-date terrorist and criminal lookout system, and until the fugitive masterminds of September 11 are brought to justice, no more visas should be issued to citizens of al Qaeda strongholds.

In addition, Congress ought to bar Muslim clerics from receiving religious visas, end all visa-for-sale schemes (investor visa programs), and scrap the H-1B visa program, which terrorism-linked Muslim charities have attempted to exploit. Finally, all those who enter on temporary visas and wish to change their status (from tourist to student, for example, or to permanent legal resident) must be required to go back to their native lands for screening and wait for approval there. Terrorists shouldn't be able to hang around inside our country, planning havoc as Mohamed Atta and numerous other al Qaeda operatives did, while their change-of-status paperwork is processed.

Scrap Visa-Free Travel

No more potential hijackers and shoe-bombers should be able to follow in the footsteps of suspected al Qaeda operatives Ramzi Yousef, Zacarias Moussaoui, and Richard Reid. All flew legally into our country without a visa under the profit-driven Visa Waiver program.

The entire enterprise should be scrapped, as should the Transit Without a Visa program. We can no longer afford to allow millions of people from all over the world to enter our country without first being screened. The airline and tourism industry will say eliminating these programs would be too costly and unfair. Tell them to ask the widows and children of the September 11 victims about bearing unjust burdens.

Beef Up Seaports and Airports

At seaports, all alien crewmen should be fingerprinted and checked against lookout databases before being granted shore leave. A unified INS, Customs, and Coast Guard force must assume immediate responsibility for inspecting ships and their cargo for terrorist stowaways. We need to double the number of immigration inspectors at air ports of entry. Armed National Guardsmen should be installed *permanently* at all major international airports, from JFK and La Guardia in New York to Dulles in Washington, D.C., to Miami, and Los Angeles. We are at war. It is not business as usual. Foreign travelers must see that we are serious the moment they step off their planes.

Stop the Revolving Door
End "Catch and Release" Games

The highest-priced, most sophisticated home security system is a joke if cops don't come and take away the thieves who manage to break in. The same holds true for homeland security. We must also develop an effective system of detention and deportation to rid our collective home of uninvited guests — and keep them out.

Illegal aliens who have been ordered deported must not be allowed to run free. The voluntary departure option is an escape hatch that must be eliminated. This policy benefits no one but the aliens who eagerly volunteer to abuse our deportation system's undeserved trust. Congress should amend the Immigration and Nationality Act to eliminate voluntary departure as an option during removal proceedings before an immigration judge.

Moreover, federal law mandates that criminal aliens who reenter the United States after deportation face up to twenty years in jail. Yet, the law is followed sporadically by United States Attorney's Offices. Simply enforce the law.

Know Where to Hold 'em: Military Bases

Increased enforcement cannot succeed without greatly expanding the INS's current twenty-thousand-bed detention capacity. Even when deportation absconders are tracked down, they are often let go because there's nowhere to put them. One official of a bonding company said the INS was freeing 50 percent of the aliens he had been ordered to track down and turn in since September 11.[5] California representative Elton Gallegly's proposal from 1995 to convert closed military bases to illegal alien detention facilities should be dusted off and put into action immediately.

End Deportation Delays: Abolish the EOIR and BIA

The most under-recognized obstacle to deporting illegal aliens is the shadowy immigration court system and its unaccountable appellate body, which routinely put aliens' rights over citizens' safety. Attorney General John Ashcroft should abolish the Executive Office for Immigration Review and the Board of Immigration Appeals and transfer their functions to existing law enforcement officers within the immigration bureaucracy. The alien lawyer lobby claims that any streamlining of the deportation bureaucracy poses a "threat to the integrity of the immigration process."[6] Nonsense.

Restoring integrity to the immigration process will require closing the loopholes and black holes into which so many fugitive absconders, criminal aliens, and unwelcome guests have disappeared. "Due process" for illegal aliens has for too long resulted in too many endless delays—and too many interminable stays.

Lock the Back Door: Stop Illegal Immigration

Militarize the Borders

Homeland Security chief Tom Ridge declared that "the last thing we want to do is militarize the borders between friends."[7] But at the southern border, which has been the site of at least one confirmed incursion by Mexican soldiers who shot at a United States Border Patrol agent,[8] we must be prepared to use our own soldiers to defend against acts of aggression. At the northern border with Canada, where dozens of terrorist groups have settled at our doorstep, every rubber orange cone and measly "No Entry" sign should immediately be replaced with an armed National Guardsman—at least until 100,000 new Border Patrol and interior enforcement agents are trained and ready to be deployed.

If we are willing to send American troops to the mountains of Afghanistan and the jungles of the Philippines to defend against foreign threats, we should be prepared to dispatch them for the duration of the War on Terror to help police the vulnerable, unguarded stretches of desert, forest, valley, and sea here on the home front.

Slow Down on Asylum

The INS remains woefully ill-equipped to keep out, track down, and remove deceptive alien opportunists—including terrorists and human rights abusers—claiming to be oppressed. Our immigration system can't afford to expand asylum benefits until it can get a handle on the tens of thousands who have already filed applications, skipped their hearings, and eluded authorities as a result of misguided compassion.

The same goes for the Temporary Protected Status program, which is supposed to grant short-term humanitarian relief to illegal aliens from selected countries in turmoil, but has turned into a special-interest, permanent-asylum program. Unless the agency demonstrates the commitment to track down those who scam the asylum system or overstay their welcome, America should not take in new waves of huddled masses.

Pull Up the Welcome Mat

It is time to turn off the magnets that attract hordes of illegal aliens who evade criminal background and medical checks, undermine our borders, and steal the opportunity of freedom and prosperity from millions of other people around the world waiting in line for the American Dream. Many others have issued this call over the years. But never has the moral and national security imperative been greater or more apparent.

Interior enforcement—investigating, tracking down, and removing those who violate our laws after they've come into the country—must be a top priority. Every Border Patrol agent and INS investigator must be trained in, and have access to, the INS and FBI fingerprint systems, as well as all available lookout databases. Fugitives from deportation who are caught must face stiff prison terms, followed by immediate deportation, and permanent exclusion from our country. The number of visas granted to citizens from countries with a high number of illegal visa overstayers must be sharply reduced.

States that adopt and retain pro–illegal alien policies should be denied federal reimbursements for health care, education, and other costs associated with illegal immigration. State and local law enforcement agencies that refuse to cooperate with the Justice Department in the War on Terror should be forced to bear the full cost of detaining and imprisoning criminal aliens. If states allow temporary foreign visitors to obtain driver's licenses, the licenses must be required to expire simultaneously with the driver's visa.

The feds should stop giving away taxpayer identification numbers to aliens who exploit them to work illegally. Employers who hire illegal aliens must no longer be let off the hook. Enforce federal sanctions first passed in 1986. Allow the Social Security Administration to access the INS's alien databases to verify immigration status. Dramatically increase penalties for marriage fraud involving suspected or known terrorist aliens.

Finally: No more amnesty programs, period.

Clean House at INS

The War on Terror will not be won if the generals are not prepared or willing to fight it. The current head of the INS is a man who freely joked after September 11 that "People who say I don't have any experience in the area are absolutely right"[9] and assured illegal aliens that it is "not practical or reasonable"[10] to deport them. Such utterances can only have a negative effect on morale among experienced rank-and-file agents, inspectors, and investigators trying to enforce the law.

Tough times require tough managers—and even tougher sanctions against incompetents, frauds, and sellouts. Congress must pass a law allowing the attorney general to fire at will INS employees who compromise our national security.

Remove all supervisors involved in the Miami International Airport/Krome Detention Center scandal from sensitive positions. Aggressively prosecute fraud, misconduct, theft, and incompetence at the highest levels of the agency. Publish an annual list of INS officials convicted of criminal misconduct. Strengthen federal whistleblower protections. Reward agency truth-tellers with management positions in their fields of expertise; demote or fire supervisors who retaliate against them.

Protect Our Birthright

American citizenship is one of the most sought-after privileges in the world. But we have doled it out carelessly to terrorists, torturers, and criminals—and it is almost impossible to take back. Congress must reform the process to allow speedy denaturalization of America's enemies and amend federal law to automatically strip citizenship from naturalized Americans convicted of terrorism. Immigration authorities convicted of fraud involving citizenship scams should face harsh penalties. Individuals who express anti-American sentiments abroad must be barred from receiving green cards leading to eventual citizenship. Those convicted of human rights atrocities in their native countries, and found to have lied to American immigration officials about past criminal records, must be immediately stripped of United States citizenship if they have been naturalized here, then prosecuted, jailed, and deported.

Entry into this country—either as an immigrant or a visitor—is a privilege, not a right. The safety of our citizens must come before the comfort and convenience of foreigners. To prevent another September 11, tourism dollars, ethnic votes, diplomatic kowtowing, and political cronyism must once and for all take a back seat to national security.

There will be howling protestations from the usual suspects. But this is no moment to give in to the homegrown abettors of anti-Americanism. It's time to take out the trash, fix the holes in our fences, and defend Lady Liberty from all those who would trespass against her.

Invasion by Any Means Necessary

Name	Place of Origin	Immigration Status
2001: Shoe-bombing attempt		
Richard Reid	United Kingdom	En route to United States without a visa (through the Visa Waiver program)
2001: September 11 hijackers		
Mohamed Atta	Egypt	Tourist; awaiting student visa, allowed in despite previous overstay
Marwan Al Shehhi	United Arab Emirates	Tourist; awaiting student visa, allowed in despite previous overstay
Hani Hanjour	Saudi Arabia	Illegal alien; overstayed student visa
Nawaf al Hazmi	Saudi Arabia	Illegal alien; overstayed tourist visa
Satam al Suqami	Saudi Arabia	Illegal alien; expired business visa
Ahmed al Ghamdi	Saudi Arabia	Tourist
Waleed al Shehri	Saudi Arabia	Tourist
Wail al Shehri	Saudi Arabia	Tourist
Abdulaziz Alomari	Saudi Arabia	Tourist
Fayez Ahmed Banihammad	Saudi Arabia	Tourist
Mohand al Shehri	Saudi Arabia	Tourist
Hazma/Hamza al Ghamdi	Saudi Arabia	Tourist
Majed Moqed	Saudi Arabia	Tourist
Salem al Hazmi	Saudi Arabia	Tourist
Ahmed al Haznawi	Saudi Arabia	Tourist
Ahmed Alnami	Saudi Arabia	Tourist

Name	Place of Origin	Immigration Status
2001: September 11 hijackers (cont'd)		
Ziad Jarrah	Lebanon	Tourist
Saaed al Ghamdi	Saudi Arabia	Tourist
Khalid Almihdhar	Saudi Arabia	Business
Zacarias Moussaoui The alleged "20th hijacker"	France	Illegal alien; violated Visa Waiver program rules
1999: The Millennium conspirators		
Ahmed Ressam	Algeria	Illegal alien; fraudulent passport; stopped at the U.S.-Canadian border
Abdelghani Meskini	Algeria	Illegal alien; stowaway landed in Boston
Abdel Hakim Tizegha	Algeria	Illegal alien; stowaway landed in Boston; snuck back and forth across the U.S.-Canadian border
1998: Plotters involved in U.S. Embassy bombings in Africa		
Wadih el Hage	Lebanon	Student; married American; became naturalized American citizen
Ali Mohammed	Egypt	Married American; became naturalized American citizen
Khalid Abu al Dahab	Egypt	Student; married three different Americans; became naturalized American citizen
Essam al Ridi	Egypt	Student; naturalized American citizen
1997: New York subway bombing conspirators		
Gazi Ibrahim Abu Mezer	Palestine	Illegal alien; multiple crossings at the U.S.-Canadian border
Lafi Khalil	Palestine	Illegal alien; violated transit visa; mistakenly issued tourist visa stamp; overstayed

Name	Place of Origin	Immigration Status
1993: The World Trade Center bombers		
Ahmed Ajaj	Palestine	Illegal alien; fraudulent passport
Mahmud Abouhalima	Egypt	Illegal alien; expired tourist visa; granted farmworker amnesty
Mohammed Abouhalima	Egypt	Illegal alien; expired tourist visa; granted farmworker amnesty
Mohammed Salameh	Jordan	Illegal alien; overstayed tourist visa; rejected for farmworker amnesty, but stayed anyway
Eyad Ismoil	Jordan	Illegal alien; overstayed student visa
Ramzi Yousef	Pakistan	Claimed asylum; freed without hearing
Nidal Ayyad	Kuwait	Naturalized American citizen
1993: New York landmark bombing conspiracy		
Sheik Omar Abdel Rahman	Egypt	Tourist (multiple visas issued); legal permanent resident (under bogus name); legal permanent resident status revoked, but applied for asylum
El Sayyid Nosair	Egypt	Tourist; married American; became naturalized American citizen
Amir Abdelgani	Sudan	Tourist; married American; became legal permanent resident
Fadil Abdelgani	Sudan	Overstayed tourist visa; married American; became legal permanent resident
Siddig Ibrahim Siddig Ali	Sudan	Married American; became legal permanent resident
Ibrahim Elgabrowny	Egypt	Legal permanent resident
Tarig Elhassan	Sudan	Married American; became legal permanent resident
Abdo Mohammed Haggag	Egypt	Married American; became legal permanent resident

— Appendix A —

Name	Place of Origin	Immigration Status
1993: New York landmark bombing conspiracy (cont'd)		
Fares Khallafalla	Sudan	Married American; became legal permanent resident
Matarawy Mohammed Said Saleh	Egypt	Married American; became legal permanent resident
Mohammed Saleh	Palestine	Married American; became legal permanent resident

Sources: Immigration and Naturalization Service; Federal Bureau of Investigation; Center for Immigration Studies

Illegal Immigration Is a Crime

Hard to believe this is necessary, but here for the record are just a few of the federal citations that spell out the crime and punishment for aliens who trespass against our borders, and those who assist them. It *is* illegal.

Violating the Borders Is Against the Law
United States Code. TITLE 8, CHAPTER 12 , SUBCHAPTER II, Part VIII, Sec. 1325.

Sec. 1325. - Improper entry by alien

(a) Improper time or place; avoidance of examination or inspection; misrepresentation and concealment of facts

Any alien who (1) enters or attempts to enter the United States at any time or place other than as designated by immigration officers, or (2) eludes examination or inspection by immigration officers, or (3) attempts to enter or obtains entry to the United States by a willfully false or misleading representation or the willful concealment of a material fact, shall, for the first commission of any such offense, be fined under title 18 or imprisoned not more than 6 months, or both, and, for a subsequent commission of any such offense, be fined under title 18, or imprisoned not more than 2 years, or both.

Overstaying a Visa Is Against the Law
United States Code. TITLE 8, CHAPTER 12, SUBCHAPTER II, Part IV, Sec. 1227(a)(1)(C)

(i) Nonimmigrant status violators

Any alien who was admitted as a nonimmigrant and who has failed to maintain the nonimmigrant status in which the alien was admitted or to which it was changed under section 1258 of this title, or to comply with the conditions of any such status, is deportable.

Hiring, Recruiting, and Harboring Illegal Aliens Are All Federal Felony Offenses
United States Code. TITLE 8 , CHAPTER 12, SUBCHAPTER II, Part VIII.

Sec. 1323. Unlawful bringing of aliens into United States: "It shall be unlawful for any person ... to bring to the United States from any place outside thereof ... any alien who does not have a valid passport and an unexpired visa ..."

Sec. 1324. Bringing in and harboring certain aliens: Any person "knowing or in reckless disregard of the fact that an alien has come to, entered, or remains in the United States in violation of law, conceals, harbors, or shields from detection, or attempts to conceal, harbor, or shield from detection, such alien in any place" shall be "fined" or "imprisoned ..."

Sec. 1324a. Unlawful employment of aliens: "It is unlawful for a person or other entity to hire, or to recruit ... for employment in the United States an alien knowing the alien is an unauthorized alien ..."

Alien Registration: An International Comparison

Country	Registration required at time of entry?	Periodic registration?	Registration at other times?	Where registration occurs	What alien must bring to register	Identification card/papers required on person while in country?
Switzerland	Yes, within eight days.	Yes, every twelve months.	Yes, whenever alien changes address, university, or job.	Cantonal police station.	Passport, visa, address information, proof of enrollment or employment.	Not required.
United Kingdom	Yes, within seven days.	No.	Yes, whenever alien changes address, university, or job.	Local police station.	Passport, visa, proof of financial means, proof of enrollment or employment, proof of accommodation.	Required.
Germany	Yes, when alien establishes residence.	No.	Yes, whenever alien changes address.	Local police station.	Passport, documentation of intended activities while in country.	Yes, must carry registration papers on person at all times.

Alien Registration: What Other Countries Require

Country	Registration required at time of entry?	Periodic registration?	Registration at other times?	Where registration occurs	What alien must bring to register	Identification card/papers required on person while in country?
Spain	Yes, within ten days to six months, depending on nationality.	Yes, every twelve months.	No.	Local division of national police.	Passport, address, proof of financial means, letter from university or contract from employer.	Yes, student must carry student identification card; worker must carry work permit.
France	Yes, within seven days.	Yes, every twelve months.	Yes, whenever alien changes address, school, or employer.	Local prefecture of national police.	Passport, visa, birth certificate, letter from university or employer, photograph.	Yes, alien must carry carte de séjour on person at all times.

Country	Registration required at time of entry?	Periodic registration?	Registration at other times?	Where registration occurs	What alien must bring to register	Identification card/papers required on person while in country?
Netherlands	Yes, within three days (to obtain residence permit).	Yes, every twelve months.	Yes, whenever alien changes address, school, or employer.	Local division of national police (alien police division).	Passport, birth certificate, apostille stamp on documents, photograph, proof of enrollment or employment, results of TB test, police report from home country.	Not required.
United States	Yes, but only enforced for certain aliens deemed national security risks.	Yes, every twelve months.	Yes, whenever alien changes address and before departure from the U.S.	INS office.	Proof of tenancy, enrollment (for students) or employment (for workers).	Not required.

Source: Department of Justice

A Technology Primer

At the INS, the main repository for information about aliens who should not be allowed into the U.S. is called **NAILS** (National Automated Immigration Lookout System). It's available to inspectors at land, sea, and air ports of entry and contains very basic data on individuals and some criminal histories. State Department employees also use the system to conduct background checks on visa applicants abroad.

The Customs Service runs **TECS** (the Treasury Enforcement Communication System), which also tracks suspicious travelers, plus businesses and vehicles. TECS is linked to the NCIC database, and contains information on federal, state, and local arrest warrants. The system, which is equipped with fingerprinting capabilities, can be accessed by Customs agents and INS inspectors.

The State Department's Consular Lookout and Support System, **CLASS**, contains data used to screen nonimmigrant applicants. CLASS includes about 4 million names and other biographical data on known or suspected terrorists, drug traffickers, and other international criminals. Another State Department database, **TIPOFF**, focuses exclusively on monitoring known and suspected terrorists. The classified data—gathered from the CIA, NSA, and FBI and administered by the Bureau of Intelligence and Research—are fed to the INS's NAILS system, which in turn is uploaded to CLASS on a daily basis. State also maintains a terrorist reporting channel known as the **VISAS VIPER** program, which allows consular posts to flag suspected terrorists even before they apply for visas, and shares names from a Canadian government database under a program called **TUSCAN**. Another program, **TIPPIX,** scans photographs of suspected terrorists into the TIPOFF/ VIPER counterterrorism database.

The granddaddy of lookout programs is **IBIS** (the Interagency Border Inspection System), which is shared by INS, the Customs Service, all major law enforcement agencies, and State Department consular offices and American embassies. Information from NAILS, CLASS, The Advance Passenger Information System (APIS), and TIPPIX is fed to IBIS, which runs on the TECS mainframe. IBIS, which can be accessed on more than twenty-four thousand computer terminals at air, land, and seaports of entry across the country, also connects to the NCIC database.

INS employees can tap into a dizzying array of automated programs designed to track unwanted visitors, suspicious travelers, foreign criminal suspects, defrauders, and other aliens who have come into contact with immigration authorities. Here's a brief dip into the agency's alphabet soup of text-based and biometric databases, as well as other related programs to which immigration officials have access:

CIS: The Central Index System, the agency's master records management system, contains information on approximately 45 million aliens, including legal permanent residents, naturalized citizens, violators of immigration laws such as deportees and smugglers, and others of interest who have crossed paths with the INS since 1960. The database tells users the physical location of an alien's hard-copy "A-file" (opened by local district offices across the country whenever an alien applies for benefits, legal permanent resident status, or citizenship, or when an alien is involved in an INS investigation or enforcement action). CIS provides the alien's date of birth, alien number, country of birth, citizenship, dates of INS actions against the alien, and selected data from other INS databases.

DACS: The Deportable Alien Control System is the central clearinghouse for tracking aliens through the detention and deportation process. It contains information about aliens who have been detained or placed on a docket for deportation or exclusion. DACS tells users the status or disposition of individual deportation cases, and also provides statistical and summary data of deportation cases by type, status, and other characteristics of the case, as well as biographical data about the alien.

APIS: The Advance Passenger Information System, which targets high-risk and suspicious travelers, is a collaboration of the INS, the Customs Service, and the airline industry. It allows airlines to collect biographical information on passengers at foreign ports and transmit it to the United States before they land. The data—including full legal name, gender, date of birth, nationality, and travel document number—are stored on machine-readable travel documents. Once uploaded, the information is checked against the FBI's National Crime Information Center database of wanted persons and a network of lookout databases (see below). Some 57 million foreign passengers who entered the United States in 2001 were entered into APIS.

SAVE: The Systematic Alien Verification for Entitlements program is an intergovernmental, information-sharing initiative used by public agencies to determine an alien's immigration status and ensure that only entitled aliens receive federal, state, or local tax-subsidized benefits. The system can electronically verify the status of lawful permanent residents and aliens in other categories.

IDENT: The INS's Automated Biometric Fingerprint Identification System collects photos and fingerprints on recidivist aliens caught entering the country multiple times, and maintains a lookout database on those who have been previously deported or who have significant criminal histories. The recidivist database includes more than one million illegal aliens who had been apprehended by the INS; the lookout database contains records on about 400,000 aliens who have been previously deported or who have significant criminal histories. IDENT also holds a database of applicants for asylum and a database of applicants for the new biometric Border Crossing cards. Last summer, the INS obtained some 8,600 fingerprint records on aliens wanted by the U.S. Marshals Service for the IDENT lookout database.

By June 2002, the system still did not include ten-print records and photos of known or suspected terrorists in its lookout database. Nor did IDENT contain lookout information on an estimated seventy thousand foreigners previously arrested by the INS and targeted by the FBI's "wants and warrants" list. Also missing are any prints on previously deported aliens or criminal aliens arrested before 1995.

IAFIS: The FBI's Integrated Automated Fingerprint Identification System is the king of fingerprint databases. With more than 40 million digitized ten-print fingerprint records, it's the world's largest biometric repository of any kind. The $640 million IAFIS project was launched in 1999, five years after IDENT. It can locate aliases if the same prints are filed under different names, and it can search for matches for latent fingerprints collected at crime scenes. The bureau processes checks on an estimated forty-two thousand prints each day in response to requests from some eighteen thousand state and local law enforcement agencies, as well as the Defense Department, the Office of Personnel Management, and the INS. Integration with IDENT continues to proceed slowly.

WIN/AFIS: In addition to the IDENT fingerprint system, the INS has access to a separate, centralized fingerprint database called the Western Identification Network/Automated Fingerprint Identification System. The high-speed computer system includes some 2.5 million arrest records and millions of fingerprint images and text data from ten-print fingerprint cards submitted by seven western states and the INS.

ENFORCE: The Enforcement Case Tracking System is the agency's main alien arrest processing system. It was created to document and track the investigation, identification, apprehension, detention, and/or removal of immigration law violators. The system standardizes the collection and reporting of enforcement data across the INS, and is being integrated with the IDENT fingerprint system. It will consolidate several existing databases, and reach out to databases from other agencies. Users will be able to determine immediately whether an apprehended illegal alien is a first-time or repeat offender. INS officers will also be able to cross-reference an alien's previous arrest record, if any, and perform instant searches based on information such as name, date of birth, place of birth, or even variations in name spelling. Congress funded ENFORCE in 1995 as part of a $2.2 billion automation project, and expected the program to be up and running in two years. Seven years later, the agency has yet to meet the deadline for full operation.

NCIC: The FBI's National Crime Information Center database contains criminal history information on millions of individuals, including wanted persons, deported felons, sexual offenders, gangsters, and terrorists. An enhanced version, NCIC 2000, was introduced three years ago. It allows agents in the field to use mobile NCIC equipment to transmit a single fingerprint for comparison against wanted, missing, and unidentified person files. The system links to some twenty-two databases containing 60 million records for criminal interrogations and investigations. In contrast to the apathy and ignorance of INS employees toward IDENT, the NCIC database is ingrained in the law enforcement culture. "We use it as a matter of habit," Chicago police detective Wayne Lipsey told *Federal Computer Week*. "It is one of our basic tools. It would be like what a hammer, screw-driver or saw is to a carpenter," added Alexandria, Virginia, police captain Michael Clancy.[1] Investigators have used NCIC to identify criminals small and large, from Martin Luther King Jr.'s assassin, James Earl Ray, to Oklahoma City bomber Timothy McVeigh.

The largest of NCIC's files, the Interstate Identification Index (III), holds information on criminal arrests and dispositions of cases involving persons arrested for felonies or serious misde-meanors under state or federal law. Under the USA Patriot Act signed into law by President Bush in the fall of 2001, both the INS and the State Department gained access to the III files.

The House Immigration Reform Caucus
Membership list as of June 2002

Congressman Robert Aderholt (R-AL)

Congressman Todd Akin (R-MO)

Congressman Richard Baker (R-LA)

Congressman James Barcia (D-MI)

Congressman Bob Barr (R-GA)

Congressman Roscoe Bartlett (R-MD)

Congressman Michael Bilirakis (R-FL)

Congressman John Boozman (R-AR)

Congressman Allen Boyd (D-FL)

Congressman Henry Brown (R-SC)

Congressman Eric Cantor (R-VA)

Congressman John Cooksey (R-LA)

Congresswoman Barbara Cubin (R-WY)

Congressman John Culberson (R-TX)

Congresswoman Jo Ann Davis (R-VA)

Congressman Nathan Deal (R-GA)

Congressman Jim DeMint (R-SC)

Congressman John Doolittle (R-CA)

Congressman John Duncan (R-TN)

Congressman J. Randy Forbes (R-VA)

Congressman Virgil Goode (I-VA)

Congressman Lindsey Graham (R-SC)

Congressman Jim Greenwood (R-PA)

Congressman Felix Grucci (R-NY)

Congressman Gil Gutknecht (R-MN)

Congressman Ralph Hall (D-TX)

Congressman Tony Hall (D-OH)

Congressman Robin Hayes (R-NC)

Congressman J. D. Hayworth (R-AZ)

Congressman Joel Hefley (R-CO)

Congressman Henry Hyde (R-IL)

Congressman Peter Hoekstra (R-MI)

Congressman Duncan Hunter (R-CA)

Congressman Johnny Isakson (R-GA)

Congressman Ernest Istook (R-OK)

Congressman Sam Johnson (R-TX)

Congressman Walter Jones (R-NC)

Congressman Brian Kerns (R-IN)

Congressman Gary Miller (R-CA)

Congressman Jeff Miller (R-FL)

Congressman Charlie Norwood (R-GA)

Congressman Butch Otter (R-ID)

Congressman David Phelps (D-IL)

Congressman Dana Rohrabacher (R-CA)

Congresswoman Marge Roukema (R-NJ)

Congressman Ed Royce (R-CA)

Congressman Bob Schaffer (R-CO)

Congressman Pete Sessions (R-TX)

Congressman John Shadegg (R-AZ)

Congressman Chris Shays (R-CT)

Congressman Michael Simpson (R-ID)

Congressman Lamar Smith (R-TX)

Congressman Nick Smith (R-MI)

Congressman Bob Stump (R-AZ)

Congressman John Sullivan (R-OK)

Congressman Tom Tancredo (R-CO)*

Congressman Patrick Tiberi (R-OH)

Congressman Fred Upton (R-MI)

Congressman David Vitter (R-LA)

Congressman Zach Wamp (R-TN)

Congressman Dave Weldon (R-FL)

Congressman Roger Wicker (R-MS)

---

*Chairman

Appendix F

Immigration Resources on the Internet

These Web sites, offering information and views from all per-
spectives (official, legal, grassroots, employee, restrictionist,
and pro–open borders), were helpful in my research.

Government

U.S. Immigration and Naturalization Service
http://www.ins.gov

U.S. State Department, visa services
http://travel.state.gov/visa_services.html

U.S. Justice Department, Office of the Inspector General
http://www.usdoj.gov/oig

U.S. Executive Office for Immigration Review
http://www.usdoj.gov/eoir

Attorney General and Board of Immigration Appeals Precedent Decisions
http://www.usdoj.gov/eoir/efoia/bia/biaindx.htm

United States Code, Title 8, Chapter 12, "Immigration and Nationality"
http://www4.law.cornell.edu/uscode/8/ch12.html

Grassroots activism/news/opinion

American Patrol (CA)
http://www.americanpatrol.com

Stein Report
http://www.steinreport.com

Americans for Better Immigration (keeps scorecards on Congress)
http://www.betterimmigration.com/

Numbers USA
http://www.numbersusa.com

Project USA
http://www.projectusa.com

Sachem Quality of Life Organization (NY)
http://www.sqlife.org

California Coalition for Immigration Reform
http://www.ccir.net

The American Cause
http://www.theamericancause.org

VDARE
http://www.vdare.com

Migration News
http://migration.ucdavis.edu/mn/index.html

Citizens Lobby
http://www.citizenslobby.com

Immigration lawyers

The Immigration Portal
http://www.ilw.com

Carl Shusterman, Immigration News
http://www.shusterman.com

Latour and Lleras, Immigration News
http://www.usvisanews.com

Greg Siskind's Immigration Bulletin
http://www.visalaw.com/bulletin.html

Research

Center for Immigration Studies
http://www.cis.org

U.S. Commission on Immigration Reform (reports and testimony, 1990–1997)
http://www.utexas.edu/lbj/uscir/

Federation for American Immigration Reform
http://www.fairus.org

The Labor Condition Application Database (contains more than one million records filed to the Department of Labor by American companies seeking to obtain H-1B, H-2B, and green card visas for foreign nationals)
http://www.zazona.com

Watchdogs

Deport Aliens (anonymous Web site monitoring the Executive Office for Immigration Review and Board of Immigration Appeals)
http://www.deportaliens.com

Government Accountability Project
http://www.whistleblower.org

The Center for Justice and Accountability
http://www.cja.org

Notes

Introduction

1 Steven A. Camarota, *The Golden Door: How Militant Islamic Terrorists Entered and Remained in the United States, 1993–2001*, Washington, D.C.: Center for Immigration Studies, 22 May 2002.

2 The INS budget increased 230 percent between 1993 and 2001.

3 August Gribbin, "GAO Says Border Still Vulnerable to Terrorist Infiltrators," *Washington Times*, 21 February 2002: A6.

4 The low-end figure comes from the United States Census Bureau's January 2002 estimate of the illegal alien population in 2000; the high-end figure comes from Northeastern University's Center for Labor Market Studies. See D'Vera Cohn, "Illegal Residents Exceed Estimate," *Washington Post*, 18 March 2001: A1.

5 Available from http://www.ins.usdoj.gov/graphics/aboutins/thisisins/overview.htm; Internet: accessed 5 May 2002.

6 Testimony of Joseph Greene, acting deputy executive associate commissioner for field operations, INS, before the

261

House Committee on Government Reform, 13 November 2001.

7 Dan Eggen, "Deportee Sweep Will Start with Mideast Focus," *Washington Post*, 8 February 2002: A1.

8 Immigration and Naturalization Service. Available from http://www.ins.gov/graphics/services/natz/oath.htm; Internet: accessed 26 June 2002.

Chapter 1: What Would Mohamed Do?

1 Bob Woodward, "In Hijacker's Bags, a Call to Planning, Prayer and Death," *Washington Post*, 28 September 2001: A1.

2 Patrick J. McDonnell, "Memo Angers INS Agents," *Los Angeles Times*, 18 February 2002: 1.

3 Ibid.

4 Ibid.

5 Blake Morrison, "Weapons Slip Past Airport Security," *USA Today*, 25 March 2002: 1A.

6 Blake Morrison, "Airport Security Failures Persist," *USA Today*, 1 July 2002: 1A.

7 "Hawaiian Authorities Search for Missing China Crew," Reuters, 11 April 2002.

8 "Report: Port Alert for Dangerous Stowaways," United Press International, 13 May 2002.

9 Frank Davis and Jay Weaver, "Terrorist Stowaway Alert Called a Mystery," *Miami Herald*, 22 May 2002: A9.

10 Richard Owen and Daniel McGrory, "Business-Class Suspect Caught in Container," *The Times* (of London), 25 October 2001.

11 "Security Breach: Who's Looking for Stowaways at N.J. Ports?" *Bergen Record*, 7 May 2002: 14.

12 Quoted in Mitchel Maddux, "Stowaways Find It Easy to Enter at N.J. Ports," *Bergen Record*, 5 May 2002: A1. The Brookings Institution Project on Homeland Security report is available

at http://www.brook.edu/dybdocroot/fp/projects/homeland/report.htm; Internet; accessed 9 May 2002.

13 James V. Grimaldi, Steve Fainaru, and Gilbert M. Gaul, "Losing Track of Illegal Immigrants," *Washington Post*, 7 October 2001: A1.

14 Mark Johnson, "For Every Agent, Miles of Border," *Milwaukee Journal Sentinel*, 26 March 2002: 1A.

15 Testimony of Eugene R. Davis, United States Senate Governmental Affairs Committee, 13 November 2001.

16 Tamara Audi and David Zeman, "Release of Pakistani Wanted for Questioning Illustrates Border Problems," *Detroit Free Press*, 19 September 2001.

17 Dan Herbeck, "Hit-or-Miss Security Leaves Borders Exposed," *Buffalo News*, 21 April 2002: A1.

18 Ibid.

19 Steve Miller, "Families of 11 Dead Illegals to Sue U.S.," *Washington Times*, 11 May 2002: A1.

20 Foster Klug, "INS Announces Six Rescue Beacons," Associated Press, 24 May 2002.

21 Melissa Manware, "Officials: Suspect Had Two Fake Marriages," *Charlotte Observer*, 28 July 2000: 1A.

22 Lynne Duke and Pierre Thomas, "Since His 'Conversion,' N.Y. Terrorism Suspect Has Led Life of Turmoil," *Washington Post*, 17 October 1993: A22.

23 Lance Williams and Erin McCormick, "Bin Laden's Man in Silicon Valley," *San Francisco Chronicle*, 21 September 2001: A1.

24 "Canton Man Being Deported," *Akron Beacon Journal*, 17 April 2002: 1.

25 Irwin Speizer, "Sting Followed Byzantine Path on 4 Continents," *Raleigh News and Observer*, 25 July 2000: A1.

26 Manware, "Officials: Suspect Had Two Fake Marriages."

27 Dan Chapman, "A Tobacco Road to Terror?" Cox News Service, 2 May 2002.

28 Tim Whitmire, "Brothers Guilty on All Counts in Hezbollah-Smuggling Case," Associated Press, 22 June 2002.

29 United States General Accounting Office, "Immigration Benefit Fraud: Focused Approach Is Needed to Address Problems," GAO-02-66.

30 Seth Hettena, "Prosecutors: Yemeni Student Spoke of Hatred for United States After Sept. 11 Attacks," Associated Press, 9 May 2002.

31 Greg Gordon, "Borders Far from Secure," *Minneapolis Star-Tribune*, 9 December 2001: 1A.

32 See 8 United States Code 1255 (adjustment of status of nonimmigrant to that of person admitted for permanent residence) and 8 United States Code 1227 (deportable aliens).

33 "The Truth Behind 245(i) Amnesty," Federation for American Immigration Reform, Washington, D.C., June 2002.

34 Murray Weiss, "I.N.S.ult: New York Cops' Fury as Feds Free Aliens," *New York Post*, 30 May 2002: 1.

35 Testimony of Mark Hall, President, Local 2499, National Border Patrol Council, and Senior Border Patrol Agent, U.S. Border Patrol, Detroit, Michigan, before the Permanent Investigations Subcommittee of the Senate Governmental Affairs Committee, 13 November 2001.

36 Joseph A. D'Agostino, "U.S. Has Given 50,000 Visas Since 9-11 to New Visitors from the Middle East," *Human Events*, 8 April 2002: 1.

37 Ibid.

38 Gordon, "Borders Far from Secure."

39 Philip Shenon, "Justice Dept. Wants to Query More Foreigners," *New York Times*, 21 March 2002: A19.

40 United States Department of State, Nonimmigrant visa application, available at http://travel.state.gov/DS-0156.pdf; Internet; accessed 6 May 2002.

41 Mary Beth Sheridan and Dan Eggen, "Arab, Muslim Men to Get Tougher U.S. Visa Screening," *Washington Post*, 14 November 2001: A24.

42 Edward T. Pound, "The Easy Path to the United States for Three of the 9/11 Hijackers," *U.S. News and World Report,* 12 December 2001.

43 On 17 June 2002, three days after Joel Mowbray's article "Catching the Visa Express" appeared on www.National Review.com, the American Embassy in Riyadh removed all references to the name "Visa Express" from its Web site. (See http://usembassy.state.gov/riyadh/wwwhvzxp.html; Internet: accessed 1 July 2002.) But Saudi travel agents continue to use the "Visa Express" moniker. (See, for example, the Fursan Travel & Tourism Web site available from http://www.fursan.com.sa/English/default.html; Internet: accessed 1 July 2002.)

44 John Burnett, "FBI Launches Investigation into Illegal Selling of Visas," National Public Radio, 25 April 2002.

45 Amy Westfeldt, "Consulate Employee Held without Bail in Bribery Case," Associated Press, 29 November 2001; Robert Rudolph, "Consulate Worker's Visa Scam Worries Probers of Terror Links," *New Jersey Star-Ledger*, 22 May 2002; available from http://www.nj.com/news/ledger/index.ssf?/base/news-2/10220586256151.xml; Internet: accessed 22 May 2002.

46 Christopher Newton, "FBI Searches for Middle East Nationals Who Might Have Bribed Embassy Employees for Visas," Associated Press, 9 July 2002. See also Pierre Thomas, "Illegal Entry: State Dept. Workers Suspected of Selling Visas to Middle Easterners," ABCNews.com, 9 July 2002. Available from http://abcnews.go.com/sections/wnt/DailyNews/visas020709.html; Internet: accessed 9 July 2002.

47 "Last Laughs: Late Night Political Humor," *Bulletin's Frontrunner*, 18 March 2002.

48 Ross Kerber, "Businesses Say They're Unlikely to Oppose Tougher Visa Rules," *Boston Globe*, 10 April 2002: C3.

49 Tom Brazaitis, "Proposed Visa Changes Worry Foreign Travelers, U.S. Kin," *Cleveland Plain Dealer*, 25 April 2002: A7.

50 United States Department of Labor, Labor Condition Applications; data available through the Labor Condition

Applications Database, available from http://www.zazona.com/ LCA-Data/; Internet: accessed 1 February 2002.

51 Lisa Getter, "Islamic American Nonprofits Face Increased Scrutiny in U.S.," *Los Angeles Times*, 4 November 2001: A1.

52 See United States Immigration and Naturalization Services, H Classification Supplement to Form I-129; available from http://www.ins.usdoj.gov/graphics/formsfee/forms/files/i-129form.pdf (page 4); Internet: accessed 10 May 2002.

53 See Peter Schrag, "Feinstein's Rule," *The American Prospect*, Vol. 12, No. 22, 17 December 2001.

54 United States General Accounting Office, "H-1B Foreign Workers: Better Controls Needed to Help Employers and Protect Workers," GAO/HEHS-00-157, September 2000. See also testimony of Richard M. Stana before the House Judiciary Committee, 17 October 2001.

55 "Three Held on Trade Theft Charges," *Facts on File World News Digest*, 3 May 2001: 413F3.

56 Ashley Dunn, "U.S. Plans Lottery with Jackpot of Legal Residency," *Los Angeles Times*, 6 May 1991: A1.

57 Gordon, "Borders Far from Secure."

58 "Results of the Diversity Immigrant Visa Lottery," United States Department of State, press release, 18 June 2002. Available from http://travel.state.gov/DV-2003results.html; Internet: accessed 1 July 2002.

59 Aldrin Brown, Jeff Collins, and Monica Valencia, "Airport Shooter Described as Dedicated Father, Aloof Neighbor," *Orange Country Register*, 7 July 2002: 1. Hadayet successfully applied for 245(i) amnesty in order to stay in the U.S., instead of returning to Egypt, while his permanent residency application was processed.

60 Interview with Kelly Shannon, United States Department of State, Bureau of Consular Affairs, 9 May 2002.

61 Tim McGlone, "9/11 Ties Suspected in Visa Fraud," *Virginian-Pilot*, 9 May 2002: A1.

62 Jerry Seper, "Saudi Accused of Taking English Tests for Illegals," *Washington Times*, 26 June 2002: A1.

63 David Washburn and David Hasemyer, "Terrorists May Have Exploited Student Visas," *San Diego Union-Tribune*, 21 September 2001: A1.

64 Hillary Mann, *Open Admissions: U.S. Policy Toward Students from Terrorism-Supporting Countries in the Middle East*, Policy Focus No. 34, Washington: The Washington Institute for Near East Policy, 1997.

65 Cheryl Thompson, "Visa Panel Will Focus on Science," *Washington Post*, 8 May 2002: A19.

66 "Open Doors Report on the Web," Higher Education Resources Group, Institute of International Education. Available from http://www.opendoorsweb.org/2001%20Files/2Table_edited.htm; Internet: accessed 30 May 2002.

67 Marcus Stern, "Student Visa Safeguards Might Leave Some Holes," Copley News Service, 29 March 2002.

68 United States Department of Justice, Office of the Inspector General, "The Immigration and Naturalization Service's Contacts with Two September 11 Terrorists: A Review of the INS's Admissions of Mohamed Atta and Marwan Alshehhi, Its Processing of Their Change of Status Applications, and Its Efforts to Track Foreign Students in the United States," 20 May 2002: 14.

69 Steve McGonigle and Jeffrey Weiss, "Deportation Sought for 4 Palestinians," *Dallas Morning News*, 18 July 2001: 21A.

70 United States General Accounting Office, "Visa Issuance: Observations on the Issuance of Visas for Religious Workers," GAO/T-NSIAD-00-207: 7; available from http://www.gao.gov/archive/2000/ns00207t.pdf; Internet: accessed 9 May 2002.

71 Ibid.

72 Walter F. Roche, "New Probe Weighed for Investor Visa Program," *Baltimore Sun*, 10 June 2002: 1A.

73 Walter F. Roche and Gary Cohn, "Cashing In: Former Immigration Officials Siphon Millions from a Program to Entice Foreign Investors with the Promise of Green Cards," *Baltimore Sun*, 20 February 2000: 1A; Michelle Malkin, "U.S. Citizenship for Sale?" *Washington Times*, 26 January 2001: A16.

74 Ibid.

75 United States Immigration and Naturalization Service, Report to Congress on the EB-5 Investor Program, March 1999.

76 Available from http://can-law.com/default_usaimg.htm; Internet; accessed 9 May 2002.

77 United States Department of Justice, Office of the Inspector General, "Follow-up Report on Improving the Security of the Transit Without Visa Program," Report No. I-2002-005, December 2001: Introduction.

78 Ibid.

79 Patrick J. McDonnell, Rich Connell, and Greg Krikorian, "Smuggling by Airline Guards Feared," Los Angeles Times, 6 May 2002: 1.

80 Hil Anderson, "Inspector Helped Smuggle Aliens through LA," United Press International, 11 June 2002.

81 United States Department of Justice, Office of the Inspector General, "Follow-Up Report on Improving the Security of the Transit Without Visa Program": Conclusion.

82 Ibid.

83 Jo Craven McGinty, "Rude Awakening: Attacks Open Eyes to Weaknesses in Visa-Waiver Program," Newsday, 9 October 2001: A39.

84 Alfonso Chardy, "Security Gaps Found in Airport Screenings," Miami Herald, 30 January 2002: 1A.

85 Glenn A. Fine, Inspector General, U.S. Department of Justice, Testimony before the Immigration and Claims Subcommittee of the House Judiciary Committee Concerning the Implications of Transnational Terrorism for the Visa Waiver Program, 28 February 2002.

86 Available from http://travel.state.gov/vwp.html; Internet: accessed 4 May 2002.

Chapter 2: Pandering While Osama Plots

1 Ruben Navarrette Jr., "Immigration/Terrorism Link Not Clear." Available from http://www.postwritersgroup.com/archives/nava1129.htm; Internet: accessed 8 May 2002.

2 Camarota, *The Golden Door.*

3 "Experts Say Marietta Can Legally Open Labor Shelter," *Marietta Daily Journal,* 12 September 2001. Available from http://www.mdjonline.com/StoryDetail.cfm?id=10033606; Internet: accessed 12 September 2001.

4 See 8 United States Code 12, Subchapter II, Part VIII, Sec. 1325-1327. Available from http://www4.law.cornell.edu/uscode/8/ch12.html; Internet: accessed 1 June 2002.

5 Karina Ioffee and Tim Steller, "Mass Deportation Effort Unlikely, INS Chief Says," *Arizona Daily Star,* 24 May 2002: B4.

6 *U.S. v. Luis A. Martinez-Flores,* Affidavit of Jesus H. Gomez. Available from http://news.findlaw.com/cnn/docs/terrorism/usmartinezflores92801.pdf; Internet: accessed 9 March 2002.

7 Ibid.

8 Ibid.

9 Ibid.

10 Virginia Department of Motor Vehicles. Available from http://www.dmv.state.va.us/webdoc/citizen/drivers/resproof.asp; Internet: accessed 9 March 2002.

11 Statement of Senator Richard Durbin, Senate Subcommittee on Oversight of Government Management, "A License to Break the Law, Protecting the Integrity of Drivers' Licenses and State IDs," 16 April 2002.

12 Tennessee Code, Public Chapter 158. Available from http://www.state.tn.us/sos/acts/102pub/pc0158.pdf; Internet: accessed 12 March 2002.

13 Bryan Mitchell, "Easing of Driver's License Hurdles Praised," *Knoxville News-Sentinel,* 9 May 2001: A4.

14 Tim Funk, "Drivers May See New Rule: Legislature Looks at Licenses Issued to Illegal Immigrants," *Charlotte Observer,* 2 September 2001: 1A.

15 David Firestone, "In U.S. Illegally, Immigrants Get License to Drive," *New York Times*, 4 August 2001: A1.

16 Allen G. Breed and Bill Poovery, "Was a Mysterious Death in Tennessee Linked to Terrorism?" Associated Press, 15 February 2002. See also, Michael Moss, "A Nation Challenged: A Suspicious Death: Memphis Fraud Case Is Long on Clues but Short on Answers," *New York Times*, 18 February 2002: A9.

17 Ibid.

18 Ibid.

19 Woody Baird, "ID Worker Burned to Death," Associated Press, 5 March 2002.

20 Mark Bixler, "Immigrants' Rights at Risk?" *Atlanta Journal-Constitution*, 27 February 2002: 1E.

21 Mark Hollis and Jody A. Benjamin, "State Imposes License Checks," *Sun-Sentinel*, 15 December 2001: 10B.

22 Christopher Kirkpatrick, "Lawmakers: DM5 License Criteria Too Lax," *Herald Sun*, 8 October 2001: B1.

23 Deborah Kong, "Utah Among 3 States That Let Illegal Aliens Drive Legally," Associated Press, 29 January 2002.

24 Thomas Frank, "Terror Fears Hit Road: License Curbs on Noncitizens," *Newsday*, 4 March 2002: A6.

25 Available from http://legis.state.nm.us/Sessions/02%20Regular/firs//HB0135.html; Internet: accessed 6 June 2002.

26 Greg Jonsson, "Illegal Immigrants Seek License to Drive," *St. Louis Post-Dispatch*, 28 April 2002: C1.

27 Deborah Sharp, "Immigrants Encounter Red Lights at State DMVs," *USA Today*, 10 May 2002: 7A.

28 Ibid.

29 "State Sued Over Immigrant Driver's Licenses Law," Associated Press, 3 May 2002. California's Democratic

governor, Gray Davis, had been set to sign the bill just days before the September 11 attacks.

30 James W. Brosnan, "Govs Cool to Standardized Driver License," *Commercial Appeal*, 25 February 2002: A1.

31 D. F. Weyermann, "Tennessee Finds a Cost to Easing Driver's License Rules," *Boston Globe*, 11 February 2002.

32 Conrad deFiebre, "Immigrants Oppose Security Proposal," *Minneapolis Star-Tribune*, 16 February 2002: 5B.

33 Sharp, "Immigrants Encounter Red Lights at State DMVs."

34 James Risen, "Sept. 11 Hijackers Said to Fake Data on Bank Accounts," *New York Times*, 9 July 2002: A1.

35 Lee Romney and Karen Robinson-Jacobs, "Wells Fargo to Accept ID Cards Issued by Mexico," *Los Angeles Times*, 8 November 2001: Business 1.

36 Ibid.

37 Mike Comerford, "Banks Loosen ID Guidelines," *Chicago Daily Herald*, 18 November 2001: Business 1.

38 K. Oanh Ha, "Banks Make Pitch to Illegal Immigrants," *San Jose Mercury News*, 27 February 2002: 1.

39 Seema Mehta, "L.A. to Honor ID Cards from Mexico," *Los Angeles Times*, 15 May 2002: 4.

40 Jennifer Mena, "Mexican ID Card Gains Status, and Long Lines of Applicants," *Los Angeles Times*, 20 January 2002: Part II, 6.

41 Maria-Belen Moran, "Mexican Consular IDs Are Officially Recognized by San Francisco Agencies," Associated Press, 6 December 2001.

42 Kathy Gambrell, "Bank Loophole Despite Terror War," United Press International, 8 February 2002.

43 Mary Beth Sheridan, "Visa Tracking Limited by Lack of Personnel," *Washington Post*, 25 February 2002: A03.

44 Anabelle Garay, "New Law Makes College More Affordable for Illegal Immigrants," Associated Press, 26 June 2001.

45 Mae M. Cheng, "Tuition Bill Passed," *Newsday*, 26 June 2002: A23.

46 Mexican American Legal Defense and Educational Fund press release, "MALDEF Applauds Passage of Legislation to Remove Obstacle to Higher Education for Immigrant Students," 11 October 2001. Available from http://www.maldef.org/ news/press.cfm?ID=86; Internet: accessed 8 May 2002.

47 In late June 2002, the Senate Judiciary Committee approved the "DREAM Act," sponsored by Utah Republican senator Orrin Hatch, which would permit all fifty states to subsidize in-state tuition for illegal aliens. It would also rescind deportation orders for some illegal alien students and allow them to jump the line for permanent legal residency.

48 See Division C of PL 104-208; 110 Stat 3009-672; 8 U.S.C. 1623.

49 Mann, *Open Admissions*.

50 Ibid.

51 Paul Mulshine, "Student Visas? Why Bother?" *Newark Star-Ledger*, 26 March 2002.

52 Dan Seligman, "Illegals with Legal Rights," *Forbes*, 7 January 2002: 128.

53 Heather Mac Donald, "Keeping New York Safe from Terrorists," *City Journal,* Autumn 2001: 11(4).

54 See Section 642 of the 1996 immigration reform bill and Section 424 of the 1996 welfare reform bill (Public Law No. 104-193).

55 See Section 133 of the 1996 immigration reform bill passed into law (Public Law No. 104-208).

56 Shawn Zeller, "Inside Job," *Government Executive*, 1 December 2001.

57 Susan Sachs, "Long Resistant, Police Start Embracing Immigration Duties," *New York Times*, 15 March 2002: A11.

58 Marcus Stern and Mark Arner, "Justice Department Eyes Local Cops to Enforce Immigration Laws," Copley News Service, 2 April 2002.

59 Dennis Daily, "Urban News," United Press International, 4 June 2002.

60 Michelle Mittelstadt and Alfredo Corchado, "U.S. May Let State, Local Authorities Enforce Federal Immigration Laws," *Dallas Morning News*, 4 April 2002.

61 Alex Brown, "City Offers Sanctuary but It Won't Stop Feds," *San Francisco Examiner*, 4 January 2002.

62 "Underground Bus Line: Local Government Turns a Blind Eye to Illegal Immigration," *Los Angeles Daily News*, 12 December 2001: N16.

63 Hal Netkin, letter to Tom Ridge, Office of Homeland Security, 8 December 2001. Available from http://www.mayorno.com/ TomRidgeLetter1d09.html; Internet: accessed 1 February 2002.

64 U.S. Newswire, "Gephardt Delivers Democratic Hispanic Radio Response," 2 February 2002.

65 "Kennedy Calls for Enactment of Immigration Reforms," CongressDaily, *National Journal*, 1 February 2002.

66 See 8 United States Code 1255(i). Available from http://www4.law.cornell.edu/uscode/8/1255.html; Internet: accessed 25 May 2002.

67 See 8 United States Code 1255(c)(6) and 8 United States Code 1227(a)(4)(B). Available from http://www4.law.cornell.edu/ uscode/8/1255.html and http://www4.law.cornell.edu/uscode/8/ 1227.html; Internet: accessed 25 May 2002.

68 Mike Robinson, "Government Says Muslim Charity Had Contact with Bin Laden Secretary," Associated Press, 27 March 2002.

69 Interview with the author, 5 June 2002.

70 Lawrence Porter, "Muslim Cleric the Target of Bush 'Anti-Terror' Dragnet," World Socialist Web site, 26 March 2002. Available from http://www.wsws.org/articles/2002/mar2002/ haddm26.shtml; Internet: accessed 5 June 2002.

71 "President Bush's Remarks to Hispanic Chamber of Commerce," Federal News Service, 6 March 2002.

72 Immigration and Naturalization Service, U.S. Department of Justice, "Questions and Answers: Section 245(i) Provision of the LIFE Act." Available from http://www.ins.usdoj.gov/graphics/publicaffairs/questsans/life245iq&a.htm; Internet: accessed 13 March 2002.

73 Available from http://www.ilw.com/lawyers/colum_article/articles/2002,0408-Klasko.shtm; Internet: accessed 13 June 2002.

74 Ibid.

75 "The Truth Behind 245(i)," FAIR.

76 See the Immigration and Nationality Act, Section 212(a)(9)(b).

77 National Immigration Forum, "Immigrants Who Would Be Helped by Restoration of Section 245(i)," September 2000. Available from http://www.immigrationforum.org/currentissues/articles/090100_245i.htm; Internet: accessed 13 March 2002.

78 Immigration and Naturalization Service, U.S. Department of Justice, Employer Information Bulletin 25; LIFE Act/245(i) Adjustment (Rev. 03/02/2001), "Adjustment of Status under Section 245(i) in Context of the Legal Immigration Family Equity (LIFE) Act Amendments' (enacted 12/21/00)." Available from http://www.ins.usdoj.gov/graphics/services/residency/obl25.htm#anchor157549; Internet: accessed 13 March 2002.

79 Stephen Dinan, "Byrd to Delay Senate Vote on Border Security," *Washington Times,* 19 March 2002: A1.

80 "Remarks by President George W. Bush at Signing of Enhanced Border Security and Visa Entry Reform Act," Federal News Service, 14 May 2002.

81 "Uniting Families Act of 2002," S. 2493, introduced 9 May 2002.

82 Dena Bunis, "Mass Mailing Will Push Legalization of Immigrants," *Orange County Register,* 15 May 2002.

83 Robert Warren, Office of Policy and Planning, Immigration and Naturalization Service, U.S. Department of Justice, *Annual Estimates of the Unauthorized Immigration*

Population Residing in the United States and Components of Change: 1987 to 1999, September 2000. Available from http://wwwa.house.gov/lamarsmith/INSreport.pdf; Internet: accessed 13 March 2002.

84 Richard Behar, "The Secret Life of Mahmud the Red," *Time,* 4 October 1993: 54.

85 Alfredo Corchadom, "Harvesting a Dream," *Dallas Morning News,* 29 October 1996: 1A.

86 "INS to Upgrade Border Detection with Hovercraft, Debilitating Pepper Substance," Associated Press, 22 May 2002.

87 Mitchel Maddux, "Two Accused of People Smuggling," *Bergen Record,* 22 May 2002.

88 Sam Dillon, "Iraqi Accused of Smuggling Hundreds in Mideast to U.S.," *New York Times,* 25 October 2001: A18.

89 Douglas Waller, "The Global Search for Osama bin Laden," *Time,* 13 November 2001. Available at http://www.time.com/time/columnist/waller/article/0,9565,184253,00.html; Internet: accessed 25 March 2002.

90 Available at http://www.terrorismfiles.org/organisations/revolutionary_armed_forces_colombia.html and http://www.terrorismfiles.org/organisations/national_liberation_army.html; Internet: accessed 25 March 2002.

91 Julie Watson, "Despite Security Worries, Remote Crossing Still an Open Door along U.S.-Mexico Border," *San Francisco Chronicle,* 20 March 2002. Available from http://www.sfgate.com/cgi-bin/article.cgi?f=/news/archive/2002/03/20/international1149EST0615.DTL; Internet: accessed 25 March 2002.

Chapter 3: The Profiteers

1 Pound, "The Easy Path to the United States for Three of the 9/11 Hijackers."

2 See Public Law 101-515.

3 Ibid.

4 Patrick Pizarro, e-mail to colleagues, 14 September 2001.

5 "Immigration and Naturalization Service Underfunded and Overtasked by Congress and Special Interest Groups," *Morning Edition*, National Public Radio (NPR), 20 March 2000.

6 Ibid.

7 See Public Law No: 107-173, the Enhanced Border Security and Visa Reform Act of 2002, Title 4, Section 403(b).

8 Remarks by Senate Democratic Leader Tom Daschle to the Travel Industry Association of America's 18th Annual Travel and Tourism Unity Dinner, 1 March 2000.

9 Glenn A. Fine, Inspector General, U.S. Department of Justice, Testimony before the Immigration and Claims Subcommittee of the House Judiciary Committee Concerning the Implications of Transnational Terrorism for the Visa Waiver Program, 28 February 2002.

10 Ibid.

11 Glenn A. Fine, Inspector General, U.S. Department of Justice, Testimony before the Senate Judiciary Committee Subcommittee on Technology, Terrorism, and Government Information, 12 October 2001.

12 Dave Williams, "The Bombing of the World Trade Center in New York City," *International Criminal Police Review*, No. 469-471, 1998. Available from http://www.interpol.int/ Public/Publications/ICPR/ICPR469_3.asp; Internet: accessed 4 May 2002.

13 William Norman, Testimony before the Immigration and Claims Subcommittee, House Judiciary Committee, 28 February 2002.

14 Bob Norman, "Admitting Terror: The Immigration Service's Own Describe How America Failed to Protect Its Borders from the September 11 Terrorists," *Miami New Times*, 18 October 2001.

15 Ibid.

16 George Borjas, "Rethinking Foreign Students: A Question of the National Interest," *National Review*, 17 June 2002: Vol. LIV, No. 11.

17 "Open Doors 2000," Institute of International Education, cited in "Facts in Brief," American Council on Education, 20 November 2000, Vol. 49, No. 21. Available from http://www.acenet.edu/hena/facts_in_brief/2000/11_20_00_fib.cfm; Internet: accessed 30 May 2002.

18 "INS Imposes Tougher Rules for Foreign Students," Associated Press, 9 April 2002. Available from http://www.arizonarepublic.com/news/articles/0409visa09.html; Internet: accessed 4 May 2002.

19 Mark Clayton, "Open Doors?" *Christian Science Monitor*, 18 December 2001: 11.

20 Marc J. Ambinder, "New Laws Complicate Foreign Students' Lives," University Wire, 24 November 1997.

21 "U.S. Commission on Terrorism Urges Close Scrutiny of All Foreign Students," *Chronicle of Higher Education*, 15 December 2000: A53.

22 Ibid.

23 Available from http://www.acacamps.org/publicpolicy/cipris4_01.htm; Internet: accessed 4 May 2002.

24 "U.S. Commission on Terrorism Urges Close Scrutiny of All Foreign Students."

25 Nicholas Confessore, "Borderline Insanity," *Washington Monthly*, May 2002. Available from http://www.washingtonmonthly.com/features/2001/0205.confessore.html; Internet: accessed 4 May 2002.

26 James V. Grimaldi, "Planned INS Probes of Students Blocked: Schools Opposed In-Depth Checks," *Washington Post*, 16 March 2002: A12.

27 Marlene M. Johnson, "International Students and Terrorism," *San Diego Union-Tribune*, 19 March 2002: B9.

28 Office of Senator Dianne Feinstein, "Senator Feinstein Urges Major Changes in U.S. Student Visa System," 27 September 2001. Available from http://feinstein.senate.gov/releases01/stvisas1.htm; Internet: accessed 17 May 2002.

29 Cindy Rodriguez, "Proposed Visa Ban Dropped," *Boston Globe*, 23 November 2001: A48.

30 Clayton, "Open Doors?"

31 Megan Carroll, "Restrictions on International Students Face Opposition," University Wire, 8 February 2002.

32 Andrew Tilghman, "Foreign Student Tracking Stalled," *Albany Times Union*, 23 February 2002: B1.

33 Joel Budd, "Higher Education: Border Patrol: As America Imposes Restrictions and Surveillance on Foreign Students, Academics Are Worried about the Impact on Their Roles— and on Enrollments," *The Guardian* (U.K.), 14 May 2002: 12.

34 Wayne Washington, "Tracking of Foreign Students Set," *Boston Globe*, 11 May 2002: A1.

35 Available from http://www.uschamber.com/NR/exeres/ 12853A11E00C-4DF3-9709-37C0662DB7EF.htm?NRMODE= Unpublished&NRNODELOCKED=False; Internet: accessed 4 May 2002.

36 Jack Lucenti, "Repeal INS Law, Group Requests," *Journal of Commerce,* 8 October 1999: 13.

37 Statement of Representative Lamar Smith, Week of 5 June 2000. Available from http://wwwa.house.gov/lamarsmith/ c-060500.html; Internet: accessed 4 May 2002.

38 AILA press release, 19 May 2000. Available from http:// www.aila.org/newsroom/00051803_press39se0005.html; Internet: accessed 4 May 2002.

39 "The Report of the Special Senate Committee on Security and Intelligence," Parliament of Canada, January 1999. Available from http://www.parl.gc.ca/36/1/parlbus/commbus/ senate/com-e/secu-e/rep-e/repsecintjan99-e.htm; Internet: accessed 30 May 2002.

40 Tom Godfrey, "T.O. Money Trail Leads to Osama," *Toronto Sun,* 4 October 2001: 2.

41 Bob Mac Donald, "U.S. Security Plan Aimed at Canada," *Toronto Sun*, 27 January 2002: 28.

42 Ross Marowits, "Suicide Hijacker Didn't Live in Toronto, Mounties Say," *Hamilton Spectator*, 21 December 2001: B5; "No Links to Attack in Canada," *Gazette,* 21 December 2001: A12.

43 Gary Dimmock, "Money Transfer from Nephew Didn't Finance Attacks: Uncle," *Ottawa Citizen*, 24 October 2001: A3; Testimony of Susan M. Collins, "Immigration and Naturalization Service Processes," Senate Governmental Affairs Committee, Permanent Subcommittee on Investigations, 13 November 2001.

44 Philip Shenon and Don van Natta Jr., "U.S. Says 3 Detainees May Be Tied to Hijackings," *New York Times*, 1 November 2001: A1.

45 Available from http://www.canadianembassy.org/issues/section110/concerns.asp and http://www.canadianembassy.org/issues/border.asp; Internet: accessed 4 May 2002.

46 Greg Barrett, "When U.S., Mexico Breed a Community, Disparity Abounds," Gannett News Service, 21 February 2002; Greg Barrett, "Is Fox Trying to Get in America's Henhouse?" Gannett News Service, 21 February 2002; Vicente Fox's interview with Ray Suarez, *NewsHour with Jim Lehrer*, PBS, March 21, 2000, available from http://www.pbs.org/newshour/bb/latin_america/jan-june00/fox_3-21.html; Internet: accessed 21 May 2002; Greg Flakus, "Fox Touts Open Borders with Southern Neighbors," Hispanic Vista.com, 12 September 2000, available from http://www.hispanicvista.com/html/000912mx.html; Internet: accessed 21 May 2002.

47 Sergio Munoz, "Los Angeles Times Interview: Juan Hernandez: Mexican American Cabinet Member Looks After Mexicans Living Abroad," *Los Angeles Times*, 11 February 2001: M3.

48 Eric Schmitt, "Bush Aides Weigh Legalizing Status of Mexicans in U.S.," *Contra Costa Times*, 15 July 2001: A13.

49 Ibid.

50 Americans for Better Borders, online mission statement. Available from http://www.uschamber.org/_Political+Advocacy/Issues+Index/Immigration/American+Borders/the+solution.htm; Internet: accessed 4 May 2002.

51 Ibid.

52 Available from http://www.aila.org/; Internet: accessed 4 May 2002.

53 Available from http://www.ailapubs.com/nohumbeinisi.html; Internet: accessed 4 May 2002.

54 Available from http://www.sackskolken.com/Advocacy/ 9-11-01_advocacy.html; Internet: accessed 4 May 2002.

55 Sergio Bustos, "New INS Computer Would Track Visas, but Couldn't Enforce Law," Gannett News Service, 11 April 2002.

56 N'Gai Croal, "Visitors, Stay Home?" *Newsweek*, MSNBC Web exclusive, 6 October 2001. Available from http://www.msnbc.com/news/639088.asp; Internet: accessed 21 May 2002.

57 "Justice Department's Initiative to Crack Down on Men from the Middle East and Pakistan Who Have Received and Ignored Deportation Notices," *All Things Considered*, National Public Radio (NPR), 8 February 2002.

58 Available from http://www.adc.org/mission.html; Internet: accessed 4 May 2002.

59 Available from http://www.cair-net.org/asp/aboutcair.asp; Internet: accessed 4 May 2002.

60 Rachel Zoll, "In the Wake of September 11, Muslim Leaders Criticized for Statements on Terrorism," Associated Press, 24 October 2001.

61 CAIR, *The Price of Ignorance: The Status of Muslim Civil Rights in the United States, 1996 Report*, Washington, D.C.: American-Muslim Research Center, 1996: 9.

62 Jeff Jacoby, "Speaking Out Against Terror," Jewishworldreview.com, 25 September 2001. Available from http://www.jewishworldreview.com/jeff/jacoby092501.asp; Internet: accessed 4 May 2002.

63 Naftali Bendavid, "Ashcroft: U.S. to Interview 3,000 More Arab Nationals," *Chicago Tribune*, 21 March 2002: 13.

64 Lenny Savino, "Publicizing Terror Suspect List Troubles Civil Libertarians," *Pittsburgh Post-Gazette*, 13 April 2002: A7.

65 Eunice Moscoso, "FBI Chief: U.S. Muslims Aid War on Terrorism: Help with Translations Important," *Atlanta Journal-Constitution*, 29 June 2002: 8A.

66 Ibid.

67 James G. Gimpel and James R. Edwards Jr., *The Congressional Politics of Immigration Reform* (Needham Heights, Mass.: Allyn & Bacon, 1999) 48.

68 Michelle Malkin, "Asian-Americans Are Milking 9-11 Fund," *Virginian-Pilot*, 18 December 2001.

69 Citizens' Commission on Civil Rights Briefing, "Rights at Risk: Equality in an Age of Terrorism," Federal News Service, 12 February 2002.

70 Available from http://www.splcenter.org/intelligenceproject/ip4q2.html; Internet: accessed 21 May 2002.

71 Ted Bridis, "New Immigration Rules Announced," Associated Press, 5 June 2002.

Chapter 4: Serial Incompetence: The Angel Resendiz Case

1 Unless otherwise noted, all information in this chapter is from the Office of the Inspector General, United States Department of Justice, *The Rafael Resendez-Ramirez Case: A Review of the INS's Actions and the Operation of Its IDENT Automated Fingerprint Identification System*, 20 March 2000. Available from http://www.usdoj.gov/oig/resenrpt/resentoc.htm; Internet: accessed 12 March 2002.

2 Ibid.

3 Office of Inspector General, United States Department of Justice, *Status of IDENT/IAFIS Integration*, Report No. I-2002-003, 7 December 2001. Available from http://www.usdoj.gov/oig/inspection/I-2002-003/finger.htm#early; Internet: accessed 12 March 2002.

4 Lisa Teachey, "Maturino Resendiz Guilty of Murder," *Houston Chronicle*, 19 May 2000: A1.

5 Andale Gross, "Suspect Named in 1997 Slaying of Stark Man," *Akron Beacon Journal*, 8 June 1999: B1.

6 "I Survived with a Little Help from My Friends," *The Key*, Magazine of the National Kappa Kappa Gamma organization, Summer 1999: 11–12.

7 Gross, "Suspect Named in 1997 Slaying of Stark Man."

8 "I Survived with a Little Help from My Friends."

9 University of Kentucky public relations department, "Christopher Maier Theater Scholarship Established," 20 July 1999. Available from http://www.uky.edu/PR/News/Archives/July99/maier.htm; Internet: accessed 12 March 2002.

10 "Pass It On," *Dallas Morning News*, 3 December 1993: 6G.

11 Evan Moore, "Trains Brought Woman Woes, and Perhaps Death," *Houston Chronicle*, 4 July 1999: A1.

12 Ibid.

13 Author telephone interview with Joyce Black, business manager of the Theron Grainger Nursing Home, 5 March 2002.

14 James Pinkerton, "Town in Shock," *Houston Chronicle*, 9 May 1999: 1.

15 Michael Hall, "Evil," *Texas Monthly*, August 1999: 104.

16 Todd Vanezia, untitled article at APBNews.com. Available from: http://www.apbonline.com/msnbc/stories/msnbc0701.txt; Internet: accessed 12 March 2002.

17 Mark Babineck, "Death Penalty Sought for Rail Killer," Associated Press, 19 May 2000.

18 Lisa Sandberg, "Weimar Still Coping with Slayings: Trial of Drifter Is Set to Begin," *San Antonio Express-News*, 7 May 2000: 1B.

19 David Medina, "Memorial Service Honors Slain Rice Alumna," *Rice News*, 24 July 1999.

20 Valerie Kalfrin, "Two More Women Found Bludgeoned in Their Beds," APBNews.com, 7 June 1999. Available from http://www.apbonline.com/911/1999/06/07/kill0607_01.html; Internet: accessed 12 March 2002.

21 Mark Babineck, "Railroad Killer Jury Learns Details of Killing Spree," Associated Press, 20 May 2000.

22 Michael Pearson, "Serial Killing Suspect Charged in 2 Ill. Deaths," Associated Press, 22 June 1999.

23 Bill Torpy, "Did Barrow County Err in Murder Charge?" *Atlanta Journal-Constitution*, 10 September 2000: 1A.

24 Charles Mount and Ray Quintalilla, "1 of Missing Woodstock Pair Found Slain," *Chicago Tribune*, 2 April 1997.

25 Caroline Fox, "Ex-St. Anne Girl Missing, Friend Dead," *Daily Journal*, 11 April 1997. Available from http://www.dailyjournal.com/web_data/editorial/0411head.html#story2; Internet: accessed 12 March 2002.

26 "Serial Killer Leads Police to Bodies," Associated Press, 17 July 2000.

27 Ibid.

28 The INS defines "aggravated felonies" to include everything from running a prostitution ring, to theft and burglary offenses, to sexual abuse of a minor, money-laundering, drug trafficking, rape, and murder. See Immigration and Nationality Act, in section 101(a)(43), 8 United States Code 1101(a)(43).

29 Office of the Inspector General, United States Department of Justice, *The Rafael Resendez-Ramirez Case: A Review of the INS's Actions and the Operation of Its IDENT Automated Fingerprint Identification System,* 20 March 2000. Available from http://www.usdoj.gov/oig/i9909/i9909p2.htm#History; Internet: accessed 12 March 2002.

30 Office of the Inspector General, United States Department of Justice, *Review of the Immigration and Naturalization Service's Automated Biometric Identification System (IDENT),* Report No. I-98-10, March 1998.

31 Office of the Inspector General, United States Department of Justice, *The Rafael Resendez-Ramirez Case: A Review of the INS's Actions and the Operation of Its IDENT Automated Fingerprint Identification System.* Available from http://www.usdoj.gov/oig/resenrpt/resenp5.htm#P991_131252; Chapter 5; Internet: accessed 12 March 2002.

32 Marcus Stern, "INS Computer System in Spotlight Following Release of Wanted Man," Copley News Service, 3 July 1999.

33 Office of the Inspector General, United States Department of Justice, *The Rafael Resendez-Ramirez Case: A Review of the INS's Actions and the Operation of Its IDENT Automated Fingerprint Identification System.* Available from http://www.usdoj.gov/oig/resenrpt/resenp4.htm#P852_92182; Chapter 4(E); Internet: accessed 12 March 2002.

34 Office of the Inspector General, United States Department of Justice. *The Rafael Resendez-Ramirez Case: A Review of the INS's Actions and the Operation of Its IDENT Automated Fingerprint Identification System.* Available from http://www.usdoj.gov/oig/resenrpt/resenp4.htm#P852_92182; Chapter 4(C); Internet: accessed 12 March 2002.

35 Ibid. Available from http://www.usdoj.gov/oig/resenrpt/resenp4.htm; Internet: accessed 11 July 2002. See Chapter 4(B): The Police Attempt to Place Lookouts for Resendez.

36 Ibid. Available from http://www.usdoj.gov/oig/resenrpt/resenp4.htm; Internet: accessed 11 July 2002. See Chapter 4(E): The Weekly Intelligence Report with Information on Resendez.

37 Ibid. Available from http://www.usdoj.gov/oig/resenrpt/resenp4.htm; Internet: accessed 11 July 2002. See Chapter 4(D): A Texas Ranger Contacts Another Houston INS Investigator About Resendez.

38 "Former INS Officer Sentenced for Theft," *San Antonio Express-News,* 4 January 2000: 2B.

39 Available from http://www.usdoj.gov/oig/resenrpt/resenp6.htm; Internet: accessed 11 July 2002. See Chapter 8(E)(2): Senior Special Agent Thomas Cason.

40 Office of the Inspector General, United States Department of Justice, *The Rafael Resendez-Ramirez Case: A Review of the INS's Actions and the Operation of Its IDENT Automated Fingerprint Identification System.* Available from http://www.usdoj.gov/oig/resenrpt/resenp6.htm#P1192_166539; Chapter 8(B)(2); Internet: accessed 12 March 2002.

41 Ibid. Available from http://www.usdoj.gov/oig/resenrpt/
resenp5.htm; Internet: accessed 11 July 2002. See Chapter
5(C)(1): Initiative by Border Patrol Agent Estevis.

42 Marcia Stepanek, "Making a Killing Online," *Business Week,*
20 November 2000: EB84.

43 Office of Inspector General, United States Department of
Justice, *Status of IDENT/IAFIS Integration.*

44 Federal Bureau of Investigation, United States Department of
Justice, *National Instant Criminal Background Check System
(NICS) 2000 Operations Report.* Available from http://
www.fbi.gov/hq/cjisd/nics/oper-rpt/oper-rpt2000.pdf; Internet:
accessed 12 March 2002.

Chapter 5: In Cold Blood:
Foreign Cop-Killers on the Loose

1 Bettina Boxall, "Final Goodbye for a 'Cop's Cop,' " *Los
Angeles Times*, 16 October 1990: B2.

2 George Ramos, "Powerless to Deport Criminal, INS Says," *Los
Angeles Times*, 13 October 1990: B3.

3 Leslie Berger and Stephen Braun, "Rookie Becomes First L.A.
Policewoman Slain on Job," *Los Angeles Times*, 12 February
1991: A1.

4 Daryl Gates, "Death of LAPD Officer Kerbrat," *Los Angeles
Times*, 25 February, 1991: B4.

5 Jeff Wilson, " 'Where's Mommy?' Child of Slain Policewoman
Asks at Her Funeral," Associated Press, 15 February 1991.

6 See 8 United States Code, Section 1226(c). Available from
http://www4.law.cornell.edu/uscode/8/1226.html; Internet:
accessed April 20, 2002.

7 Diehl Rettig, interview with the author, 20 March 2002.

8 Ibid.

9 Available from http://www.gao.gov/archive/1997/gg97154t.pdf;
Internet: accessed 20 April 2002.

10 In February 2002, Vasquez was ordered to pay restitution to the Washington State agency overseeing death benefits to the Saunders family. In June 2002, Vasquez won a $7,000 settlement after filing a civil suit claiming his constitutional rights were violated by a sheriff's deputy during his arrest. Meanwhile, the Saunders family has filed suit against the INS for negligence.

11 Written testimony of Paul H. Thomson, Commonwealth's Attorney for the City of Winchester, Virginia, submitted to Congress, 17 December 2001.

12 Stephanie K. Moran, "Timbrook's Family Talks of Their Loss," *Winchester Star*, 27 January 2001.

13 Bhavna Mistry and Naush Boghossian, "Burying Their Own: Thousands Honor Lawman Shot on Duty," *Los Angeles Daily News*, 5 May 2002: N1.

14 Elton Gallegly, "Enforcing Border Laws Will Save Lives," *Los Angeles Daily News*, 29 May 2002: N13.

Chapter 6: The Torturers Next Door

1 Quoted in *The Founders' Almanac: A Practical Guide to the Notable Events, Greatest Leaders & Most Eloquent Words of the American Founding*, edited by Matthew Spalding (Washington, D.C.: The Heritage Foundation, 2001), 169.

2 See, most recently, Amnesty International, "United States of America: A Safe Haven for Torturers," April 2002. Available from http://www.aiusa.org/stoptorture/safehaven.pdf; Internet: accessed 15 May 2002.

3 Alfonso Chardy and Elisabeth Donovan, "Torture Suspects Find Haven in United States," *Miami Herald*, 1 August 2001.

4 David Adams, "Reaching for More Foreign Criminals," *St. Petersburg Times*, 9 April 2001: 1A.

5 John-Thor Dahlberg, "Alleged Torturer Now a United States Citizen," *Los Angeles Times*, 11 November 2001: A37.

6 Available from http://www.cubacenter.org/media/news_articles/darkness.html; Internet: accessed 18 May 2002. Original source is *The Persistence of Darkness* by Amaro Gomez Boix,

translated by Lilian Sotolongo Dorka; published in *El Nuevo Herald* (*Miami Herald*) on 10 February 1989.

7 David Warm, "Nowhere to Hide," *City Link*, 16 May 2001. Available from http://www.xso.com/cover/coverstory051601.html; Internet: accessed 15 May 2002.

8 United States Attorney's Office Southern District of Florida. Available from http://www.usdoj.gov/usao/fls/Mederos.html; Internet: accessed 15 May 2002.

9 Ellis Berger, "INS Lacks Explanation for Suspect's Citizenship," *Ft. Lauderdale Sun-Sentinel*, 6 September 2001: 4B.

10 "How a Torture Figure Became a Citizen," *Fulton County Daily Report*, 2 March 1998.

11 *Abebe-Jira v. Negewo*, 72 F. 3d 844 (11th Cir. 1996).

12 Elisabeth Kuryo and Bill Rankin, "Women Get $1.5 Million in Torture Case," *Atlanta Journal-Constitution*, 20 August 1993: D12.

13 Telephone interview with the author, 12 March 2001.

14 Ibid.

15 See, for example, "Fundwatch Report on the USAID Human Rights Fund in Haiti," available from http://www.igc.org/wohaiti/reports/fundwtch.html; Internet: accessed 15 May 2002. See also, "Human Rights Watch World Report 1998," available from http://www.hrw.org/worldreport/Americas-07.htm; Internet: accessed 15 May 2002.

16 Peter J. A. Riehm, "The USS Harlan County Affair," *Military Review*, 1997; Vol. LXXVII, No. 4, 31. Available from http://www-cgsc.army.mil/milrev/english/julaug97/riehm.html; Internet: accessed 15 May 2002.

17 Ian Martin, "Haiti: Mangled Multilateralism," *Foreign Policy*, 95 (Summer 1994): 73.

18 David Grann, "Giving 'The Devil' His Due," *Atlantic Monthly*, 2001; 287(6): 55–75.

19 Ibid. See also, Chardy and Donovan, "Torture Suspects Find Haven in United States."

20 Alfonso Chardy, "INS Arrests Ex-Colonel Given Life in Haiti for His Role in Massacre," *Miami Herald*, 22 June 2001: 1B.

See also, Niles Lathem, "CIA Harbors Haitian Killer in Queens," *New York Post,* 14 May 2001: 7.

21 "St. Lucie County Man Claims Half of June 28 Florida Lotto Jackpot," Business Wire, 1 July 1997.

22 Mary Ellen Flannery, "Lottery Winner from Haiti Aches for Political Asylum," *Palm Beach Post*, 3 July 1997: 1B.

23 Colleen Mastony, "INS Arrests Port St. Lucie Man Tied to '94 Slayings in Haiti," *Palm Beach Post*, 23 June 2001:1B

24 Ibid.

25 "Newspaper Deliveryman Accused of Killing in Vietnamese Camp," Associated Press, 10 June 2001.

26 Le Thuy-Doan and Daniel Yi, "INS Investigating Allegation Against Vietnam Refugee," *Los Angeles Times*, 12 June 2001: 7.

27 John Gittelsohn and Anh Do, "Refugee Accused of Beating Fellow Inmates in Vietnam," *Orange County Register*, 11 June 2001.

28 Greg Quill, "CBC Tracks War Criminals, African 'Murderers and Torturers' in Canada," *Toronto Star*, 6 October 1992: E1.

29 David Stout, "Ex-Somali Army Officer Is Arrested in Virginia," *New York Times*, 28 February 1998: A4.

30 Steve Fainaru, "Stolen Refuge: Rights Violators Exploit U.S. Immigration System," *Boston Globe*, 4 May 1999. Ali filed for asylum in 1993, but withdrew his application and obtained a green card in 1996 through alternate means after he married a United States citizen. An immigration judge ruled that since the asylum application was inactive at the time deportation charges were filed, Ali's alleged lies were not officially "documented."

31 Steve Fainaru, "Suspect in 'Cleansing' by Serbs Living in Vt.," *Boston Globe*, 3 May 1999: A1.

32 Harold R. Tyler Jr., *The Churchwomen Murders: A Report to the Secretary of State*, 2 December 1983.

33 Ibid.

34 United States Institute of Peace, "Madness to Hope: The 12-Year War in El Salvador, Report of the Commission on the Truth for El Salvador." Available from http://www.usip.org/library/tc/doc/reports/el_salvador/tc_es_03151993_casesB2ce.html; Internet: accessed 15 May 2002.

35 News briefing of Richard Boucher, State Department spokesman, 27 October 2000.

36 Marianne M. Armshaw, "Salvadoran Generals Go to Trial Again," *National Catholic Reporter*, 4 May 2001: 8.

37 United States District Court, Southern District of Florida, *Juan Romagoza Arce, Neris Gonzalez, Carlos Mauricio, and Jorge Montes, Plaintiffs, v. Jose Guillermo Garcia, an Individual, Carlos Eugenio Vides Casanova, an Individual, and Does 1 Through 50, Inclusive, Defendants*, Case No. 99-8364.

38 Sarah Finke, "Families of 4 US Churchwomen File Lawsuit Against Former Salvadoran Generals," *Central America/Mexico Report*, Volume 19, no. 3. Available from http://www.rtfcam.org/report/volume_19/No_3/article2.htm; Internet: accessed 15 May 2002.

39 Andrew Bounds, "US Catches Up with Abusers of Human Rights," *Financial Times* (London), 24 May 2001: 7.

40 "Selected Issues Relating to CIA Activities in Honduras in the 1980s," United States, Central Intelligence Agency, Office of the Inspector General, 27 August 1997.

41 *The Facts Speak for Themselves: The Preliminary Report on Disappearances of the National Commissioner for the Protection of Human Rights in Honduras,* Center for Justice and International Law (CEJIL) & Human Rights Watch/Americas, July 1994. Summary available from http://hrw.org/reports/world/honduras-pubs.php; Internet: accessed May 15, 2002.

42 Chardy and Donovan, "Torture Suspects Find Haven in United States."

43 Jody A. Benjamin, "INS Arrests Foreign Officers Linked to Atrocities Abroad," *Ft. Lauderdale Sun-Sentinel*, 30 April 2002. Available from http://www.sun-sentinel.com/news/local/

southflorida/sfl-carrest30apr30.story; Internet: accessed 15 May
2002.

44 "Summary of the Anti-Atrocity Alien Deportation Act,"
10 May 2001. Available from http://leahy.senate.gov/press/
200105/010510b.html; Internet: accessed 18 May 2002.

45 Prepared statement of Representative Mark Foley before the
House Committee on the Judiciary, Subcommittee on
Immigration and Claims, 28 September 2000.

46 Rebecca Carr, "Foreigners Who Help Terrorism Probe Could
Become Citizens," Cox News, 20 November 2001.

Chapter 7: House of Horrors: The INS Mess

1 John Ashcroft, interview with *Fox News Sunday,* 24 March
2002.

2 George W. Bush, remarks at a news conference, 13 March 2002.

3 See, for example, House Judiciary Committee Chair F. James
Sensenbrenner in "House Votes to Abolish INS, Create Two
Separate Agencies," *Federal Human Resources Week,* Vol. 9,
No. 4, 7 May 2002, and John McLaughlin, *The McLaughlin
Group,* Federal News Service, 23 November 2001.

4 Testimony of Glenn Fine, United States House Judiciary
Committee, "Immigration and Naturalization Performance
Issues," 17 October 2001.

5 Stephen Engelberg, "In Immigration Labyrinth, Corruption
Comes Easily," *New York Times*, 12 September 1994: A1.

6 David Rosenzweig, "INS Agents Accused of Ransom Scam,"
Los Angeles Times, 19 May 2000: B1.

7 Ibid.

8 David Rosenzweig, "INS Agent Admits Scheme to Ransom
Immigrants," *Los Angeles Times*, 14 September 2000: B5.

9 Charles Rappleye, "Black Eye," *Los Angeles Weekly*, 12 January 2001: 15.

10 Telephone interview with Detective Paul Hernandez, 19 February 2002.

11 Telephone interview with INS spokesman Russ Bergeron, 11 March 2002.

12 William Branigin, "Field Managers Accuse INS Operations Director of Cronyism, Seek His Ouster," *Washington Post,* 6 December 1996: A29.

13 Phillipp Oehmke, "Overwhelmed: Life at 26 Federal Plaza," from *Under the Radar: The World of the Undocumented Immigrant in New York City,* online project of the Columbia School of Journalism, available at http://www.jrn.columbia.edu/studentwork/investigative/office.shtml.

14 Catherine Wilson, "Eight-Month Sentence for INS Jailer Accused of Rape," Associated Press, 24 July 2001.

15 Alfonso Chardy, "INS Guard Given Good Referral," *Miami Herald,* 22 December 2001: 3B.

16 Telephone interview with the author, 12 February 2002.

17 "INS Inspector Is Arrested in Cocaine Case," *San Diego Union-Tribune,* 20 September 2001: B2.

18 Elaine De Valle, "INS Agent Faces Charges," *Miami Herald,* 25 September 2001: 1B. See also, United States Department of Justice, Office of the Inspector General, Semiannual Report to Congress, Investigations Division, Significant Investigations, 1 April 2001–30 September 2001.

19 "Miami Immigration Officer Pleads Guilty to Accepting Bribes," Associated Press, 25 October 2001.

20 David McLemore, "INS Officers Tied to Illegal Crossings," *Dallas Morning News,* 2 September 2001: 43A.

21 United States Department of Justice, Southern District of Texas, press release, 8 November 2001.

22 Jody A. Benjamin, "Agents Arrest Worker for INS," *Ft. Lauderdale Sun-Sentinel:* 1B. See also: U.S. Department of Justice, U.S. Attorney's Office, Southern District of Florida. Available from http://www.usdoj.gov/usao/fls/Barragan3.html; Internet: accessed 20 May 2002.

23 "Ex-INS Examiner Admits Trading Green Cards for Sex," *Chicago Tribune,* 4 January 2002: 3.

24 Ibid.

25 Interview with the author, 14 February 2002.

26 United States General Accounting Office, "Immigration Benefit Fraud: Focused Approach Is Needed to Address Problems," GAO-02-66.

27 United States Department of Justice, Office of the Inspector General, Inspections Division, Immigration and Naturalization Service, Document Fraud Records Corrections, Report Number I-96-09, September 1996.

28 Ibid.

29 Marlowe Hood, "The Taiwan Connection," *Los Angeles Times Magazine,* 9 October 1994: 20.

30 Seth Rosenfeld, "Probe of Green Card Selling Scheme Widens," *San Francisco Examiner*, 2 July 1994: A4.

31 Jerry DeMarco, "Immigration Official Sentenced," *Bergen Record*, 22 April 1997: A4.

32 Robert E. Kessler, "Leading INS Official Charged in Bribery," *Newsday*, 5 August 1996: A35.

33 DeMarco, "Immigration Official Sentenced."

34 "Immigration Official Sentenced Following Conviction for Making False Statements, Reports U.S. Attorney," P.R. Newswire, 5 August 1999.

35 United States Department of Justice, Office of the Inspector General, Semiannual Report to Congress, 1 April 1999–30 September 1999: 12.

36 "HK Cops Rearrest U.S. Immigration Official," United Press International, 25 April 1997. Stuchiner's original conviction was quashed because he was charged under the wrong ordinance, one that focused more on his actual possession of the bogus travel papers than the production of passports. Three appeals court judges had ruled that Stuchiner's original jail sentence was unsustainable.

37 Melinda Liu and Brook Larmer, "Smuggling People," *Newsweek*, 17 March 1997: 34.

38 Available from http://www.angelfire.com/nv/paladinlaw/; Internet: accessed 15 May 2002.

39 U.S. Department of Justice press release, "Attorney General Reno and INS Commissioner Meissner Announce New Naturalization Team," 25 April 1997. Available from http://www.usdoj.gov/opa/pr/1997/April97/174ag.htm; Internet: accessed 17 February 2002.

40 Ibid.

41 United States Department of Justice, Office of the Inspector General, "An Investigation of Misconduct and Mismanagement at ICITAP, OPDAT, and the Criminal Division's Office of Administration," September 2000: 41. Available from http://www.house.gov/judiciary/icitap.htm; Internet: accessed 16 May 2002.

42 Ibid., 59.

43 Ibid., 36.

44 Ibid., footnote 13.

45 Ibid., 401.

46 Ibid., 142.

47 Ibid.

48 Ibid., 401.

49 Ibid., 404.

50 Ibid., 256.

51 Ibid., 250.

52 Ibid., footnote 4.

53 United States Office of the Special Counsel, press release, 16 July 2001. Available from http://www.osc.gov/documents/press/2001/pr01_16.htm; Internet: accessed 16 May 2002.

54 Statement of Neil Jacobs before the National Security, International Affairs, and Criminal Justice Subcommittee of the House Government Reform and Oversight Committee, 24 September 1996.

55 KPMG Peat Marwick, Department of Justice Immigration and Naturalization Service, *Naturalization Quality Procedures Implementation Review*, Final Report, Washington, D.C., 17 April 1997, ii–iii. See also, United States Department of Justice Immigration and Naturalization Service, "INS and KPMG Complete Review of August, 1995–September, 1996

Naturalizations," 9 February 1998. Available from http://www.usdoj.gov/opa/pr/1998/February/052.htm.html; Internet: accessed 24 May 2002.

56 David Schippers, *Sellout: The Inside Story of President Clinton's Impeachment* (Washington, D.C.: Regnery Publishing, Inc., 2000).

57 William Branigin, "Audit Faults INS Practices," *Washington Post*, 19 April 1997: A1.

58 Michelle Mittlestadt, "INS Whistleblower Receives Settlement," Associated Press, 10 March 2000.

59 Testimony of Joyce Woods, United States House of Representatives, Government Reform and Oversight Committee, Hearing on Naturalization Fraud, 24 September 1996.

60 United States Department of Justice, Office of the Inspector General, "An Investigation of the Immigration and Naturalization Service's Citizenship USA Initiative," 31 July 2000. See "INS Employees' Allegations of Retaliation." Available from http://www.usdoj.gov/oig/cusarpt/allegations.htm#_Toc489261290; Internet: accessed 16 May 2002.

61 Testimony of Mark P. Hall, United States Senate Judiciary Committee, 14 April 1999.

62 Testimony of Robert Lindemann, United States Senate Judiciary Committee, 10 February 2000.

63 *Today Show*, NBC, 25 March 2002.

64 Tamara Audi and David Zeman, "Release of Pakistani Wanted for Questioning Illustrates Border Problems," *Detroit Free Press*, 19 September 2001.

65 James V. Grimaldi, "INS Drops Sanctions Over 2 Agents' Statements," *Washington Post*, 6 April 2002: A8.

66 "Patrol Agents Face Suspension Following Remarks to Newspaper," Associated Press, 25 September 2001.

67 Ibid.

68 Jerry Seper, "Whistleblowers Given a Reprieve," *Washington Times*, 6 April 2002: A03.

69 Testimony of Glenn Fine, United States House of Representatives, House Judiciary Subcommittee on Immigration and Claims, 17 October 2001.

Chapter 8: Welcome to Miami

1 Unless otherwise noted, all information in this chapter is from Michael R. Bromwich, "Alleged Deception of Congress: The Congressional Task Force on Immigration Reform's Fact-finding Visit to the Miami District of INS in June 1995," statement before the U.S. House of Representatives Subcommittee on Immigration and Claims Concerning Allegations of Deception and/or Office of Inspector General, U.S. Department of Justice, *Alleged Deception of Congress: The Congressional Task Force on Immigration Reform's Fact-finding Visit to the Miami District of INS in June 1995*, June 1996.

2 Correspondence with INS spokesman Russ Bergeron, 18 June 2002.

3 Marc Lacey, "New Task Force Targets Illegal Immigration," *Los Angeles Times*, 16 March 1995: A3.

4 Bob Norman, "Admitting Terror, Part 3," *Miami New Times*, 1 November 2001. Available from http://www.newtimesbpb.com/issues/2001-11-01/news.html; Internet; accessed 1 March 2002.

5 Elise Ackerman, "Agents of Deception," *Miami New Times,* 12 September 1996. Available from http://www.miaminewtimes.com/issues/1996-09-12/feature2.html/1/index.html; Internet: accessed 1 March 2002.

6 Jordan Bressler, "Congress Task Force Says Immigration Has 'Back Door Off Hinges,' " *Associated Press*, 12 June 1995.

7 Rene Sanchez, "INS Accused of Misleading Hill Task Force," *Washington Post*, 14 July 1995: A19.

8 "Be Sure INS Deception at Krome Results in Termination of Con Artist," *Ft. Lauderdale Sun-Sentinel*, 2 July 1996: 8A.

9 Carol Rosenberg, "One Fired, Others Punished in INS Inspection Scandal," *Miami Herald*, 21 February 1997.

10 Ibid.

11 Office of the Inspector General, U.S. Department of Justice, Follow-Up Report, *Alleged Deception of Congress: The Congressional Task Force on Immigration Reform's Fact-Finding Visit to the Miami District of INS in June 1995*, September 1997. Available from http://www.usdoj.gov/oig/insmiafp/miafpp1.htm; Internet: accessed 1 March 2002.

12 Sara Fritz, "INS Charade Angers Duped Delegation," *St. Petersburg Times,* 8 August 1999: 3A.

13 William Branigin, "INS Weighs Plan to Free Criminals," *Washington Post*, 4 February 1999: A2.

14 Michelle Malkin, "Lifetime Employment Guarantee," *Washington Times,* 26 November 2001: A17.

15 Correspondence with Russ Bergeron.

16 Susannah Zak Figura, "Fair Game," *Government Executive*, 1 May 1999: 41.

17 "New INS Center Will Serve Law Enforcement Agencies in Other States," Associated Press, 28 July 1999.

18 Ibid.

19 Prepared testimony of Walter D. Cadman, counterterrorism coordinator, Office of Field Operations, Immigration and Naturalization Service, before the United States Senate Committee on Judiciary, Subcommittee on Technology, Terrorism, and Government, 24 February 1998.

20 Norman, "Admitting Terror."

21 Michelle Malkin, "An INS Horror Story," *Washington Times*, 18 November 2001: B1.

Chapter 9: Fatal Errors: The Technology Boondoggle

1 *The American Heritage Dictionary of the English Language*, Fourth Edition, Joseph P. Pickett et al., eds. (Boston: Houghton Mifflin Company, 2000).

2 United States Department of Justice, Office of the Inspector General, "Follow-Up Report on the Visa Waiver Program,"

Report No. I-2002-002, December 2001. Available from
http://www.usdoj.gov/oig/inspection/I-2002-002/; Internet:
accessed 20 May 2002.

3 *60 Minutes*, CBS News, 10 March 2002.

4 Cheryl W. Thompson, "New Security Checks Swamp INS
Offices," *Washington Post*, 16 May 2002: A1.

5 Patrick J. McDonnell, "INS Mix-Up Drops 3,500 from Travel
'Watch List,'" *Los Angeles Times*, 23 May 2002: 1.

6 Tom Brune, "An Agency in Crisis: Behind Recent INS Blun-
ders, an Overwhelming Bureaucracy," *Newsday*, 24 March
2002: A6.

7 United States General Accounting Office, "Information Tech-
nology: INS Needs to Better Manage the Development of Its
Enterprise Architecture," AIMD-00-212, 1 August 2000.
Available from http://www.gao.gov/archive/2000/ai00212.pdf;
Internet: accessed 20 May 2002.

8 United States General Accounting Office, "Securing
America's Borders: INS Faces Information Technology
Planning and Implementation Challenges," testimony of
Randolph Hite, Director, Information Technology Systems
Issues, 11 October 2001. Available from http://www.gao.gov/
new.items/d02148t.pdf; Internet: accessed 19 May 2002.

9 U.S. Department of Justice, Office of the Inspector General,
"Follow-Up Review: Immigration and Naturalization Service
Management of Automation Program," Audit Report 99–19,
July 1999. Available from http://www.usdoj.gov/oig/au9919/
9919tc.htm; Internet: accessed 19 May 2002.

10 Ibid.

11 United States Department of Justice, Office of the Inspector
General, *The Rafael Resendez-Ramirez Case: A Review of the
INS's Actions and the Operation of Its IDENT Automated
Fingerprint Identification System*, 20 March 2000. Available
from http://www.usdoj.gov/oig/resenrpt/
resenp6.htm#P1286_191490; Internet; accessed 12 March 2002.

12 Testimony of Keith Olson, President, Local 2913, National
Border Patrol Council of the American Federation of

Government Employees AFL-CIO, before the United States Senate Permanent Subcommittee on Investigations, Committee on Governmental Affairs, 13 November 2001.

13 Jonathan Peterson, "Response to Terror: High Tech, Low Effort at INS," *Los Angeles Times*, 19 November 2002: A1.

14 INSpect Alert Update, Inspections Function, Immigration and Naturalization Service, Office of Internal Audit, November 1999.

15 United States Department of Justice, Office of the Inspector General, *Inspections Report: Immigration and Naturalization Service Monitoring of Nonimmigrant Overstays*, Report Number I-97-08, September 1997. Available from http://www.usdoj.gov/oig/i9708/i9708toc.htm; Internet: accessed 20 May 2002.

16 "The Immigration and Naturalization Service's Automated I-94 System," Report No. 01-18, 6 August 2001. Available from http://www.usdoj.gov/oig/au0118/; Internet: accessed 20 May 2002.

17 Available from http://www.ins.usdoj.gov/graphics/services/tempbenefits/sevphos.htm; Internet: accessed 20 May 2002.

18 Borjas, "Rethinking Foreign Students."

19 Ibid.

20 United States Department of Justice, Office of the Inspector General, "The Immigration and Naturalization Service's Contacts with Two September 11 Terrorists: A Review of the INS's Admissions of Mohamed Atta and Marwan Alshehhi, Its Processing of Their Change of Status Applications, and Its Efforts to Track Foreign Students in the United States," 20 May 2002: Executive Summary.

21 Ibid.

Chapter 10: "It Ain't Over 'Til the Alien Wins"

1 Prepared statement of Barbara Jordan, Chairwoman of the United States Commission on Immigration Reform, before the Subcommittee on Immigration and Refugee Affairs, Judiciary Committee, United States Senate, 3 August 1994.

2 Larry Keller, "As United States Seeks to Root Out Terrorists, Foreign Residents Who May Have Run Afoul of Immigration Laws Fear They'll Fall Prey to the Hunt," *Palm Beach Daily Business Review*, 5 October 2001: A13.

3 Author interview with INS spokesman Bill Strassberger, 6 June 2002.

4 It is known as the Holtzman amendment to the Immigration and Naturalization Act. See U.S. Congress, House, *PL 95-549 Immigration and Naturalization Act—Nazi Germany*, 95th Cong., 2nd sess., 1978.

5 "Audit Report of I-551 Card Processing Controls of the Immigration and Naturalization Service," No. 88-1, 1988. Available from http://www.usdoj.gov/oig/au9706/a9706ap.htm; Internet: accessed 24 May 2002.

6 See Special Audit of the Immigration and Naturalization Service, Report No. 89-09, February 1989, and testimony of Michael R. Bromwich, Inspector General, U.S. Department of Justice, before the U.S. Senate Committee on the Judiciary, Subcommittee on Immigration, 1 May 1997.

7 "Alien Fingerprint Requirement in the Immigration and Naturalization Service," Report No. I-93-13, February 1994. Available from http://www.usdoj.gov/oig/i9313.htm; Internet: accessed 25 May 2002.

8 General Accounting Office, *INS Fingerprinting of Aliens, Efforts to Ensure the Authenticity of Aliens' Fingerprints*, GAO/GGD-95-40, December 1994.

9 "INS Announces New Naturalization Process and Finger-print Policy to Ensure Integrity and Improve Customer Service," press release, PR Newswire, 14 November 1997.

10 See United States Department of Justice, Office of the Inspector General, *Special Report: An Investigation of the Immigration and Naturalization Service's Citizenship USA Initiative*, Part V, "Criminal History Checking Procedures," 31 July 2000.

11 Until 1990, both powers ultimately rested with federal district courts. That year, the Immigration Act of 1990 transferred naturalization authority to the attorney general,

who delegated it to the INS. But the act failed to spell out whether the agency also could *revoke* naturalizations, instead of sending cases through the usual judicial process. In 1996, the agency on its own issued administrative regulations for stripping aliens of citizenship in cases where the INS made a mistake in approving an application or where the application was based on fraud, misrepresentation, or concealment of disqualifying evidence. The regulations gave aliens targeted for denaturalization 60 days to respond after receiving notice from the agency, and 180 days for the agency to make a decision after receiving a response. Appeals could be referred to another legal unit inside the agency, or the case could be referred to a U.S. attorney for regular court proceedings.

12 *Gorbach v. Reno*, United States of Court of Appeals for the Ninth Circuit, No. 98-35723, 20 July 2000.

13 Ibid.

14 Statement of Representative Lamar Smith on Naturalization Reform Act of 1997, H.R. 2837, House Judiciary Committee, 5 March 1998.

15 Katharine Q. Seelye, "20 Charged with Helping 13,000 Cheat on Test for Citizenship," *New York Times,* 28 January 1998: A12.

16 Prepared Statement of Dan Stein, Executive Director, Federation for American Immigration Reform, before the United States House Judiciary Committee Immigration and Claims Subcommittee, 25 February 1999.

17 Ibid. TPS applicants, who are not screened in the United States, may be granted work authorization while their applications are pending. One noteworthy TPS beneficiary is Ingmar Guandique, a violent Salvadoran criminal serving time for assaulting two women in Washington, D.C.'s Rock Creek Park. In early 2002, he was questioned in the death of murdered intern Chandra Levy, who disappeared the same month Guandique's attack took place. Levy's remains were discovered in Rock Creek Park in May 2002.

18 Ibid.

19 Charles Lane and Hanna Rosin, "Court Limits Detention of Immigrants," *Washington Post,* 29 June 2001: A1.

20 Cheryl W. Thompson, "INS to Free 3,400 Ex-Convicts," *Washington Post,* 20 July 2001: A02.

21 Ibid.

22 Telephone interview with Kelly Shannon, United States State Department, 9 May 2002.

23 H.R. 1452, "Family Reunification Act of 2001."

24 See the Immigration Reform and Control Act (Public Law 99-603); the Anti-Drug Abuse Act of 1988 (Public Law 100-690); the Antiterrorism and Effective Death Penalty Act of 1996 (Public Law 104-132); and the Illegal Immigration Reform and Immigrant Responsibility Act of 1996 (Public Law 104-208).

25 "Criminal Aliens: INS's Efforts to Identify and Remove Imprisoned Aliens Need to Be Improved," Statement of Norman J. Rankin, Director, Administration of Justice Issues, General Government Division. Available from http://www.gao.gov/archive/1997/gg97154t.pdf; Internet: accessed 20 April 2002.

26 Suzanne Gamboa, "Names of Missing Foreigners Ordered Deported to Be Entered in Crime Database," Associated Press, 5 December 2001.

27 Joseph A. D'Agostino, "INS Lowballed Deportation Evaders," *Human Events,* 18 March 2002.

28 Mary Beth Sheridan, "INS Seeks Law Enforcement Aid in Crackdown," *Washington Post,* 6 December 2001: A25

29 William K. Rashbaum, "I.N.S. Agents Say Staffing Shortage Is Undercutting Counterterrorism," *New York Times,* 20 May 2002: B1.

30 Dan Eggen, "U.S. Search Finds 585 Deportee 'Absconders,'" *Washington Post,* 30 May 2002: A7.

31 Dan Eggen and Cheryl W. Thompson, "United States Seeks Thousands of Fugitive Deportees," *Washington Post,* 8 January 2002: A01.

32 Valerie Alvord, "INS Unprepared to Handle the Nation's Fastest Growing Prison Population," Copley News Service, 5 February 1999.

33 Gordon, "Borders Far from Secure."

34 Public Law 104-208.

35 Public Law 104-132.

36 Lena Williams, "A Law Aimed at Terrorists Hits Legal Immigrants," *New York Times*, 17 July 1996: A1.

37 See *INS v. St. Cyr*, 533 United States, 121 S.Ct. 2271 (25 June 2001) (upholding habeas jurisdiction) and *Calcano-Martinez v. I.N.S.*, 533 United States, 121 S.Ct. 2268 (25 June 2001) (dismissing petitions for review).

38 EOIR Web site available at http://www.usdoj.gov/eoir/; Internet: accessed 20 April 2002; information about BIA available at http://www.usdoj.gov/eoir/biainfo.htm; Internet: accessed 20 April 2002.

39 Kevin Murphy, "United States Overhauls Immigration Court System to Speed Deportation," *Kansas City Star*, 7 February 2002.

40 Jody A. Benjamin, " '96 Reform Law Lets INS Cast a Wide Net," *Ft. Lauderdale Sun-Sentinel*, 22 April 2001: 1A.

41 Juan Mann (alias), "It's the Fraud, Stupid!" Available at http://www.geocities.com/deportaliens/fraud.html; Internet: accessed 20 April 2002.

42 Statement of Kevin D. Rooney, Director, Executive Office for Immigration Review, House Committee on the Judiciary, Subcommittee on Immigration and Claims, Oversight Hearing, 6 February 2002.

43 Available from http://www.gottrouble.com/legal/immigration/deportation_relief.html; Internet: accessed 20 April 2002.

44 Jerry Seper, "Ashcroft Reviews Overturned Deportation," *Washington Times*, 19 December 2001: A4.

45 Ibid. See also, Jerry Seper, "Appeals Panel, Judge Differ on Fate of Nanny: Deportation Ordered Twice for Convicted Baby-Killer," *Washington Times*, 10 December 2001: A7.

46 Beverley Lumpkin, "Board of Immigration Radicals," abcnews.com, 24 August 2001. Available from http://abcnews.go.com/sections/us/HallsOfJustice/hallsofjustice92.html; Internet: accessed 20 April 2002.

47 Ted Bridis, "Ashcroft Orders Haitian Mom Deported," Associated Press, 8 May 2002. See also 23 I&N Dec.373 (AG 2002). Available from http://www.usdoj.gov/eoir/efoia/bia/decisions/revdec/pdfDEC/3472.pdf; Internet: accessed 7 July 2002.

48 23 I&N Dec. 173 (BIA 2001). Available from http://www.usdoj.gov/eoir/efoia/bia/Decisions/Revdec/pdfDEC/3455.pdf; Internet, accessed 8 May 2002.

49 Julia Malone, "Federal Review Board Charts New Course for Criminal Aliens," Cox News Service, 6 January 2002.

50 23 I&N Dec. 78 (BIA 2001). Available from http://www.usdoj.gov/eoir/efoia/bia/Decisions/Revdec/pdfDEC/3449.pdf; Internet: accessed 20 April 2002.

51 Interim Decision: #3125: Matter of Short, A-38827315, Board of Immigration Appeals, 16 November 1989: Volume 20 (page 136). Available from http://www.asylumlaw.org/docs/united_states/BIA/biavol20.pdf; Internet: accessed 1 May 2002.

52 Ibid.

53 Mike Royko, "Legal Babble OKs Travesty of Justice," *Chicago Tribune*, 22 November 1989: 3.

54 United States Department of Justice, Office of the Inspector General, Inspections Division, "Voluntary Departure: Ineffective Enforcement and Lack of Sufficient Controls Hamper the Process," Report No. I-99-09, March 1999. Available from http://www.usdoj.gov/oig/i9909/i9909toc.htm; Internet: accessed 20 April 2002.

55 Ibid.

56 Memorandum for Regional Directors from Michael A. Pearson on Criminal Indices Checks, 20 December 2001.

57 Testimony of Mark Hall before the Permanent Investigations Subcommittee, Senate Governmental Affairs Committee, 13 November 2001.

58 William Branigin, "Nation's Political Asylum System Draws Criticism from Both Sides," *Washington Post*, 7 July 1996: A3.

59 United States Department of Justice, "World Trade Center Bombing Suspect Apprehended in Pakistan," press release, 8 February 1995. Available from http://www.usdoj.gov/opa/pr/Pre_96/February95/78.txt.html; Internet: accessed 1 May 2002.

60 Mezer first attempted to enter the United States through the Ross Lake National Recreation Area in Washington State. He was unable to complete the difficult hike, and park rangers came to his rescue. After consulting with the INS, the park officials sent him back to Canada. A week later, Mezer tried to jog into the U.S. through Peace Arch Park in Blaine, Washington. Agents caught him and again returned him to Canada. A few months later, federal officials picked up Mezer at a Greyhound bus station in Bellingham, Washington. Border Patrol agent Eugene Davis notes that Mezer was trying to secure transportation for two other border-jumpers as well.

61 United States Department of Justice, Office of the Inspector General, *Bombs in Brooklyn: How the Two Illegal Aliens Arrested for Plotting to Bomb the New York Subway Entered and Remained in the United States*, March 1998. Available from http://www.usdoj.gov/oig/brookb/brbrtoc.htm; Internet: accessed 20 April 2002.

62 Sydney P. Freedberg, "Terrorists Entered the United States with Ease," *St. Petersburg Times*, 25 November 2001: 18A.

63 William Branigin, "INS Chief Highlights Reform in Political Asylum System," *Washington Post*, 5 January 1996: A2.

64 "Border Patrol: Not Enough Agents to Watch Canada's Border," Associated Press, 16 April 1999.

65 United States Department of Justice, Office of the Inspector General, *Bombs in Brooklyn*.

66 Stuart Pfeifer, "O.C. Suspect Immigrated Despite Arrest," *Los Angeles Times*, 12 March 2001: A1.

67 Ibid.

68 Ibid.

69 Patricia Hurtado, "Smuggling Scheme," *Newsday*, 12 February 2002: A3.

70 Mark Hamblett, "Attorney Pleads Guilty to Smuggling Aliens Taken Hostage," *Legal Intelligencer*, 14 February 2002: 4.

71 Ibid.

72 Larry Neumeister, "Lawyer, Wife Admit Chinese Smuggling Scheme," Associated Press, 11 February 2002.

73 Matt Hayes, "Corrupt Lawyers Aid Immigration Woes," FoxNews.com, available at http://www.foxnews.com/story/0,2933,51263,00.html; Internet: accessed 3 May 2002.

74 Branigin, "Nation's Political Asylum System Draws Criticism from Both Sides."

75 Mark Krikorian, "Who Deserves Asylum?" Center for Immigration Studies, June 1996. Available from http://www.cis.org/articles/1996/msk6-96.html; Internet: accessed 20 April 2002.

76 *Abankwah v. INS*, 185 F.3d 22 (2nd Cir. 1999).

77 William Branigin and Douglas Farah, "Asylum Seeker Is Impostor, INS Says," *Washington Post*, 20 December 2000: A1.

78 Interview with the author, 3 May 2002.

79 United States General Accounting Office, "Immigration Benefit Fraud: Focused Approach Is Needed to Address Problems," January 2002; GAO-02-66.

80 Ted Bridis, "Ashcroft Approves Rules Creating Visas for Victims of 'Human Trafficking,'" Associated Press, 24 January 2002.

Conclusion

1 Dan Eggen, "FBI Warns of Suicide Bombs," *Washington Post*, 21 May 2002: A4.

2 The law makes an exception if the secretary of state determines that the alien does not pose a threat to the safety or national security of the United States. This mechanism can be used to approve entry for a small number of diplomats,

heads of state, and so forth. See Section 306 of the Enhanced Border Security and Visa Entry Reform Act of 2002.

3 In June 2002, the INS ordered all Yemenis to be searched upon entry into and exit from the country, and asked commercial airlines and large U.S. charter flight operators to notify the agency when they have Yemeni passengers.

4 The visa moratorium should be extended to Palestinians as well. As for the Philippines and Pakistan, where al Qaeda has spread, their governments remain allies in the fight against al Qaeda. Thus they do not warrant inclusion on a moratorium list at this time. Nevertheless, all visitors and immigrants from these countries should be included in the Justice Department's pilot fingerprint plan to be launched in the fall of 2002.

5 Vincent Smith, president of Capital Bonding Corp., interview with CBS News, 28 May 2002. Available from http://www.cbsnews.com/stories/2002/05/28/eveningnews/main510335.shtml; Internet: accessed 28 May 2002.

6 T. Alexander Aleinikoff and David A. Martin, "Ashcroft's Immigration Threat," *Washington Post*, 26 February 2002: A21.

7 Michael Coleman, "Ridge Juggles Needs at Border," *Albuquerque Journal*, 1 March 2002: A1.

8 Bill McAllister, "INS Confirms Border Incident with Mexico," *Denver Post*, 22 May 2002: A17.

9 Thomas Frank, "Uphill Battle for INS Chief," *Newsday*, 24 March 2002: A6.

10 Karina Ioffee and Tim Steller, "Mass Deportation Effort Unlikely, INS Chief Says," *Arizona Daily Star*, 24 May 2002.

Appendix D

1 Louisa Shepard, "To Catch a Thief," *Federal Computer Week*, 30 March 1998.

Acknowledgments

Those mentioned here may not necessarily agree with the conclusions in the book, but their contributions were invaluable and I owe them tremendously.

My thanks go first to all those whose names I cannot name, for your tips and leads and insights and prodding and dedication to your jobs.

Thanks to José Touron, Eugene Davis, James Bonnette, Sherry Moore, Barbara Suri, and other former and current INS employees who were willing to go on the record to share their knowledge and frustrations.

Thanks also to Rob Sanchez for his invaluable research database, to Richard Krieger for his indefatigable efforts, to Steve Perlman for his accountability crusade, and to "Juan Mann" for opening my eyes.

Thanks to Larry Van Hoose, Arizona Congressman J. D. Hayworth, and members of the House Conservative Opportunity Society, who took time out of their packed schedules to listen to some of the ideas that laid the groundwork for Chapter 2.

For their quick and friendly responses to specific questions I had over the course of writing the book, and in general for their work, my thanks to the Federation for American Immigration Reform and the Center for Immigration Studies. Thanks also to staffers at the Justice Department's Office of the Inspector General, for their meticulous reports upon which I drew.

My gratitude goes to those who read all or part of the manuscript drafts: Len Stark, Jim Edwards, Carole Malkin, J. S., and especially my mentor/friend/hero, Michael Fumento.

Thanks to all my readers, from the Bronx to Miami to Houston to Los Angeles to Honolulu to Canada and Australia, who sent helpful clippings and shared their thoughts on immigration reform and their experiences with the system.

For bolstering my journalism career over the years and helping me reach a broader audience, I give special thanks to Tom Gray, Binyamin Jolkovsky and Jewishworldreview.com, Rick and Carole Newcombe and the entire staff at Creators Syndicate, John McLaughlin, and Roger Ailes. A Seattle salute to Lou Guzzo, whose correspondence and continued encouragement has buoyed me.

This book would not have been possible without the help of David Limbaugh; my thanks to him for his advice, energy, and advocacy. Deep thanks to Al Regnery, Harry Crocker, and the entire staff at Regnery for their support. A special note of appreciation to my project editor extraordinaire, Bernadette Malone. For her cheerfulness, her patience, and above all, her incredibly skillful and gifted editing, I am most grateful.

Thanks to Mom and Dad, for everything.

And finally, the best for last: For Jesse, my rock, my sounding board, my best friend, my unindicted coconspirator and unattributed coauthor in all that I do, words fail. My love for you is matched only by my bottomless debts to you. Thank you, eternally.

Index